SCOUT COMICS

FB/TW/IG:
@SCOUTCOMICS

LEARN MORE AT:
WWW.SCOUTCOMICS.COM

Brendan Deneen, *CEO*
James Haick III, *President*
Tennessee Edwards, *CSO*
Don Handfield, *CMO*
James Pruett, *CCO*
David Byrne, *Co-Publisher*
Charlie Stickney, *Co-Publisher*
Joel Rodriguez, *Head of Design*

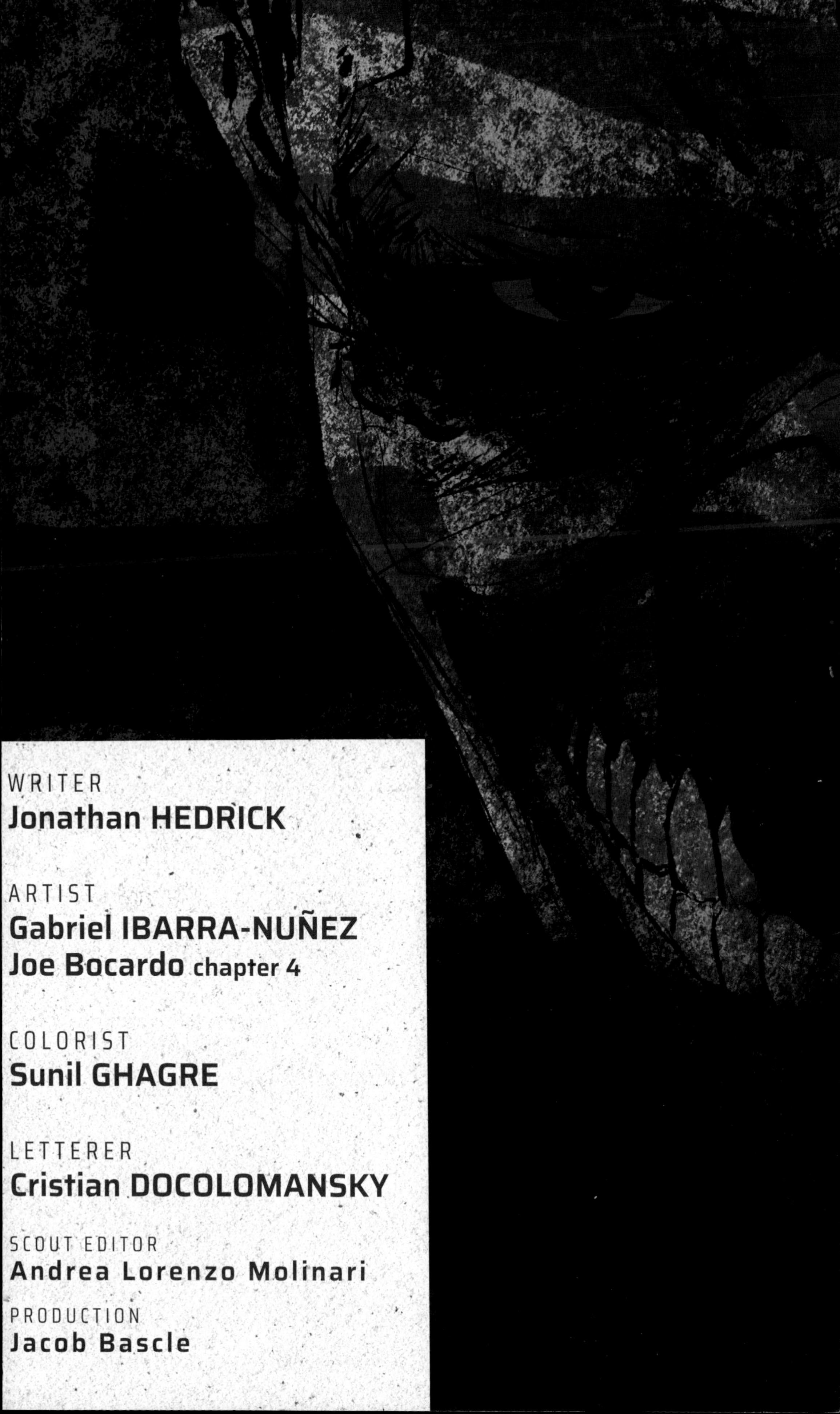

WRITER
Jonathan HEDRICK

ARTIST
Gabriel IBARRA-NUÑEZ
Joe Bocardo chapter 4

COLORIST
Sunil GHAGRE

LETTERER
Cristian DOCOLOMANSKY

SCOUT EDITOR
Andrea Lorenzo Molinari

PRODUCTION
Jacob Bascle

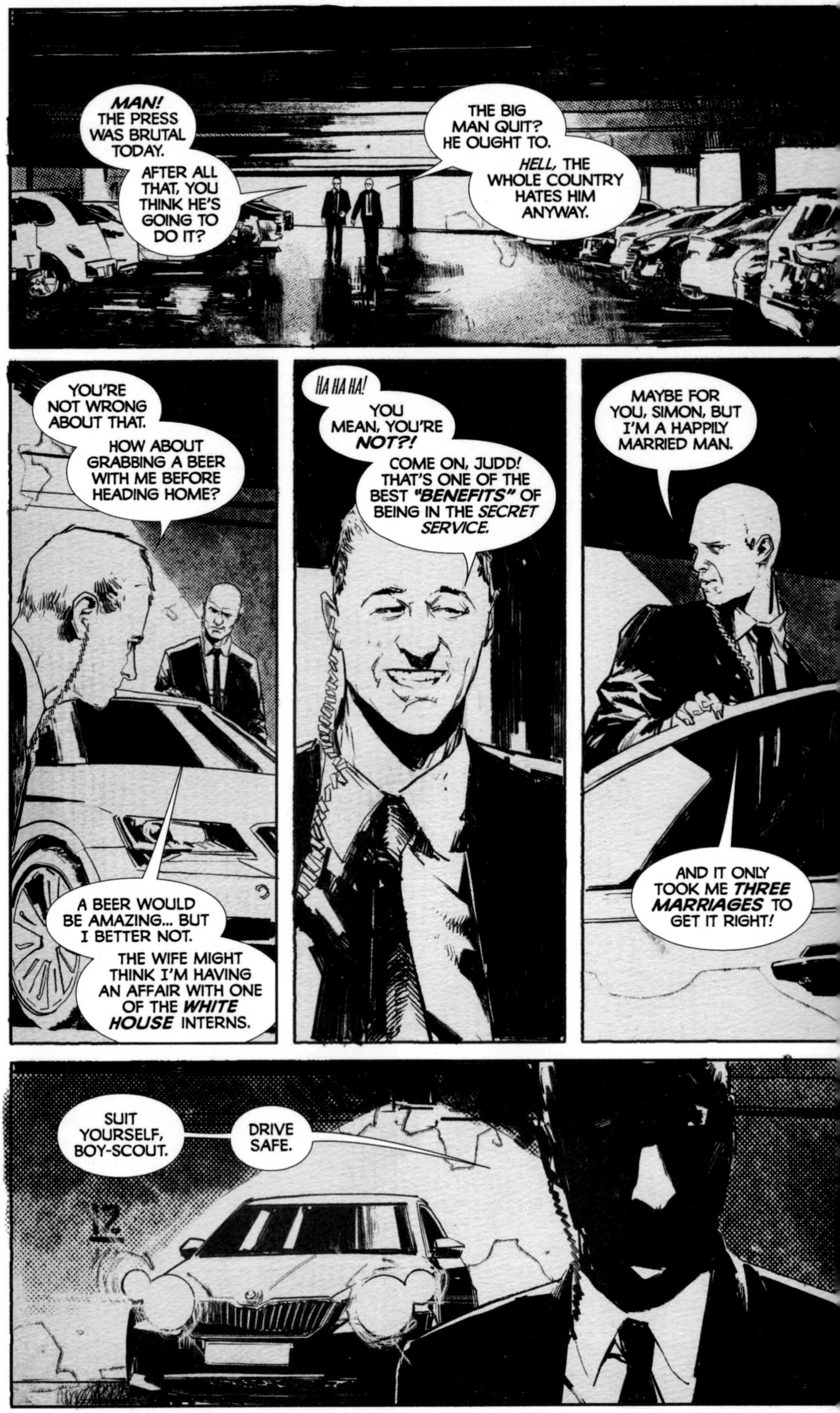
MAN! THE PRESS WAS BRUTAL TODAY.
AFTER ALL THAT, YOU THINK HE'S GOING TO DO IT?
THE BIG MAN QUIT? HE OUGHT TO.
HELL, THE WHOLE COUNTRY HATES HIM ANYWAY.
YOU'RE NOT WRONG ABOUT THAT.
HOW ABOUT GRABBING A BEER WITH ME BEFORE HEADING HOME?
A BEER WOULD BE AMAZING... BUT I BETTER NOT.
THE WIFE MIGHT THINK I'M HAVING AN AFFAIR WITH ONE OF THE WHITE HOUSE INTERNS.
HA HA HA!
YOU MEAN, YOU'RE NOT?!
COME ON, JUDD! THAT'S ONE OF THE BEST "BENEFITS" OF BEING IN THE SECRET SERVICE.
MAYBE FOR YOU, SIMON, BUT I'M A HAPPILY MARRIED MAN.
AND IT ONLY TOOK ME THREE MARRIAGES TO GET IT RIGHT!
SUIT YOURSELF, BOY-SCOUT.
DRIVE SAFE.

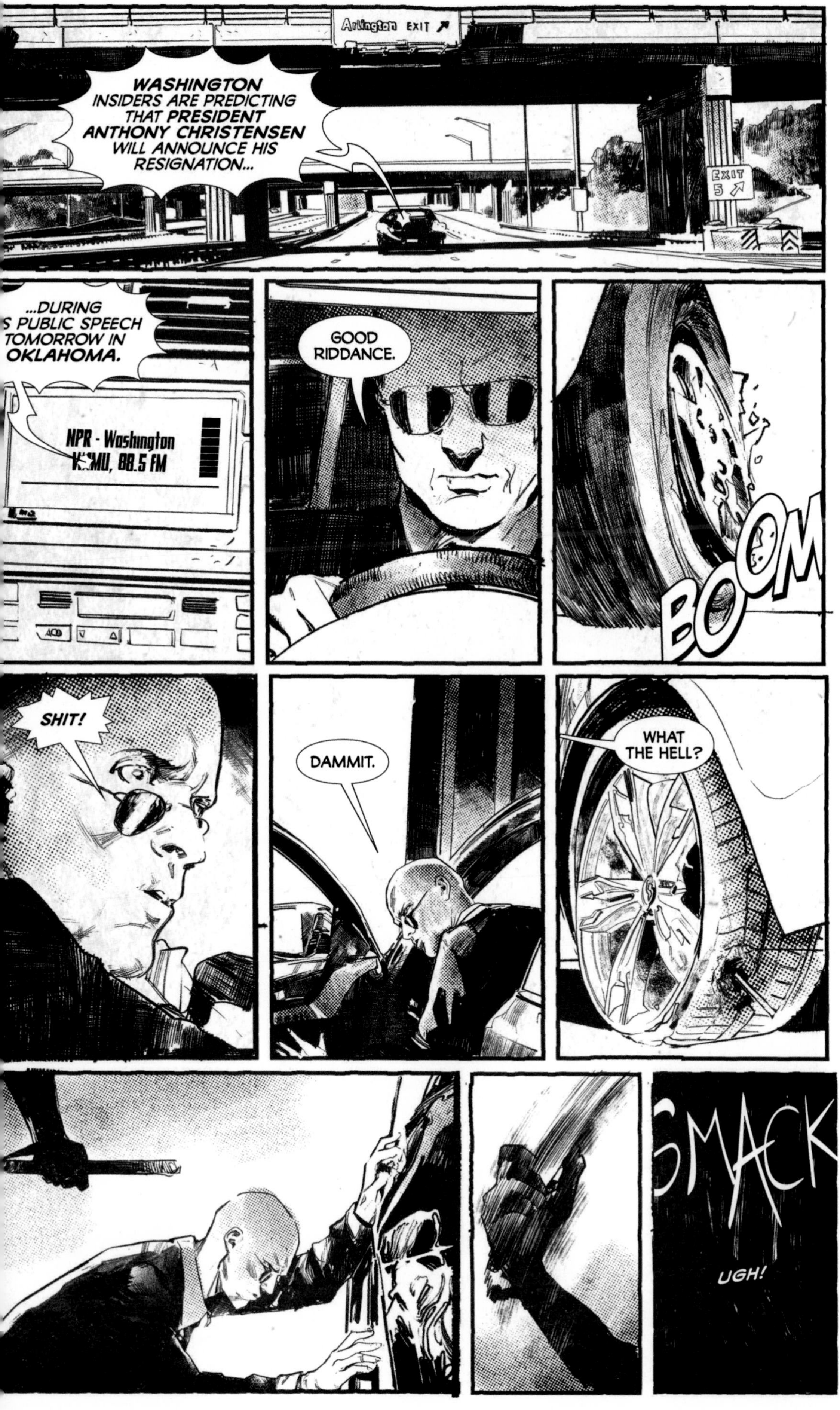

Arlington EXIT
WASHINGTON INSIDERS ARE PREDICTING THAT PRESIDENT ANTHONY CHRISTENSEN WILL ANNOUNCE HIS RESIGNATION...
EXIT 5
...DURING S PUBLIC SPEECH TOMORROW IN OKLAHOMA.
NPR - Washington
GOOD RIDDANCE.
BOOM
SHIT!
DAMMIT.
WHAT THE HELL?
SMACK
UGH!

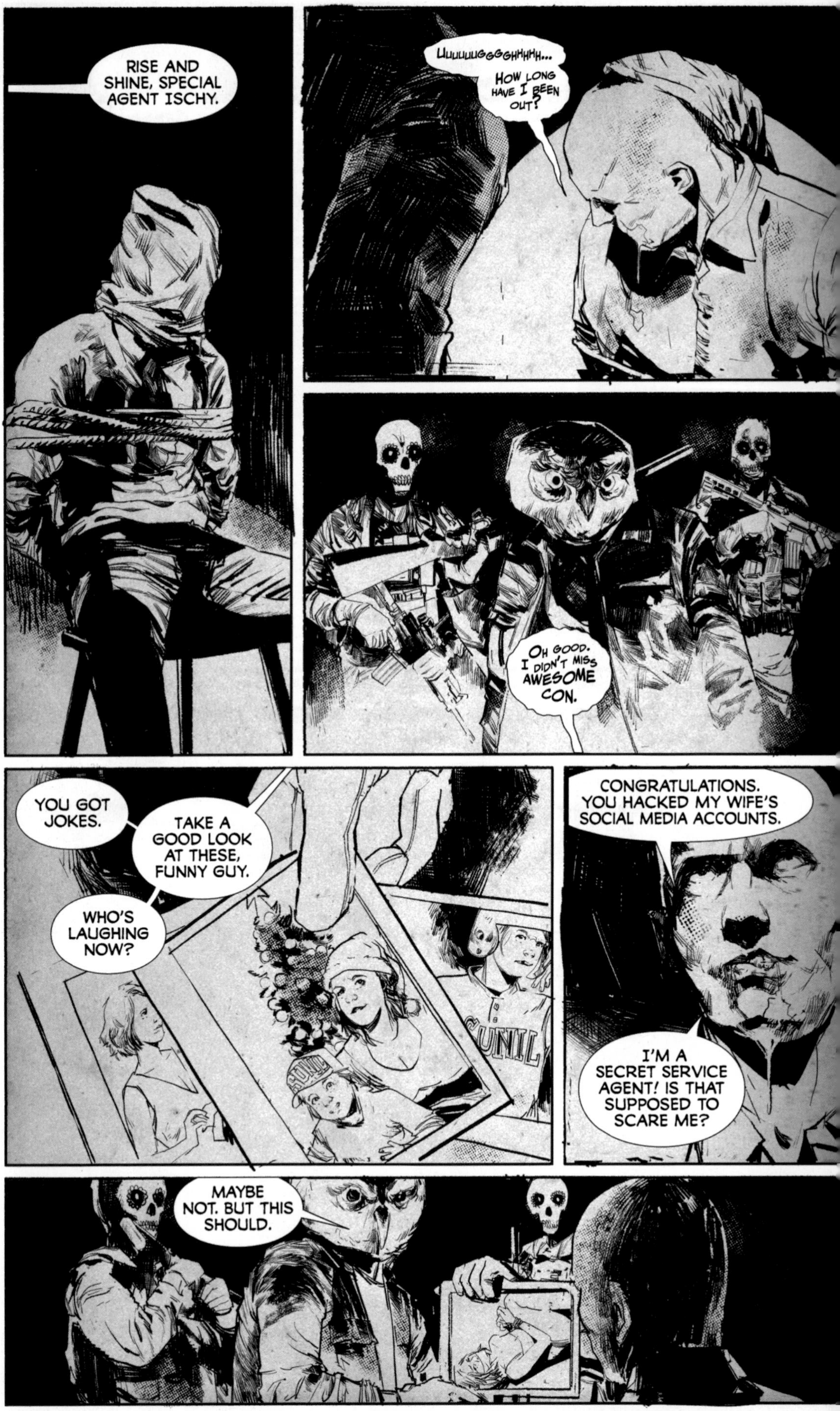
RISE AND SHINE, SPECIAL AGENT ISCHY.
UUUUUUGGGGHHHHH... HOW LONG HAVE I BEEN OUT?
OH GOOD. I DIDN'T MISS AWESOME CON.
YOU GOT JOKES.
TAKE A GOOD LOOK AT THESE, FUNNY GUY.
WHO'S LAUGHING NOW?
CONGRATULATIONS. YOU HACKED MY WIFE'S SOCIAL MEDIA ACCOUNTS.
I'M A SECRET SERVICE AGENT! IS THAT SUPPOSED TO SCARE ME?
MAYBE NOT. BUT THIS SHOULD.

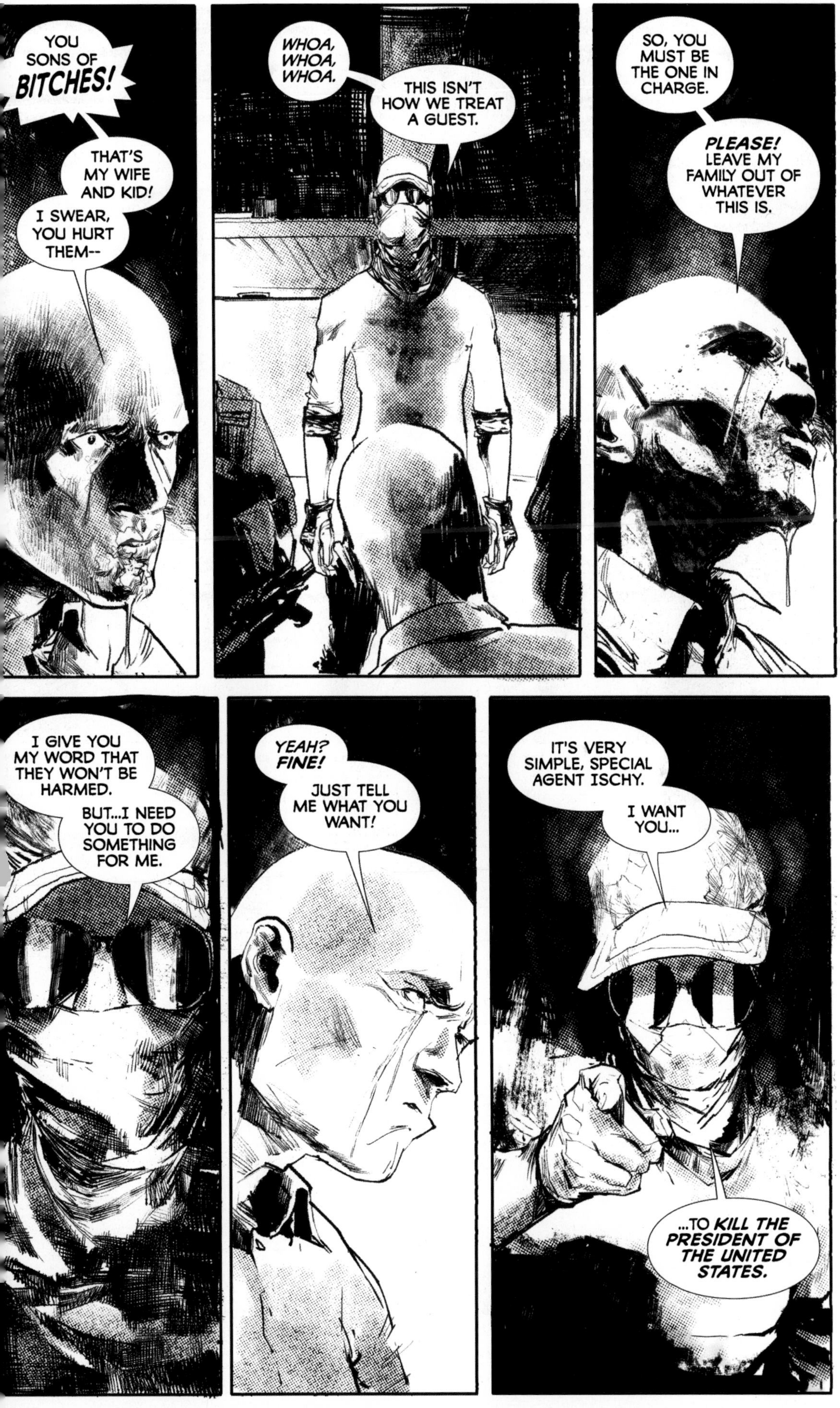
YOU SONS OF BITCHES!
THAT'S MY WIFE AND KID!
I SWEAR, YOU HURT THEM--
WHOA, WHOA, WHOA.
THIS ISN'T HOW WE TREAT A GUEST.
SO, YOU MUST BE THE ONE IN CHARGE.
PLEASE! LEAVE MY FAMILY OUT OF WHATEVER THIS IS.
I GIVE YOU MY WORD THAT THEY WON'T BE HARMED.
BUT...I NEED YOU TO DO SOMETHING FOR ME.
YEAH? FINE!
JUST TELL ME WHAT YOU WANT!
IT'S VERY SIMPLE, SPECIAL AGENT ISCHY.
I WANT YOU...
...TO KILL THE PRESIDENT OF THE UNITED STATES.

CHAPTER 1

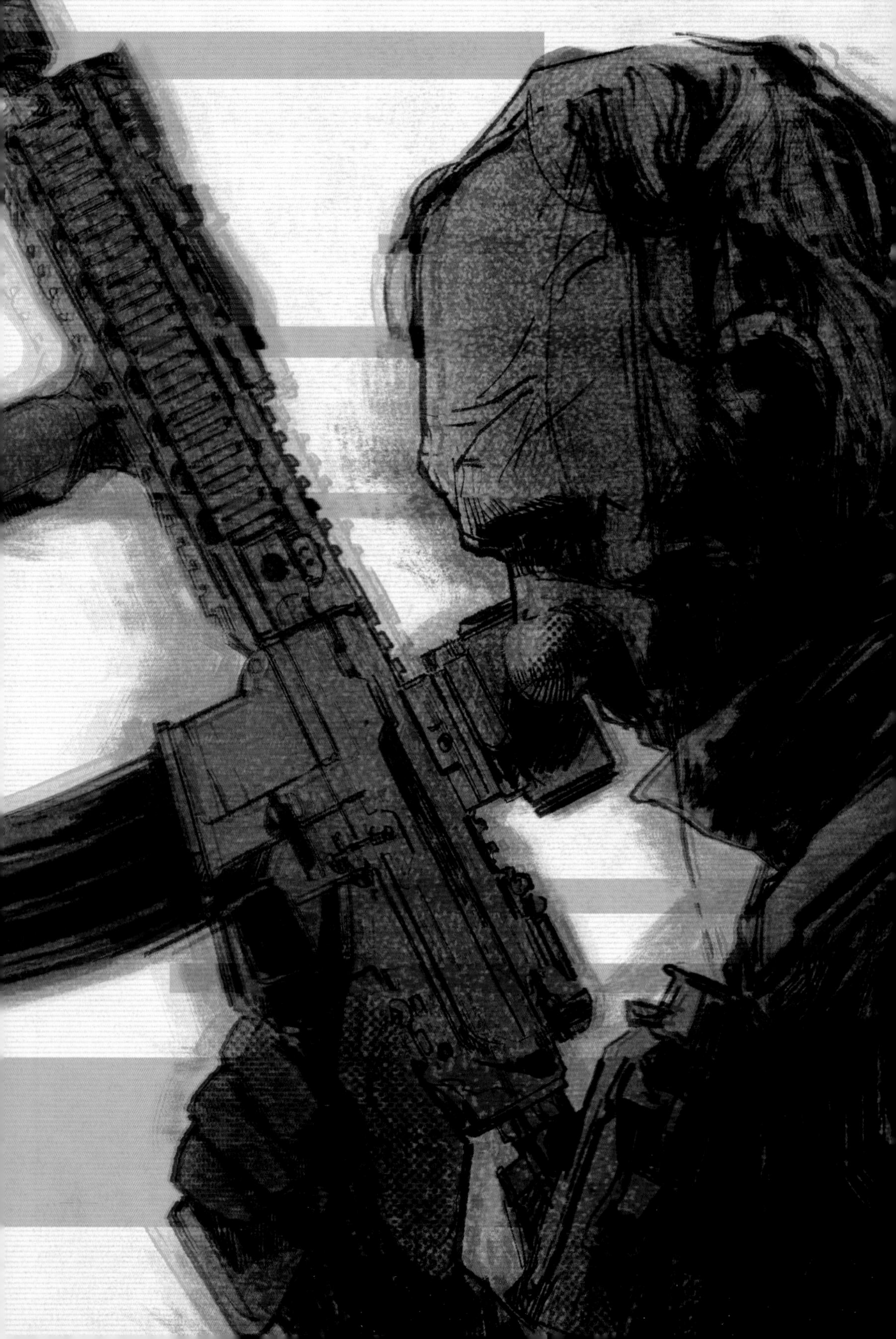

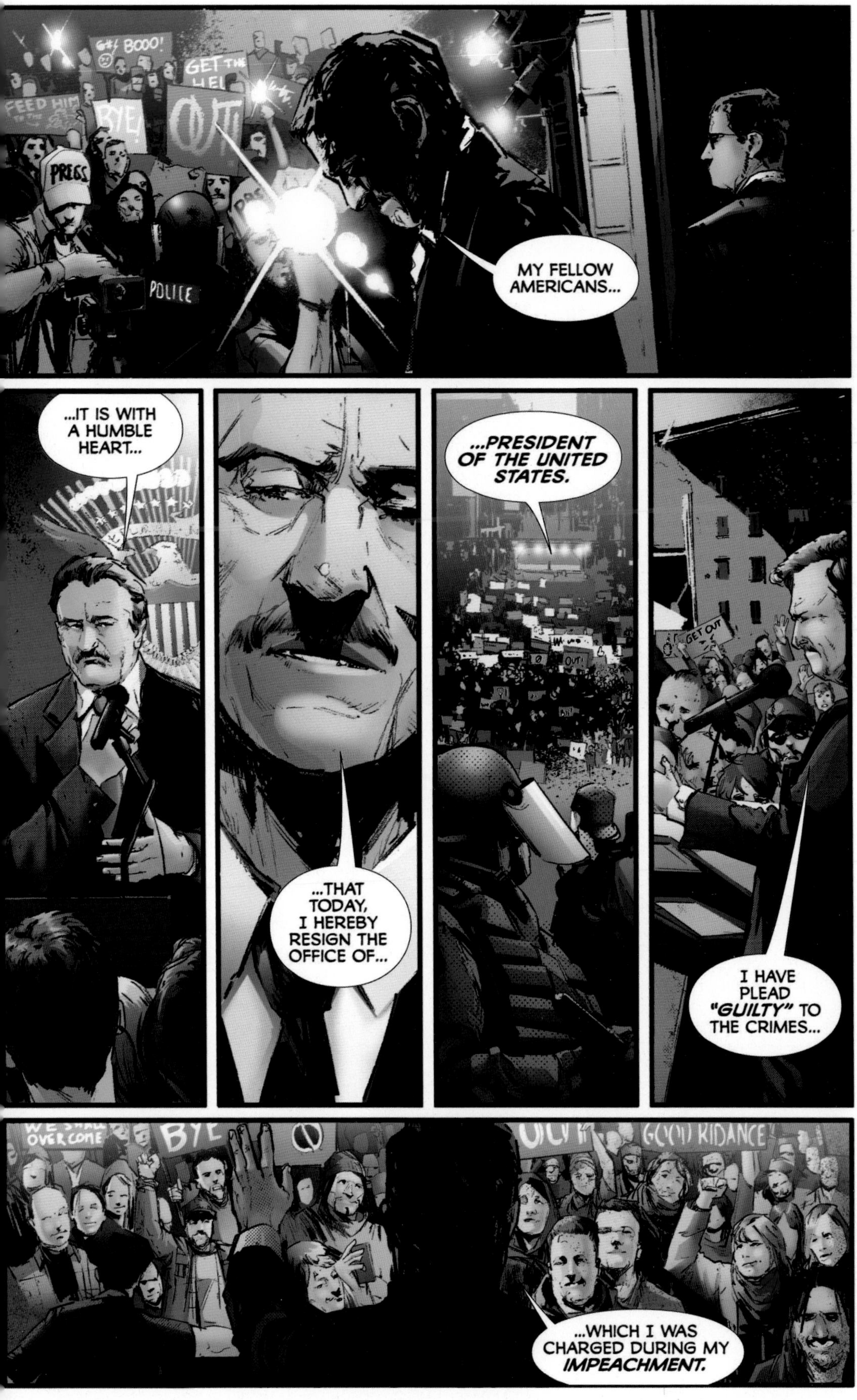

PRESS
POLICE
FEED HIM
BYE!
OUT!
GET THE HELL
MY FELLOW AMERICANS...
...IT IS WITH A HUMBLE HEART...
...THAT TODAY, I HEREBY RESIGN THE OFFICE OF...
...PRESIDENT OF THE UNITED STATES.
OUT!
GET OUT
I HAVE PLEAD "GUILTY" TO THE CRIMES...
OVERCOME
BYE
GOOD RIDANCE
...WHICH I WAS CHARGED DURING MY IMPEACHMENT.

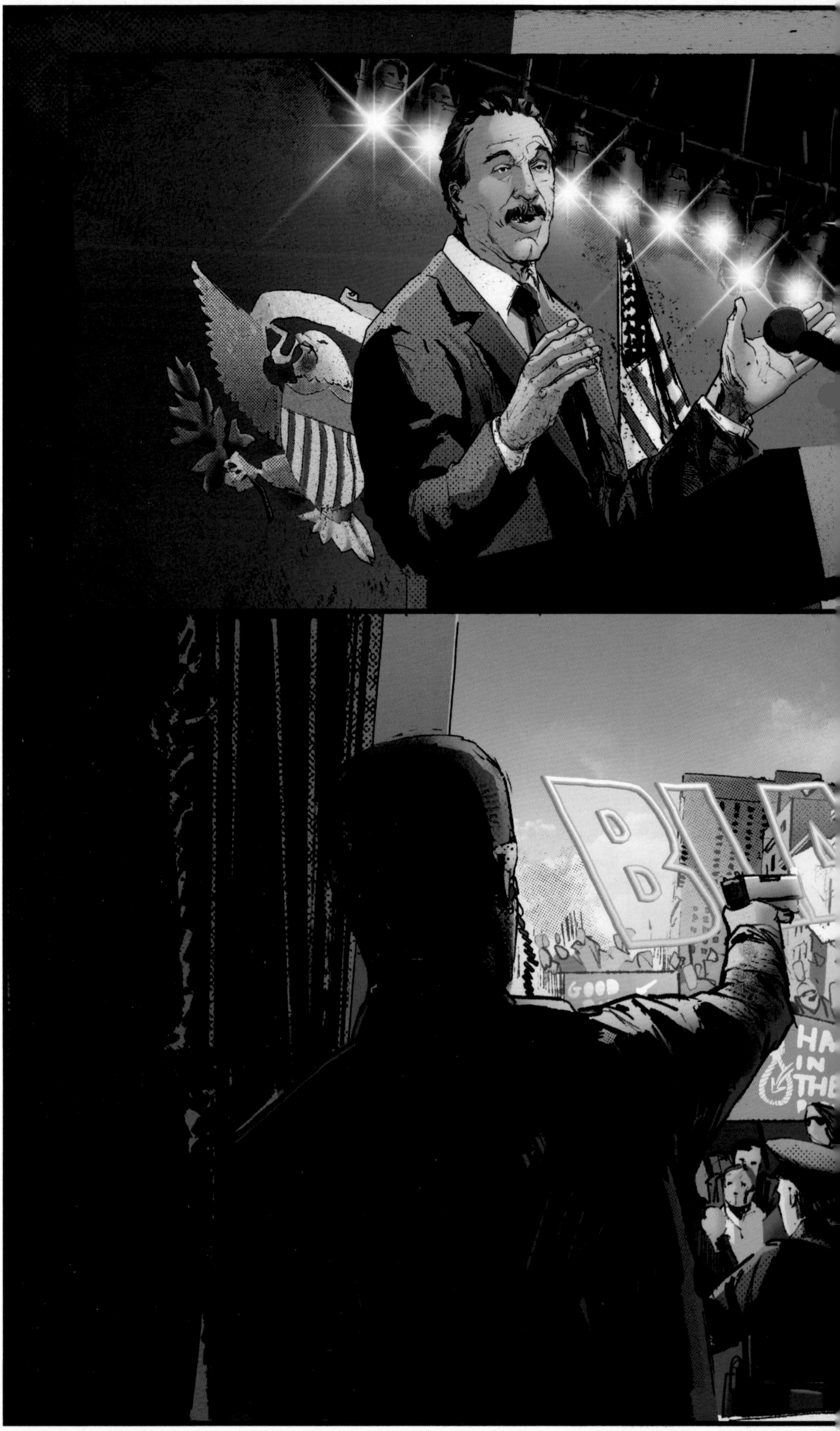
GOOD

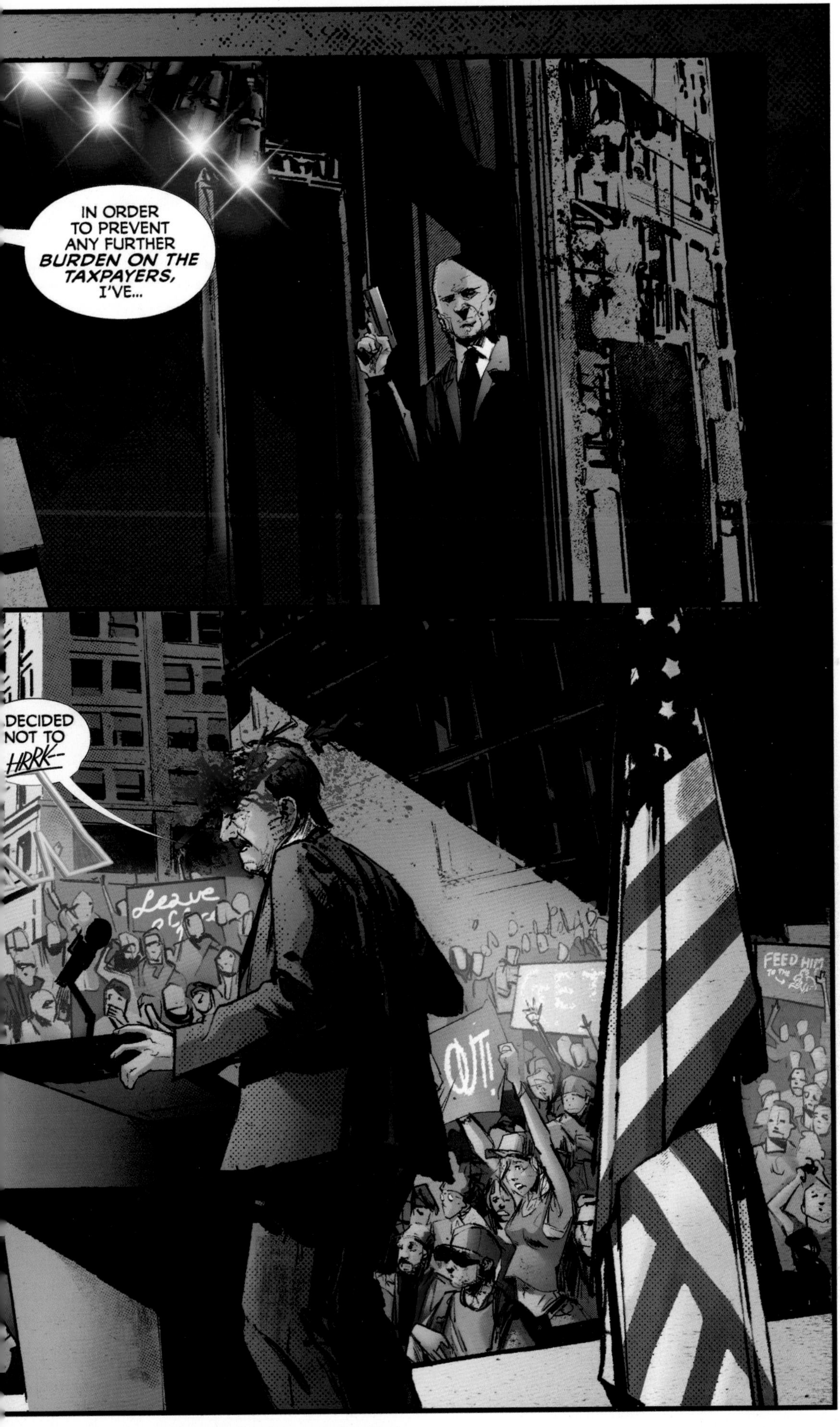
IN ORDER TO PREVENT ANY FURTHER *BURDEN ON THE TAXPAYERS,* I'VE...
DECIDED NOT TO *HRRK--*
Leave
OUT!
FEED HIM TO THE

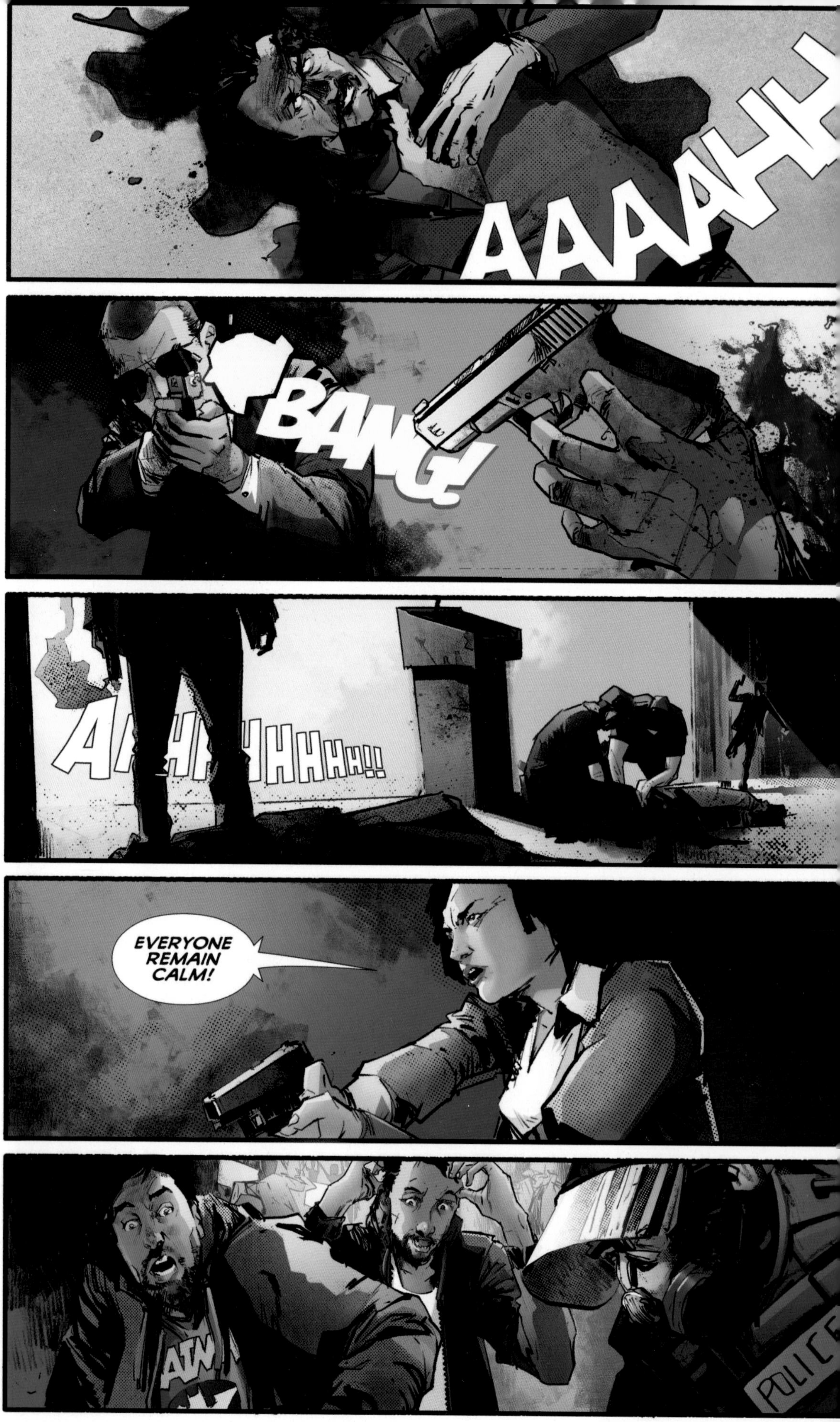
AAAAHH
BANG!
AHHHHHHH!!
EVERYONE REMAIN CALM!
POLICE

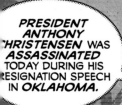

PRESIDENT ANTHONY CHRISTENSEN WAS *ASSASSINATED* TODAY DURING HIS RESIGNATION SPEECH IN *OKLAHOMA.*

SECRET SERVICE AGENT, *JUDD ISCHY,* WAS FATALLY SHOT SECONDS AFTER SHOOTING THE PRESIDENT.

THE DEPARTMENT OF *HOMELAND SECURITY* IS ON HIGH ALERT...

...AND IS CONDUCTING AN *INVESTIGATION* INTO THE SECRET SERVICE AGENCY SO AS TO DETECT ANY FURTHER *THREATS.*

A STATEMENT ISSUED BY THE *WHITE HOUSE* CONFIRMS...

...THAT *VICE PRESIDENT MEREDITH MCDEARMON* HAS BEEN SWORN IN AS THE NEW PRESIDENT.

PRESIDENT MCDEARMON'S *LOCATION,* HOWEVER, IS CURRENTLY *CLASSIFIED,* PRESUMABLY FOR HER SAFETY.

FUNERAL ARRANGEMENTS FOR THE LATE PRESIDENT CHRISTENSEN HAVE BEGUN IN HIS HOMETOWN OF *BETHANY, CONNECTICUT.*

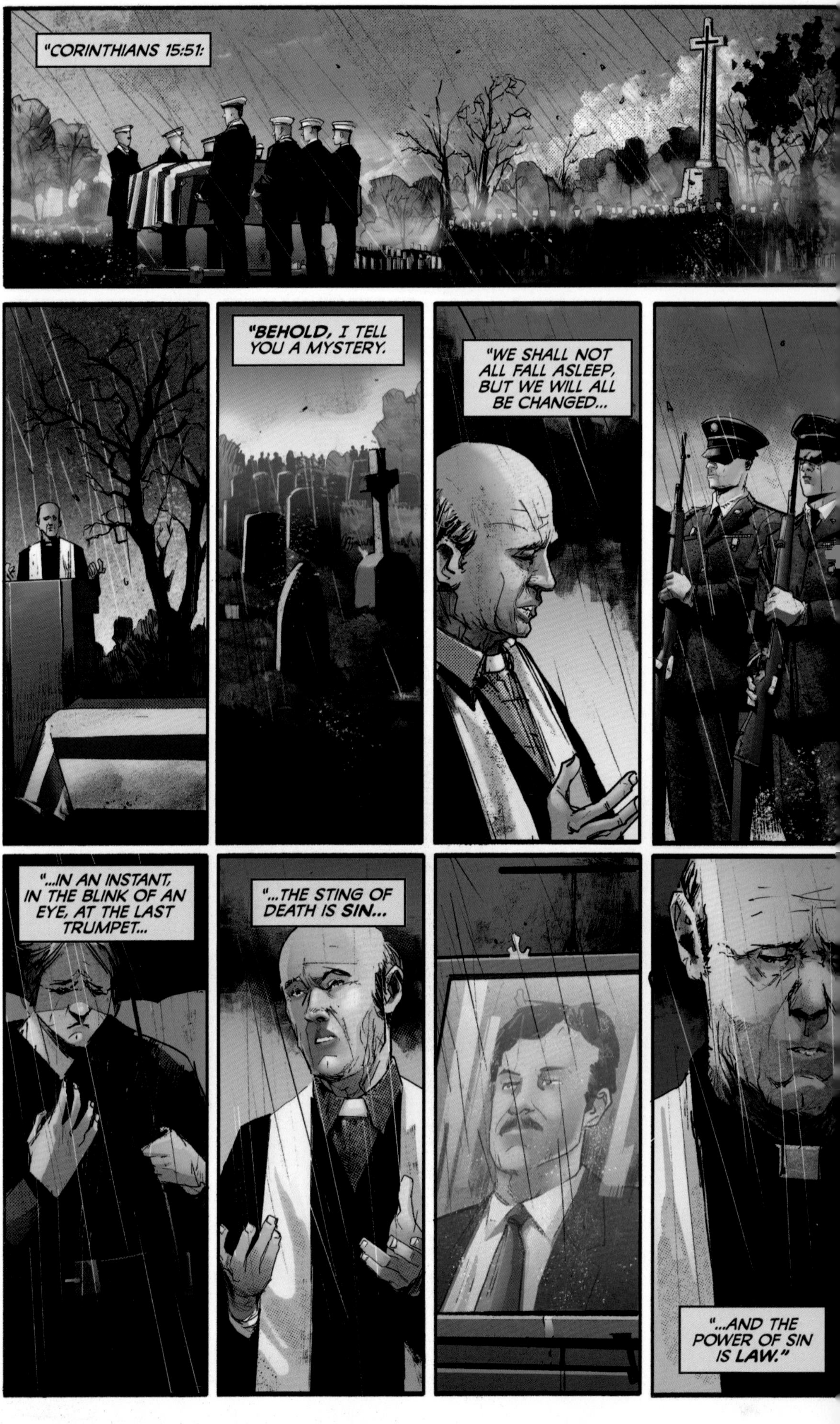
"CORINTHIANS 15:51:
"BEHOLD, I TELL YOU A MYSTERY.
"WE SHALL NOT ALL FALL ASLEEP, BUT WE WILL ALL BE CHANGED...
"...IN AN INSTANT, IN THE BLINK OF AN EYE, AT THE LAST TRUMPET...
"...THE STING OF DEATH IS SIN...
"...AND THE POWER OF SIN IS LAW."

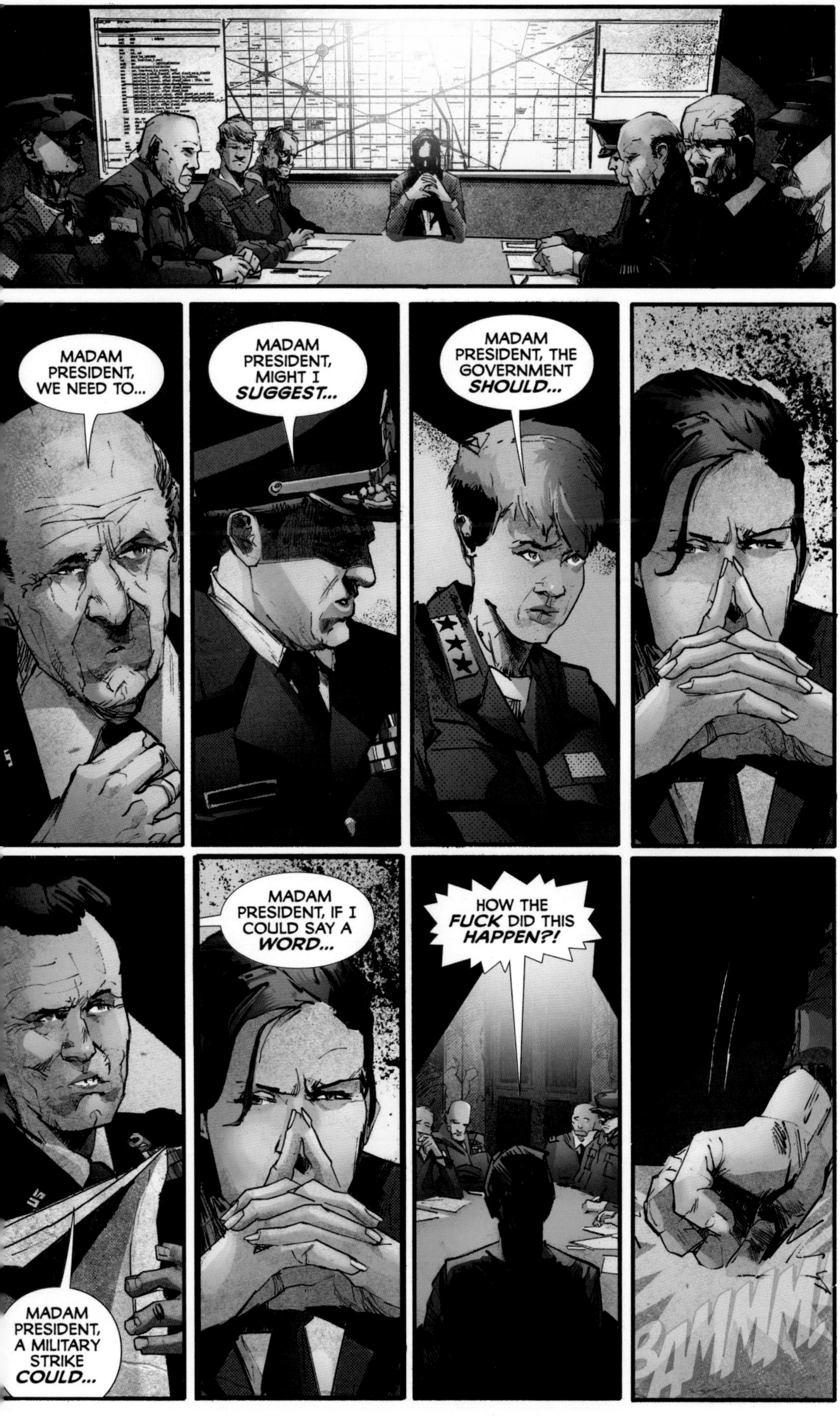
MADAM PRESIDENT, WE NEED TO...
MADAM PRESIDENT, MIGHT I *SUGGEST...*
MADAM PRESIDENT, THE GOVERNMENT *SHOULD...*
MADAM PRESIDENT, A MILITARY STRIKE *COULD...*
MADAM PRESIDENT, IF I COULD SAY A *WORD...*
HOW THE *FUCK* DID THIS *HAPPEN?!*
BAMMM!

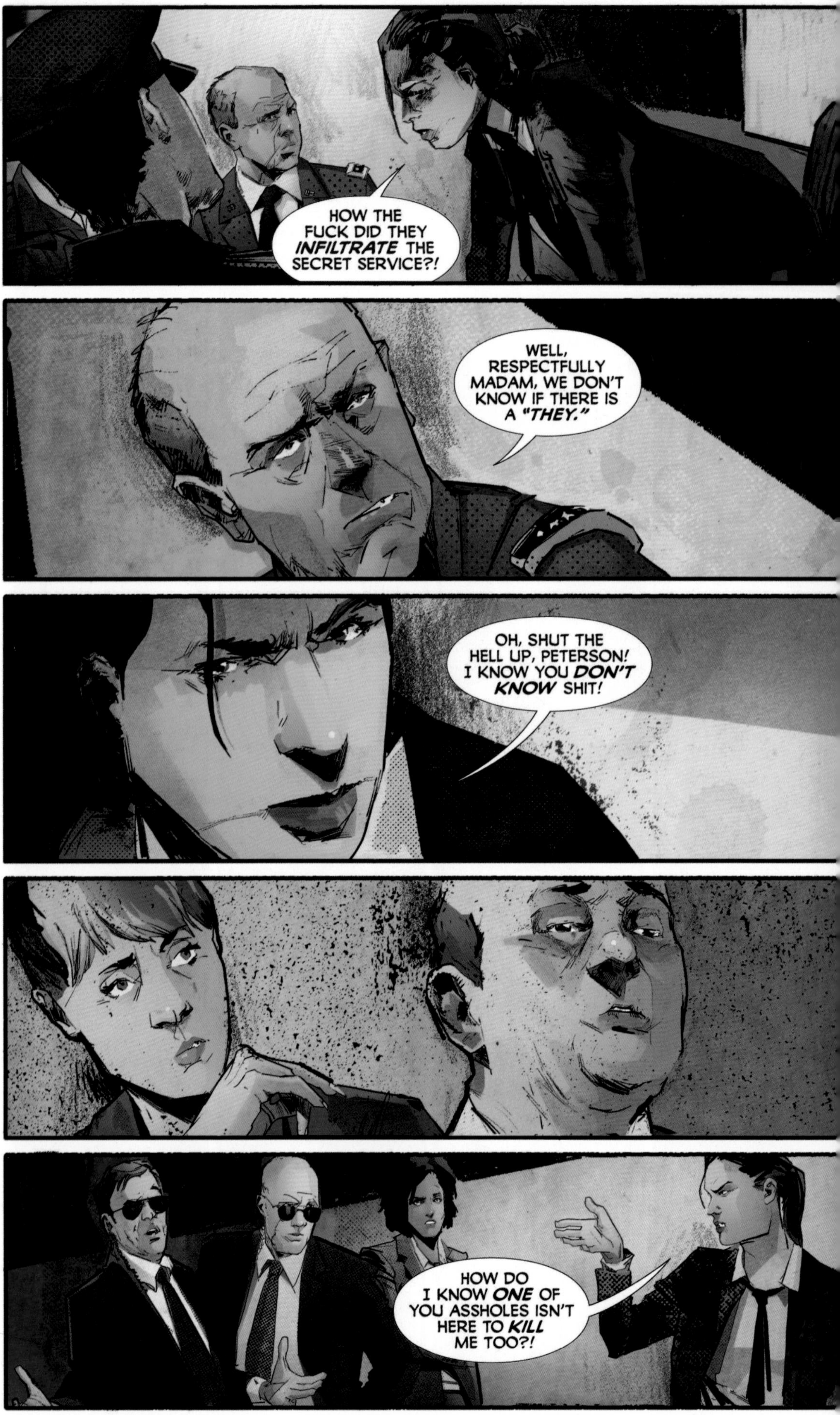
HOW THE FUCK DID THEY *INFILTRATE* THE SECRET SERVICE?!
WELL, RESPECTFULLY MADAM, WE DON'T KNOW IF THERE IS A *"THEY."*
OH, SHUT THE HELL UP, PETERSON! I KNOW YOU *DON'T KNOW* SHIT!
HOW DO I KNOW *ONE* OF YOU ASSHOLES ISN'T HERE TO *KILL* ME TOO?!

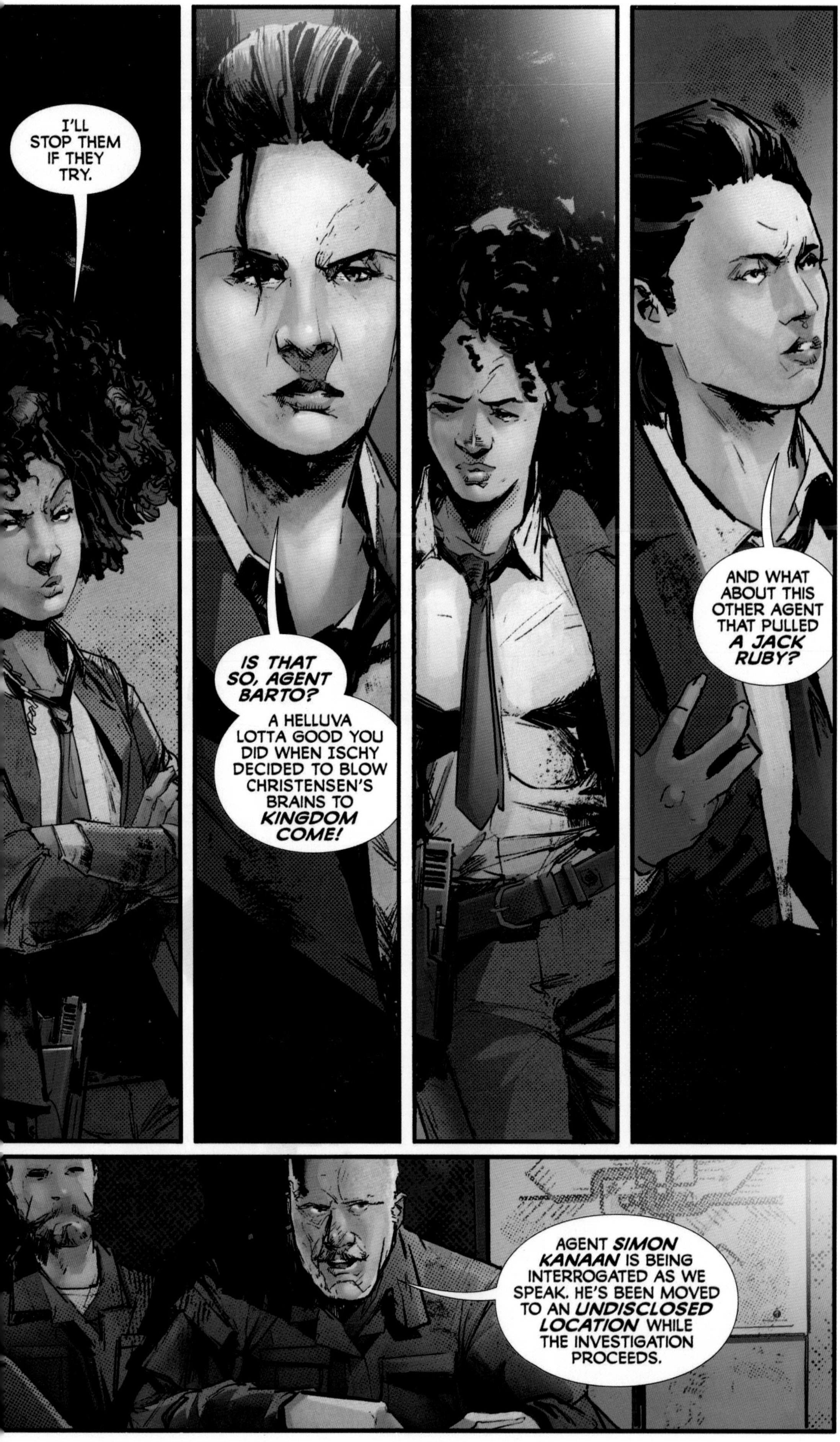
I'LL STOP THEM IF THEY TRY.
IS THAT SO, AGENT BARTO?
A HELLUVA LOTTA GOOD YOU DID WHEN ISCHY DECIDED TO BLOW CHRISTENSEN'S BRAINS TO KINGDOM COME!
AND WHAT ABOUT THIS OTHER AGENT THAT PULLED A JACK RUBY?
AGENT SIMON KANAAN IS BEING INTERROGATED AS WE SPEAK. HE'S BEEN MOVED TO AN UNDISCLOSED LOCATION WHILE THE INVESTIGATION PROCEEDS.

LET'S GO OVER THIS AGAIN. AT WHAT POINT DID YOU *DRAW* YOUR WEAPON?

LIKE I SAID BEFORE, WHEN I SAW AGENT ISCHY STEP TOWARDS THE PRESIDENT.

WHY DID YOU DECIDE TO *SHOOT* HIM INSTEAD OF *TACKLING* HIM?

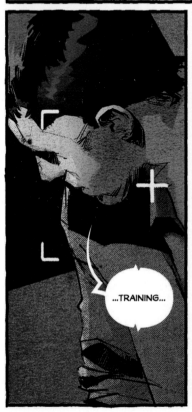

...TRAINING...

EXCUSE ME? WHAT WAS THAT? I DIDN'T *HEAR* YOU?

BECAUSE THAT'S WHAT I WAS *FUCKING TRAINED TO DO!*

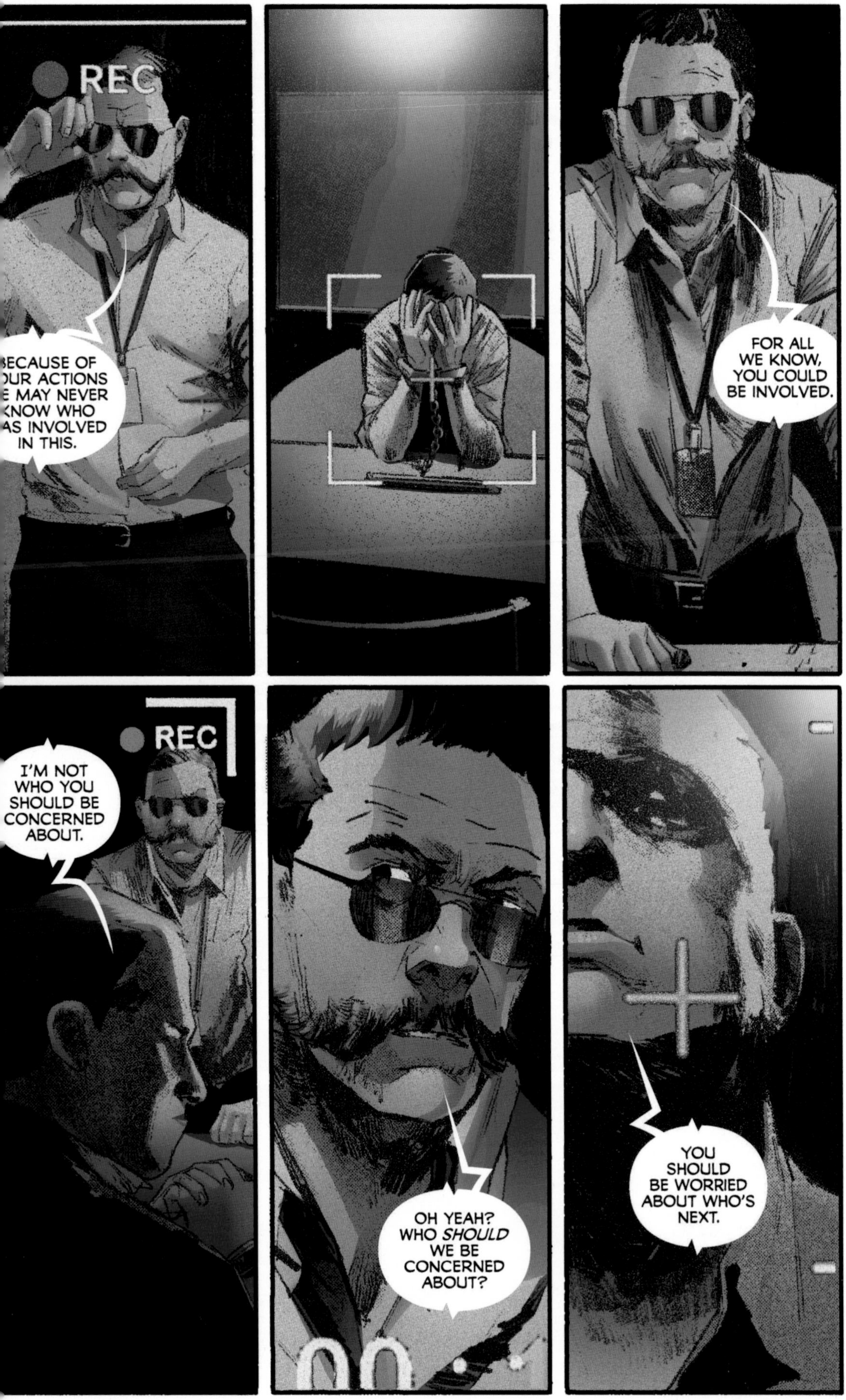
REC
ECAUSE OF UR ACTIONS E MAY NEVER KNOW WHO AS INVOLVED IN THIS.
FOR ALL WE KNOW, YOU COULD BE INVOLVED.
REC
I'M NOT WHO YOU SHOULD BE CONCERNED ABOUT.
OH YEAH? WHO *SHOULD* WE BE CONCERNED ABOUT?
YOU SHOULD BE WORRIED ABOUT WHO'S NEXT.

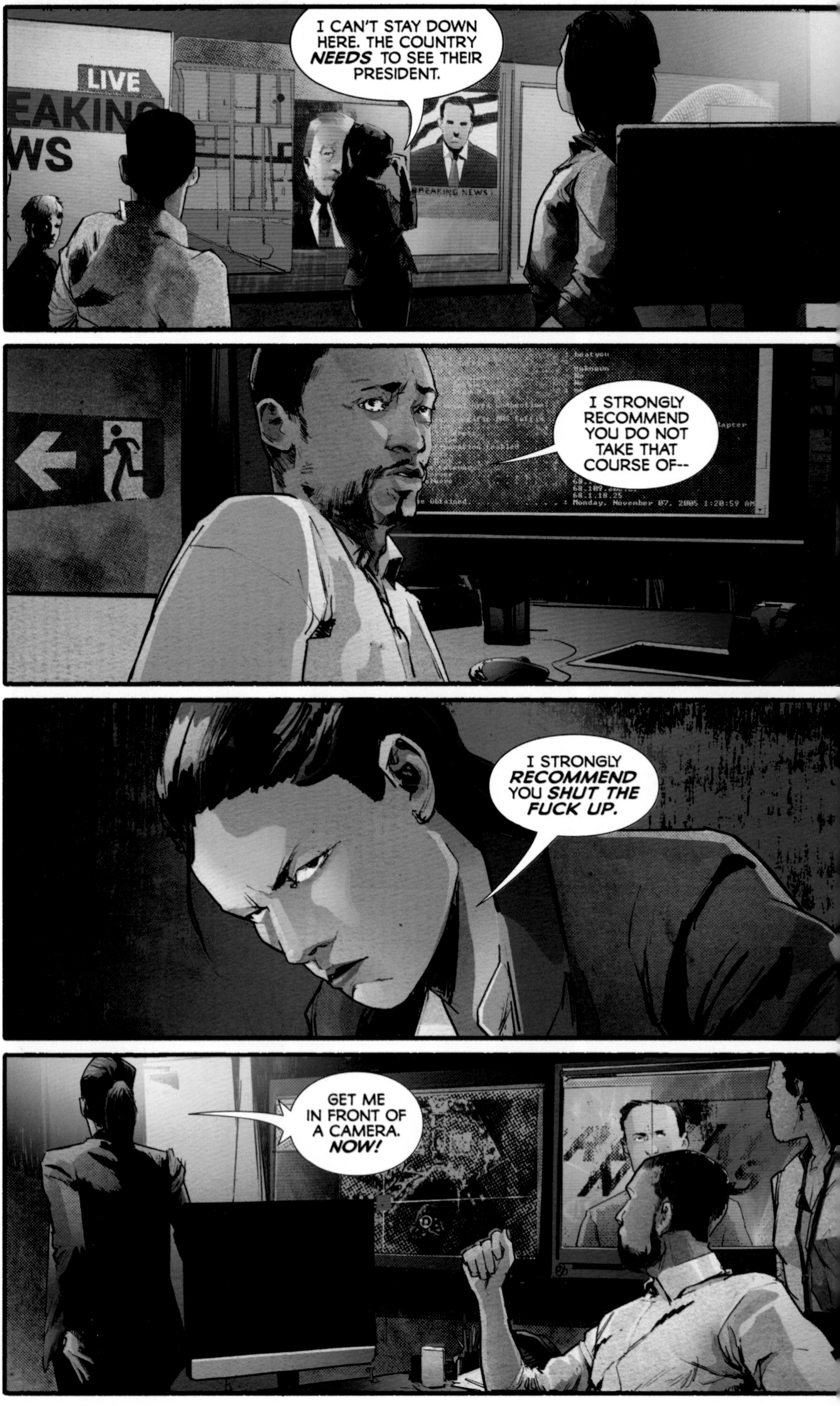
LIVE
I CAN'T STAY DOWN HERE. THE COUNTRY NEEDS TO SEE THEIR PRESIDENT.
I STRONGLY RECOMMEND YOU DO NOT TAKE THAT COURSE OF--
I STRONGLY RECOMMEND YOU SHUT THE FUCK UP.
GET ME IN FRONT OF A CAMERA. NOW!

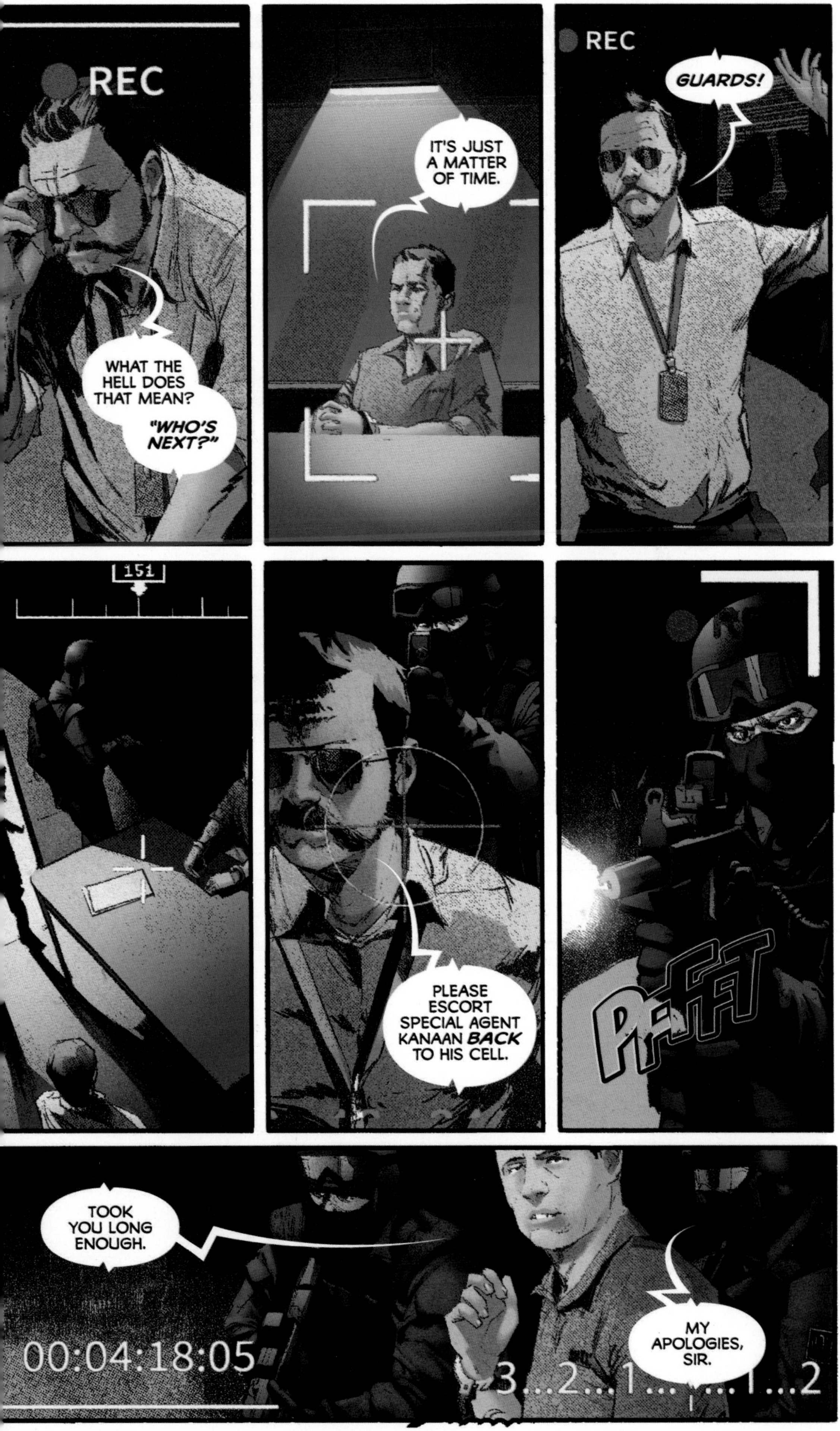
REC
WHAT THE HELL DOES THAT MEAN? "WHO'S NEXT?"
IT'S JUST A MATTER OF TIME.
REC
GUARDS!
151
PLEASE ESCORT SPECIAL AGENT KANAAN BACK TO HIS CELL.
PFFFT
TOOK YOU LONG ENOUGH.
MY APOLOGIES, SIR.
00:04:18:05
3...2...1... ...1...2

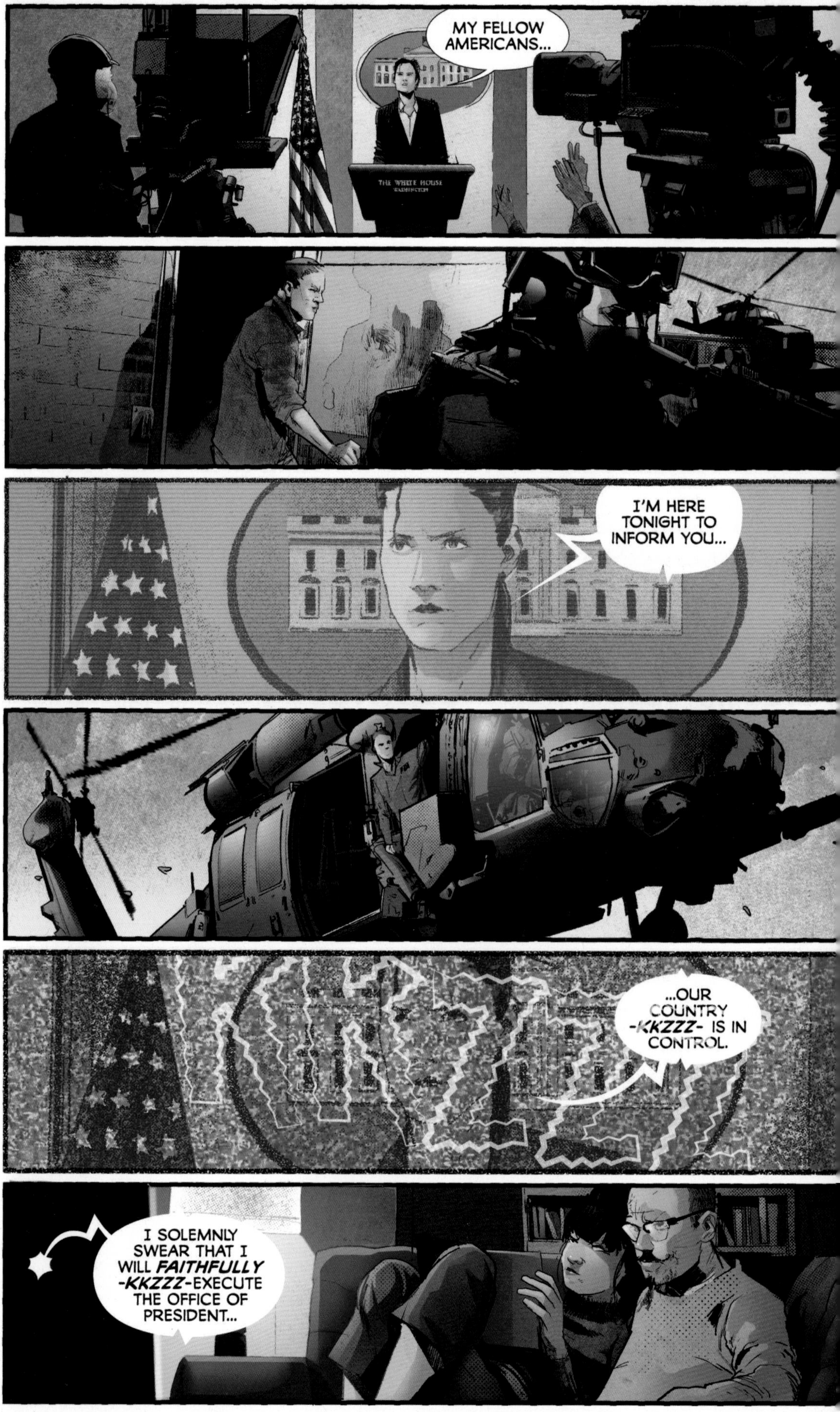

MY FELLOW AMERICANS...
THE WHITE HOUSE
I'M HERE TONIGHT TO INFORM YOU...
...OUR COUNTRY -KKZZZ- IS IN CONTROL.
I SOLEMNLY SWEAR THAT I WILL *FAITHFULLY* -*KKZZZ*-EXECUTE THE OFFICE OF PRESIDENT...

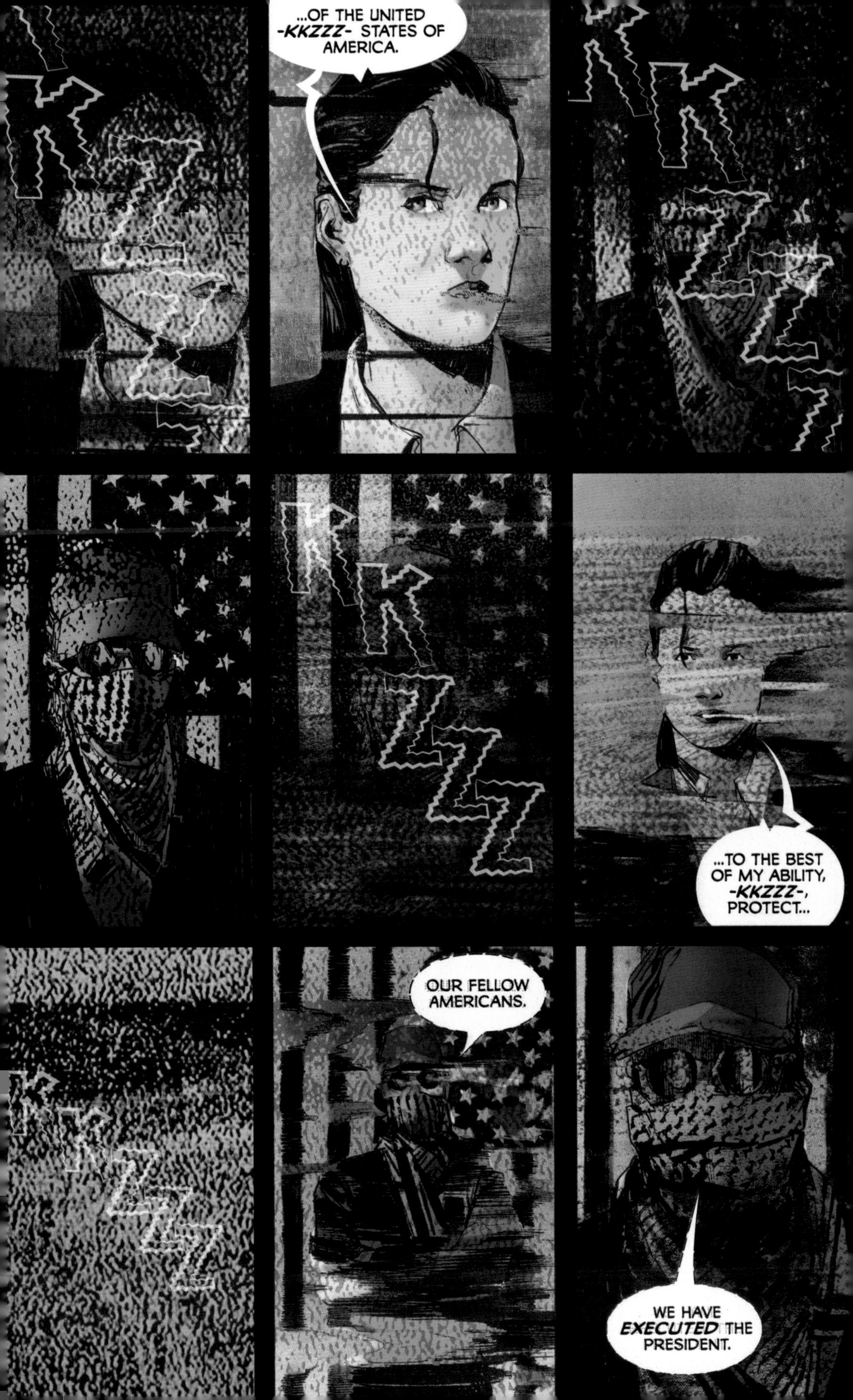
KKZZZ
...OF THE UNITED -KKZZZ- STATES OF AMERICA.
KKZZZ
KKZZZ
...TO THE BEST OF MY ABILITY, -KKZZZ-, PROTECT...
KKZZZ
OUR FELLOW AMERICANS.
WE HAVE EXECUTED THE PRESIDENT.

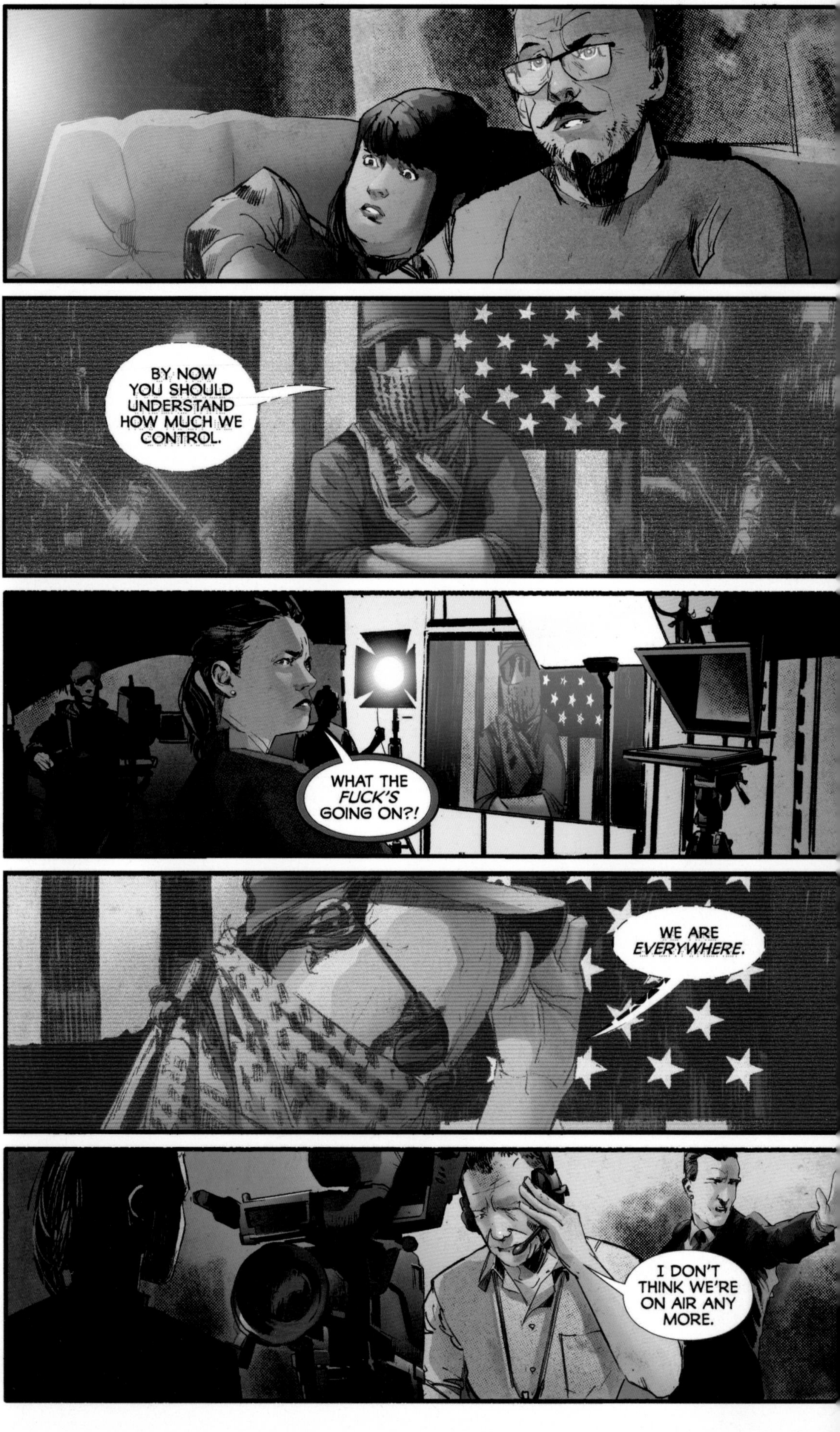
BY NOW YOU SHOULD UNDERSTAND HOW MUCH WE CONTROL.
WHAT THE *FUCK'S* GOING ON?!
WE ARE *EVERYWHERE.*
I DON'T THINK WE'RE ON AIR ANY MORE.

PRESIDENT CHRISTENSEN ADMITTED TO HIS CRIMES AND WAS PUNISHED.

JUSTICE WAS SERVED.

SHUT IT DOWN!

BUT THAT WAS ONLY THE BEGINNING.

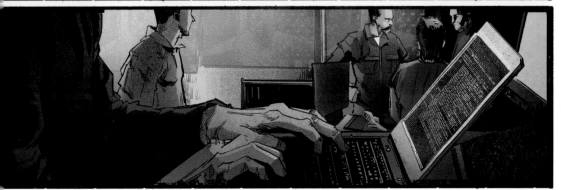

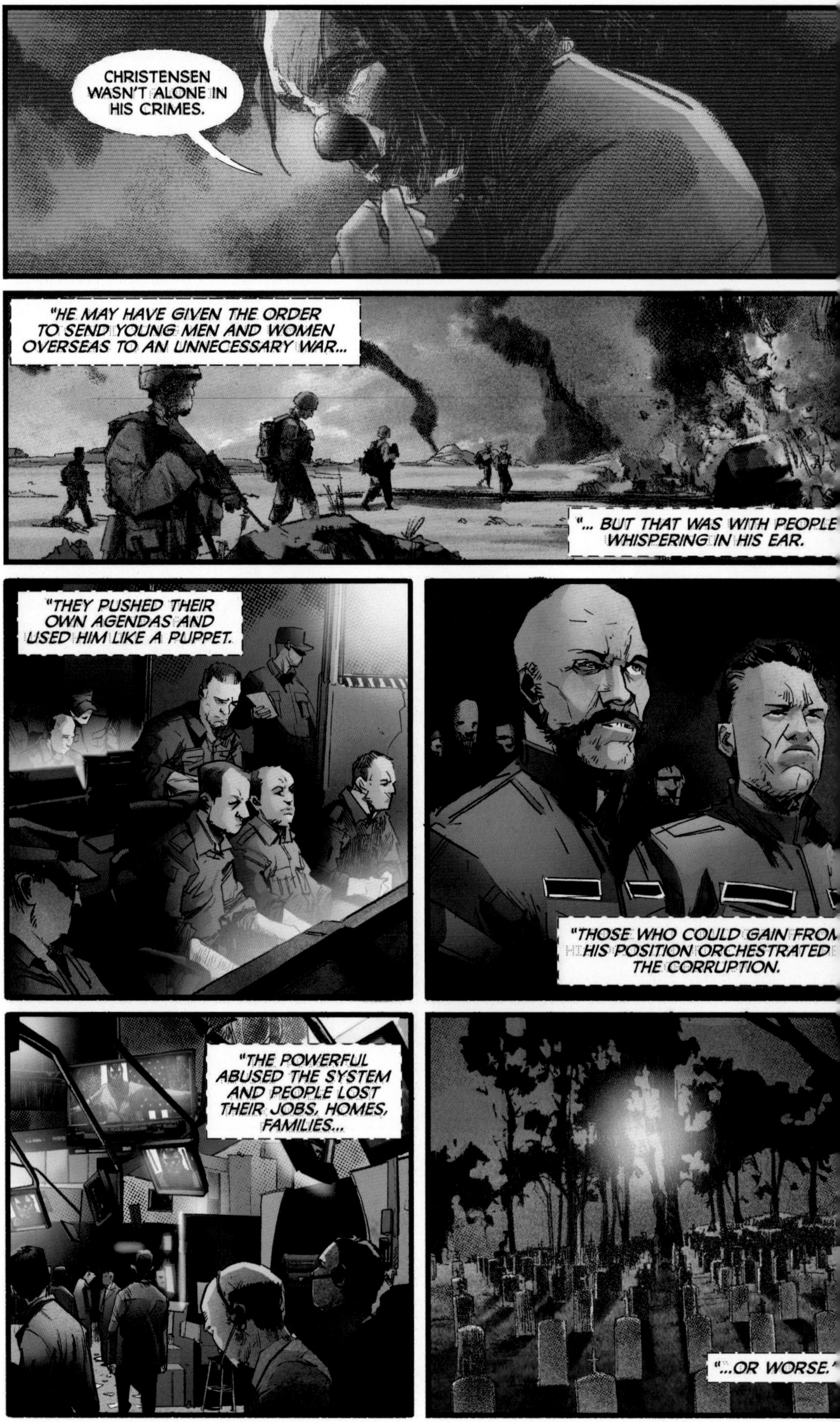
CHRISTENSEN WASN'T ALONE IN HIS CRIMES.
"HE MAY HAVE GIVEN THE ORDER TO SEND YOUNG MEN AND WOMEN OVERSEAS TO AN UNNECESSARY WAR...
"... BUT THAT WAS WITH PEOPLE WHISPERING IN HIS EAR.
"THEY PUSHED THEIR OWN AGENDAS AND USED HIM LIKE A PUPPET.
"THOSE WHO COULD GAIN FROM HIS POSITION ORCHESTRATED THE CORRUPTION.
"THE POWERFUL ABUSED THE SYSTEM AND PEOPLE LOST THEIR JOBS, HOMES, FAMILIES...
"...OR WORSE."

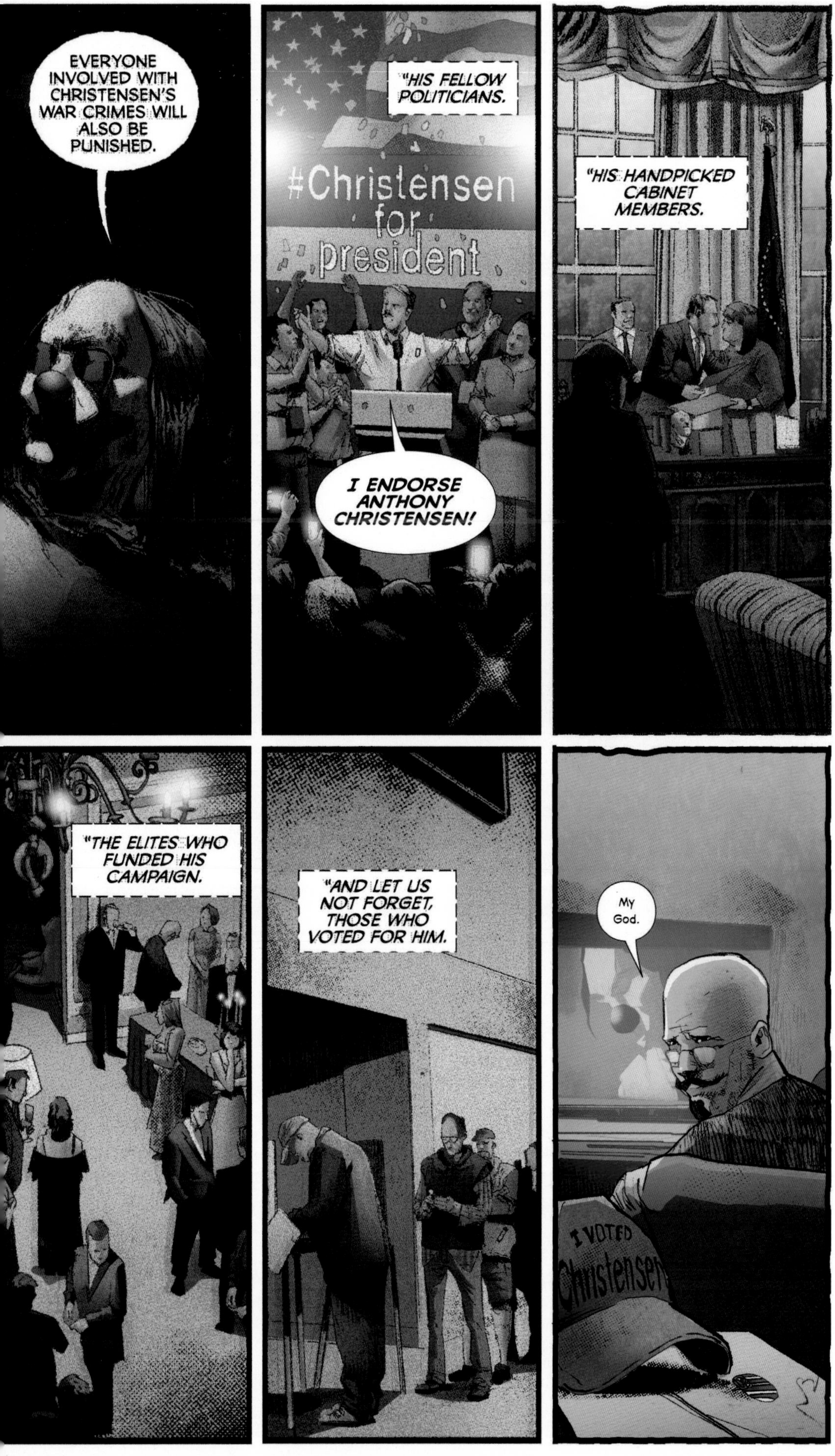
EVERYONE INVOLVED WITH CHRISTENSEN'S WAR CRIMES WILL ALSO BE PUNISHED.
"HIS FELLOW POLITICIANS.
#Christensen for president
I ENDORSE ANTHONY CHRISTENSEN!
"HIS HANDPICKED CABINET MEMBERS.
"THE ELITES WHO FUNDED HIS CAMPAIGN.
"AND LET US NOT FORGET, THOSE WHO VOTED FOR HIM.
My God.
I VOTED Christensen

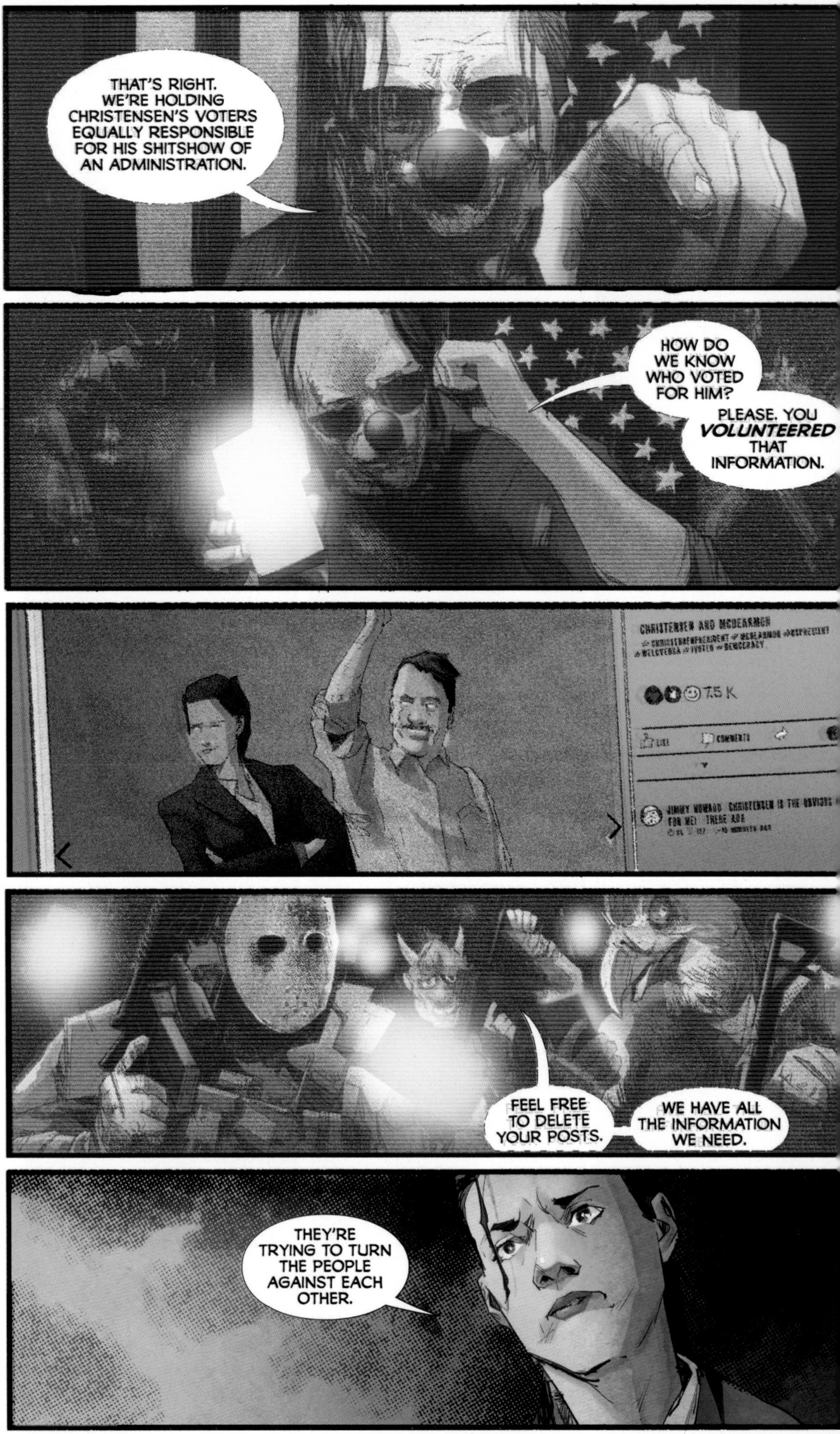

THAT'S RIGHT. WE'RE HOLDING CHRISTENSEN'S VOTERS EQUALLY RESPONSIBLE FOR HIS SHITSHOW OF AN ADMINISTRATION.
HOW DO WE KNOW WHO VOTED FOR HIM?
PLEASE. YOU *VOLUNTEERED* THAT INFORMATION.
CHRISTENSEN AND MCDEARMON
7.5 K
FEEL FREE TO DELETE YOUR POSTS.
WE HAVE ALL THE INFORMATION WE NEED.
THEY'RE TRYING TO TURN THE PEOPLE AGAINST EACH OTHER.

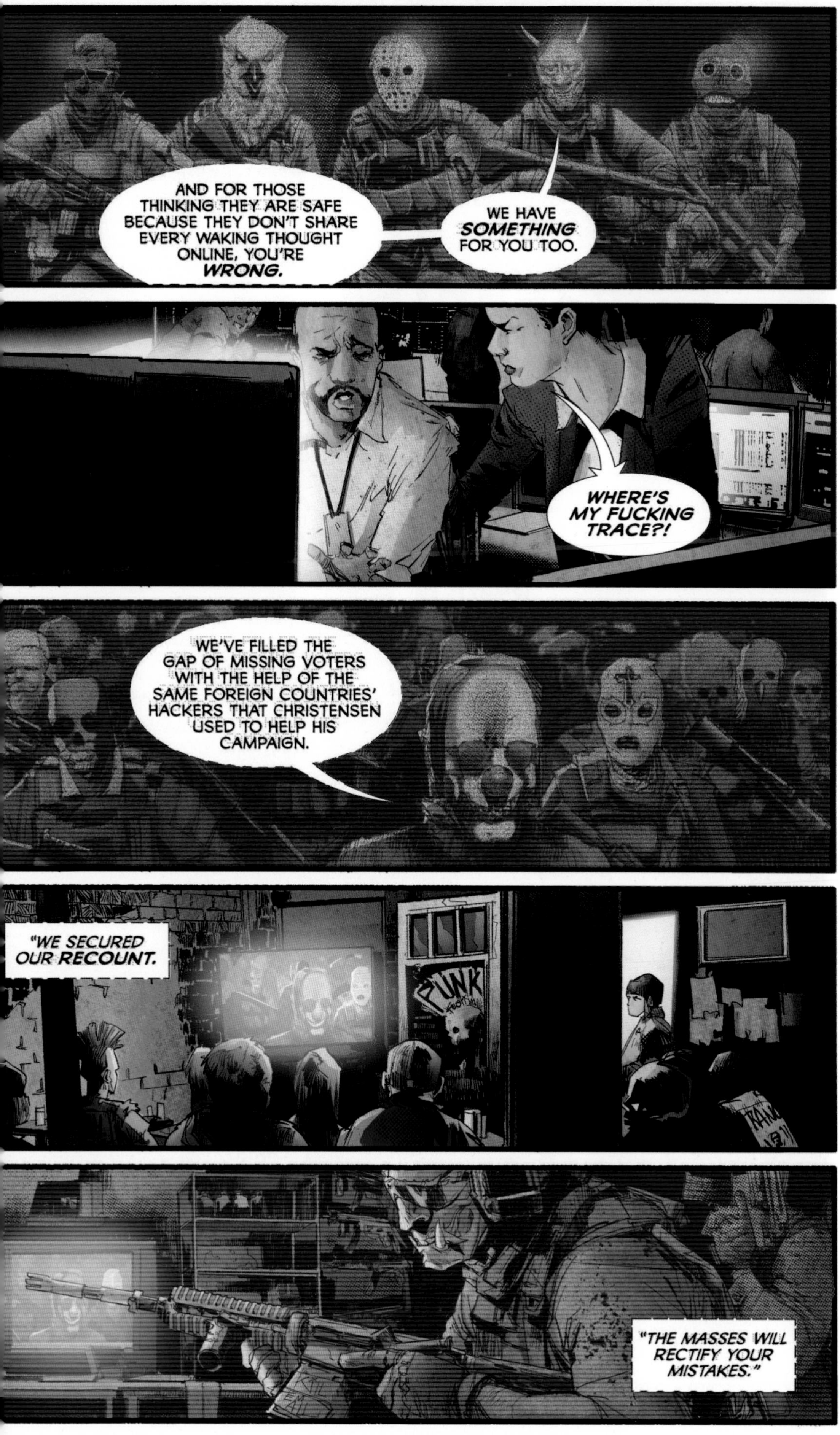

AND FOR THOSE THINKING THEY ARE SAFE BECAUSE THEY DON'T SHARE EVERY WAKING THOUGHT ONLINE, YOU'RE WRONG.
WE HAVE SOMETHING FOR YOU TOO.
WHERE'S MY FUCKING TRACE?!
WE'VE FILLED THE GAP OF MISSING VOTERS WITH THE HELP OF THE SAME FOREIGN COUNTRIES' HACKERS THAT CHRISTENSEN USED TO HELP HIS CAMPAIGN.
"WE SECURED OUR RECOUNT.
PUNK
"THE MASSES WILL RECTIFY YOUR MISTAKES."

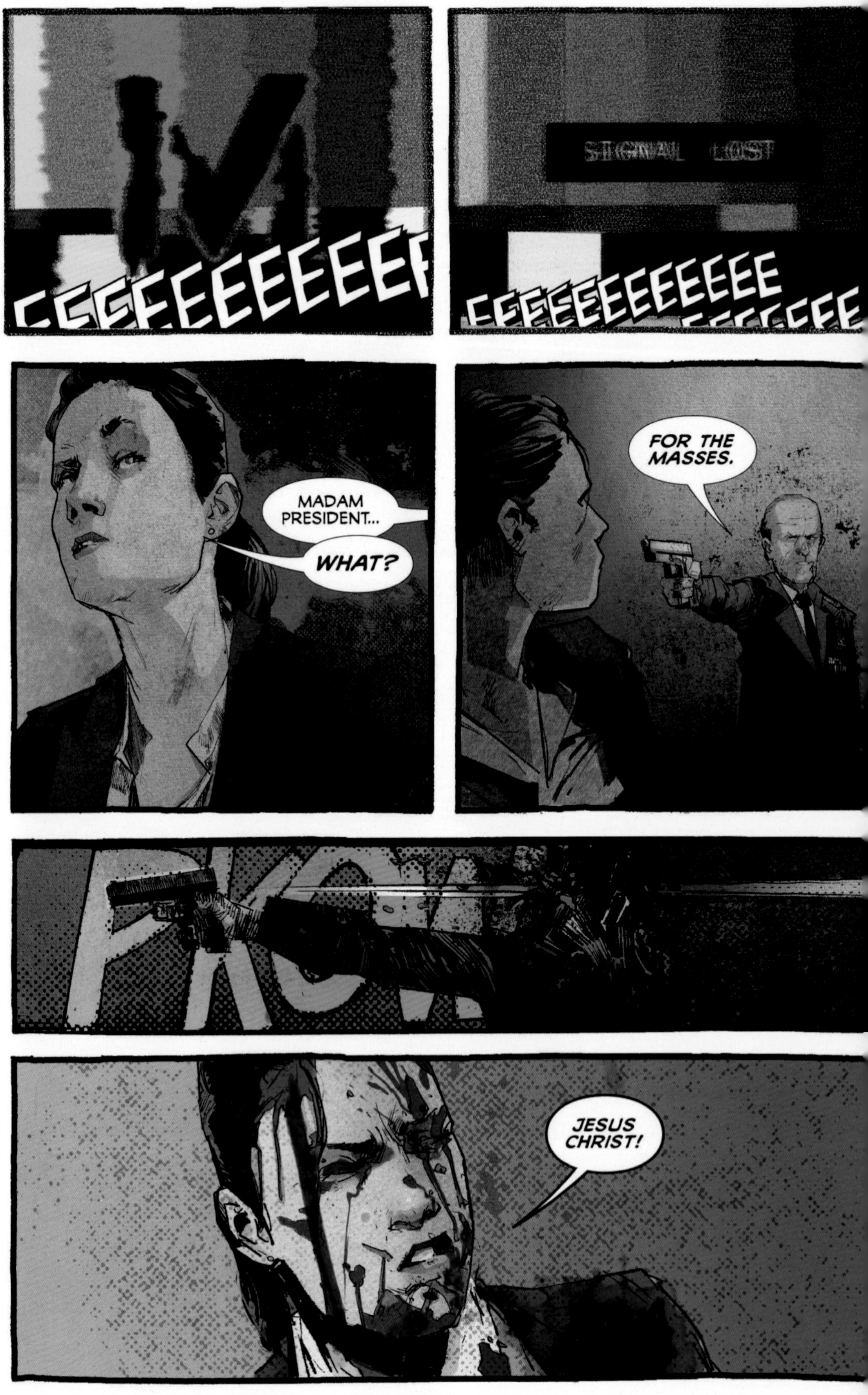
SIGNAL LOST
MADAM PRESIDENT...
WHAT?
FOR THE MASSES.
JESUS CHRIST!

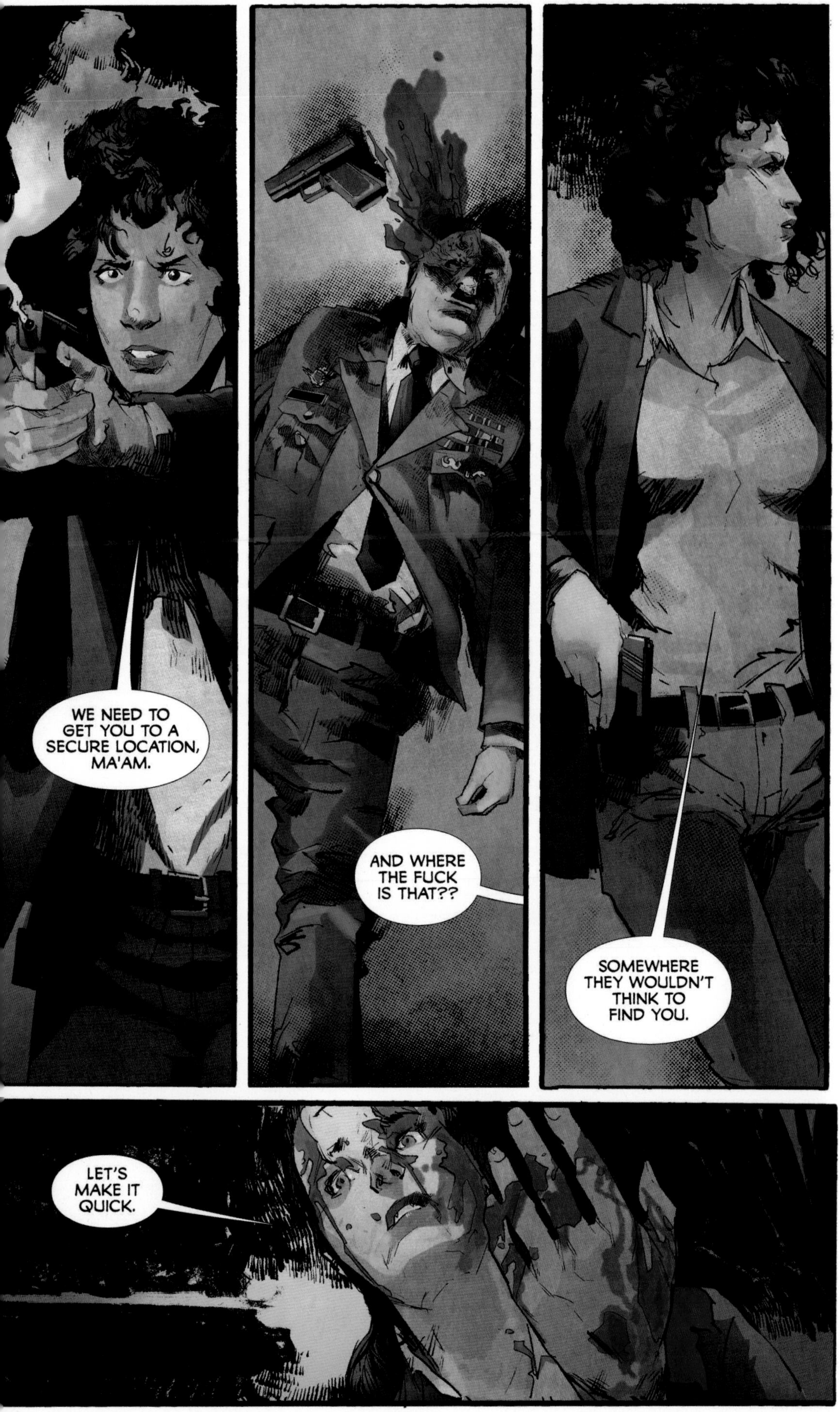
WE NEED TO GET YOU TO A SECURE LOCATION, MA'AM.
AND WHERE THE FUCK IS THAT??
SOMEWHERE THEY WOULDN'T THINK TO FIND YOU.
LET'S MAKE IT QUICK.

"THE COUNTRY IS ABOUT TO BE AT WAR."

PROUD PARENT OF A VETERAN

REELECT CHRISTMORE

VETERAN

NEXT ISSUE:

"OFF TO COLLEGE

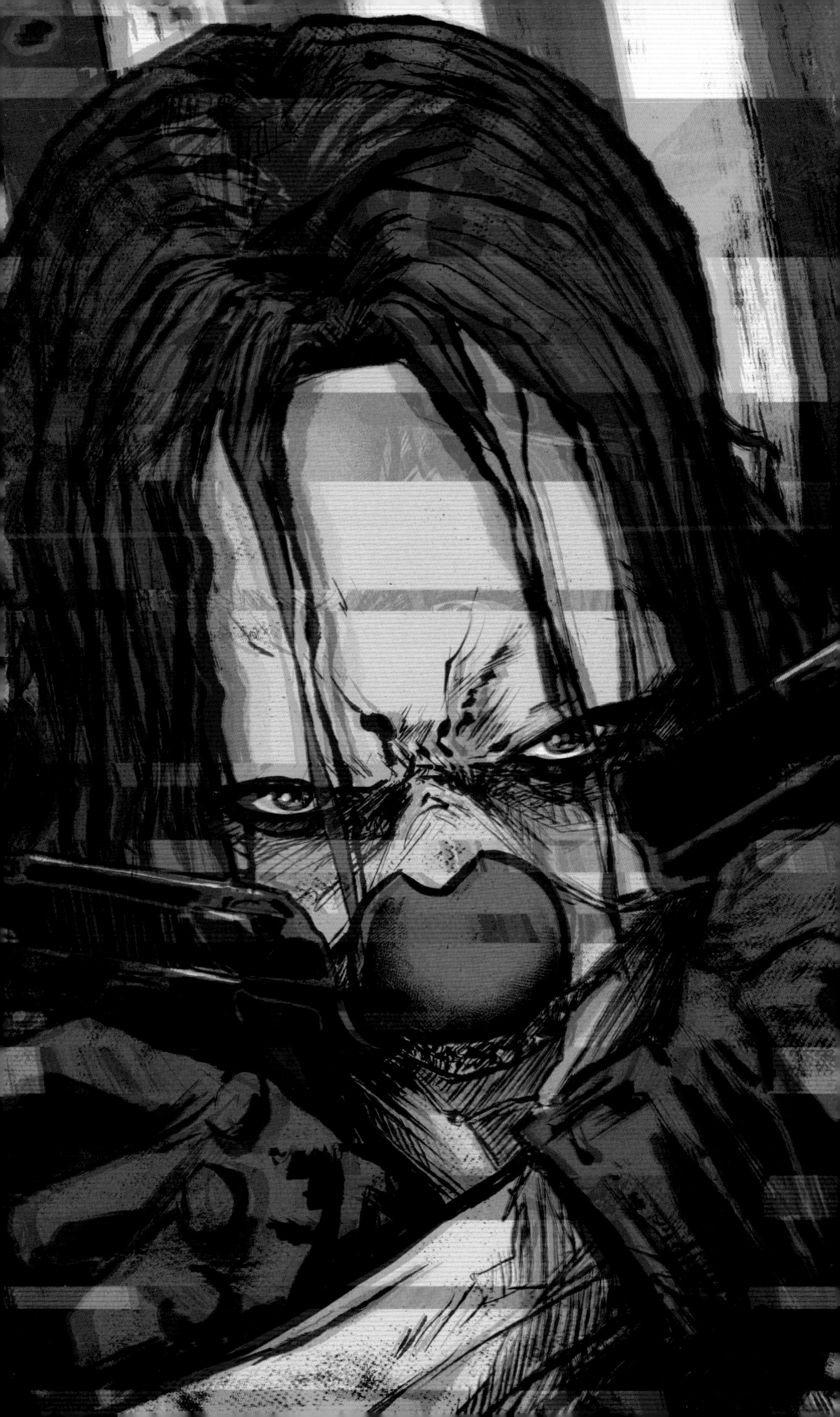

CHAPTER 2

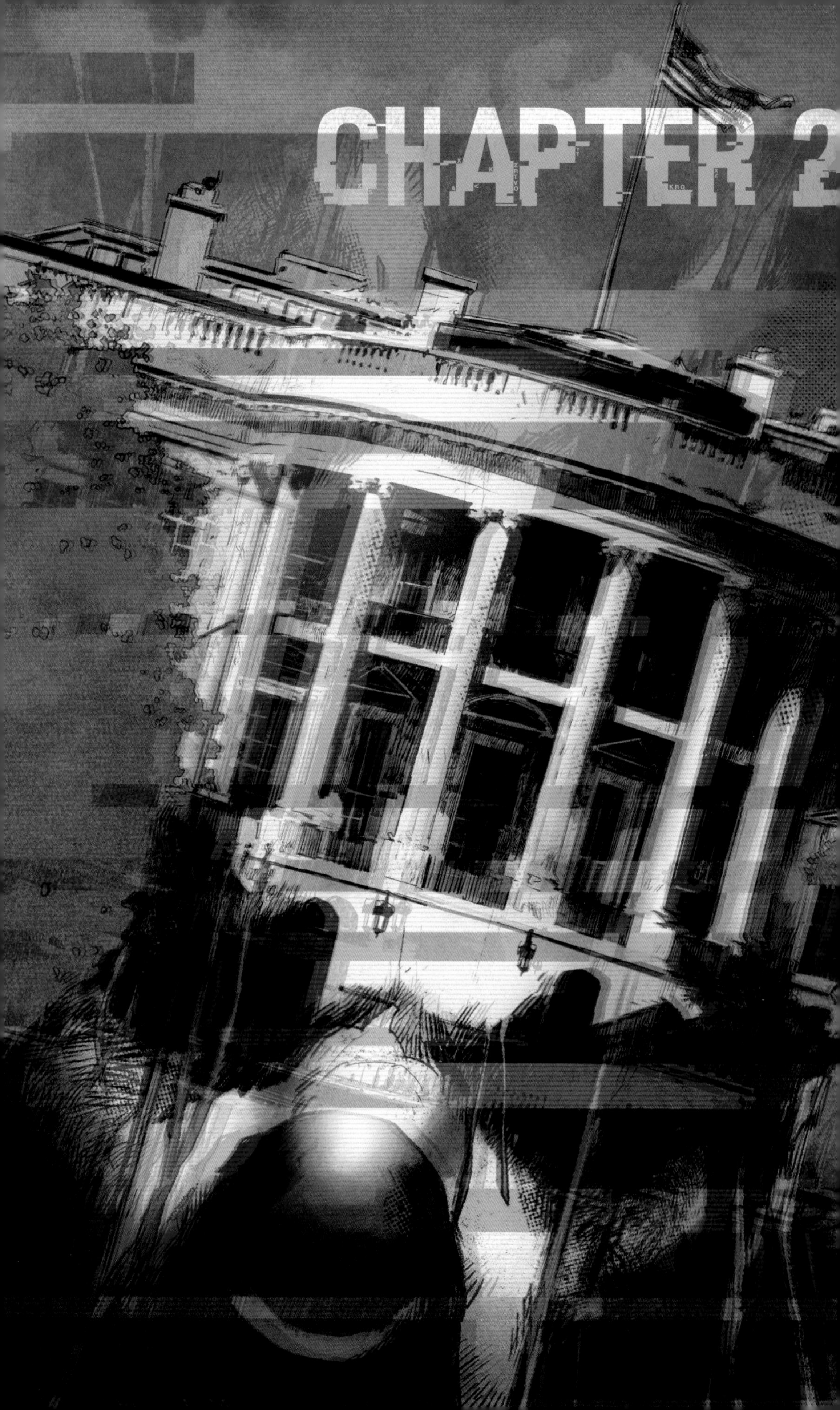

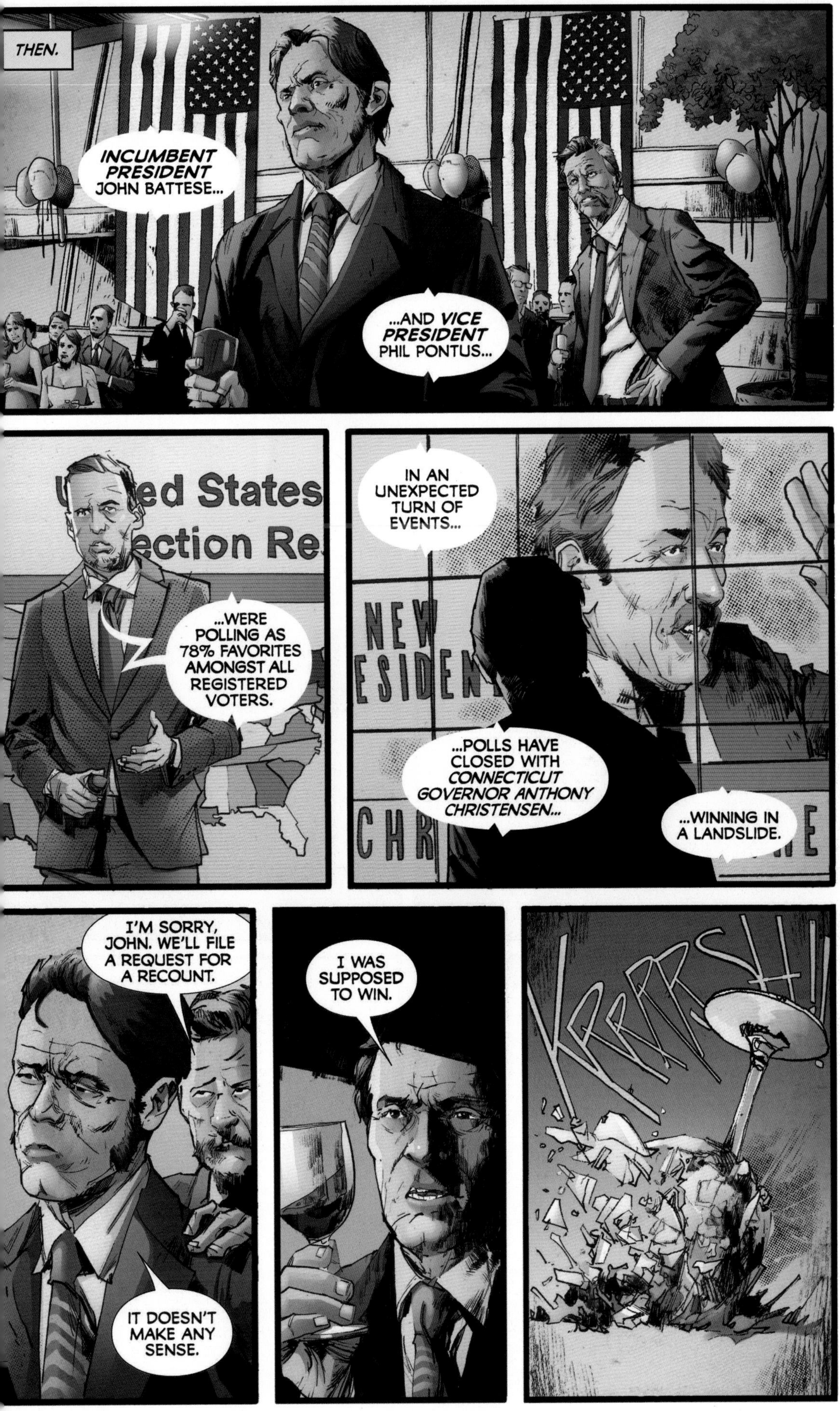
THEN.
INCUMBENT PRESIDENT JOHN BATTESE...
...AND VICE PRESIDENT PHIL PONTUS...
ed States
ection Re
...WERE POLLING AS 78% FAVORITES AMONGST ALL REGISTERED VOTERS.
IN AN UNEXPECTED TURN OF EVENTS...
NEW
ESIDEN
...POLLS HAVE CLOSED WITH CONNECTICUT GOVERNOR ANTHONY CHRISTENSEN...
CHR
...WINNING IN A LANDSLIDE.
I'M SORRY, JOHN. WE'LL FILE A REQUEST FOR A RECOUNT.
IT DOESN'T MAKE ANY SENSE.
I WAS SUPPOSED TO WIN.
KRRRRSH!!

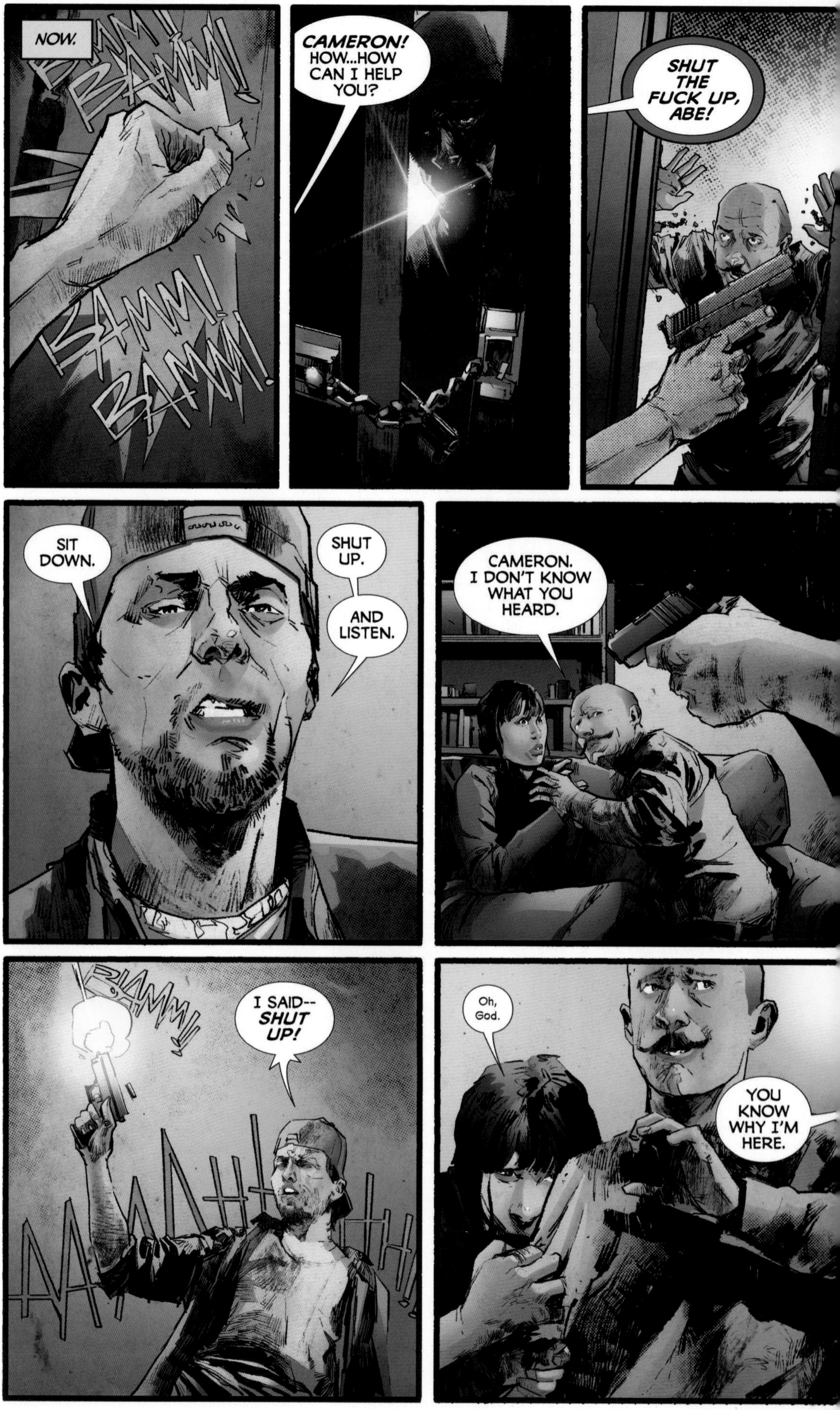
NOW.
BAMM! BAMM!
BAMM! BAMM!
CAMERON! HOW...HOW CAN I HELP YOU?
SHUT THE FUCK UP, ABE!
SIT DOWN.
SHUT UP.
AND LISTEN.
CAMERON. I DON'T KNOW WHAT YOU HEARD.
BLAMM!!
AAAHHH!!
I SAID-- SHUT UP!
Oh, God.
YOU KNOW WHY I'M HERE.

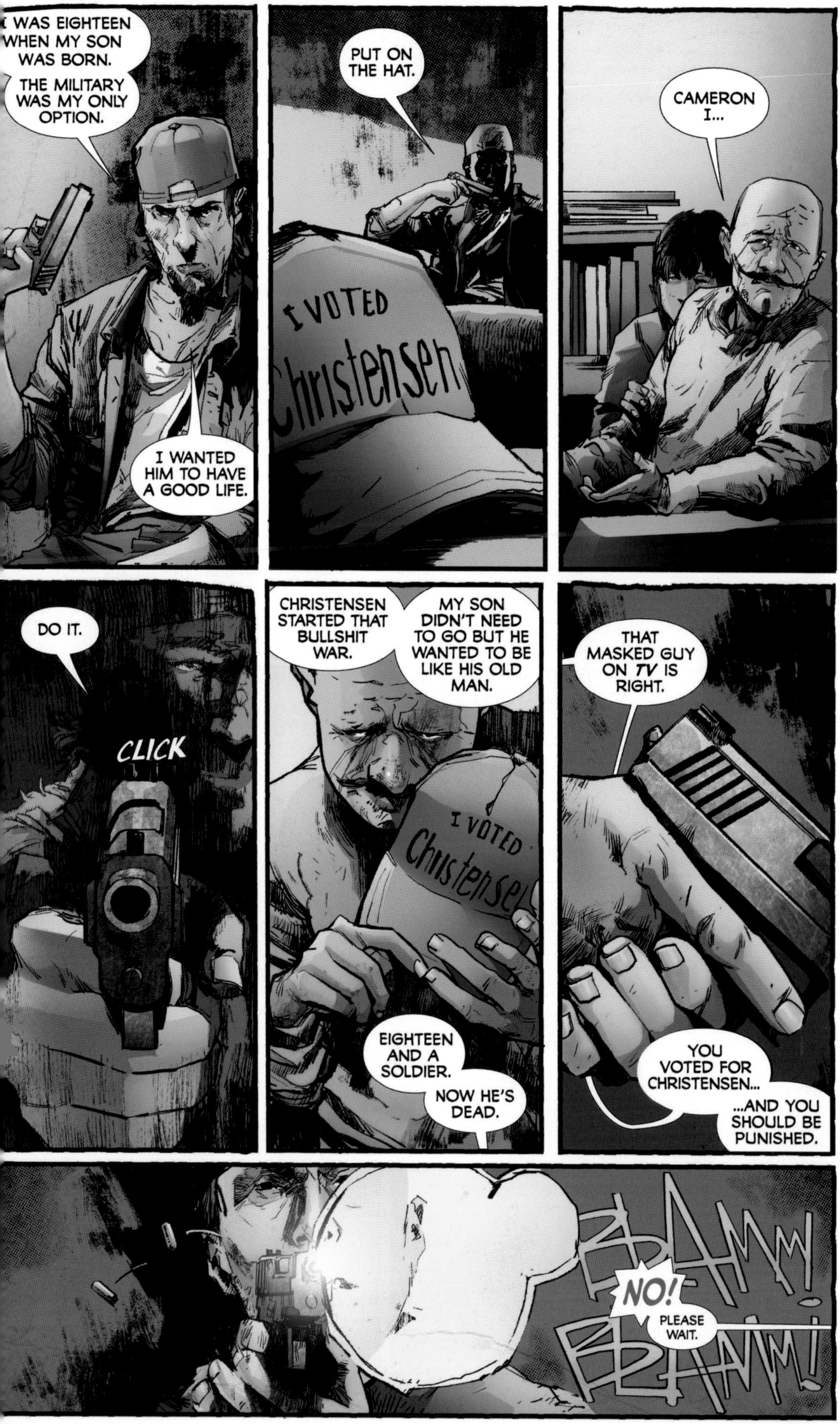
I WAS EIGHTEEN WHEN MY SON WAS BORN.
THE MILITARY WAS MY ONLY OPTION.
I WANTED HIM TO HAVE A GOOD LIFE.
PUT ON THE HAT.
I VOTED Christensen
CAMERON I...
DO IT.
CLICK
CHRISTENSEN STARTED THAT BULLSHIT WAR.
MY SON DIDN'T NEED TO GO BUT HE WANTED TO BE LIKE HIS OLD MAN.
I VOTED Christensen
EIGHTEEN AND A SOLDIER.
NOW HE'S DEAD.
THAT MASKED GUY ON TV IS RIGHT.
YOU VOTED FOR CHRISTENSEN...
...AND YOU SHOULD BE PUNISHED.
BLAMM
NO!
PLEASE WAIT.
BLAMM!

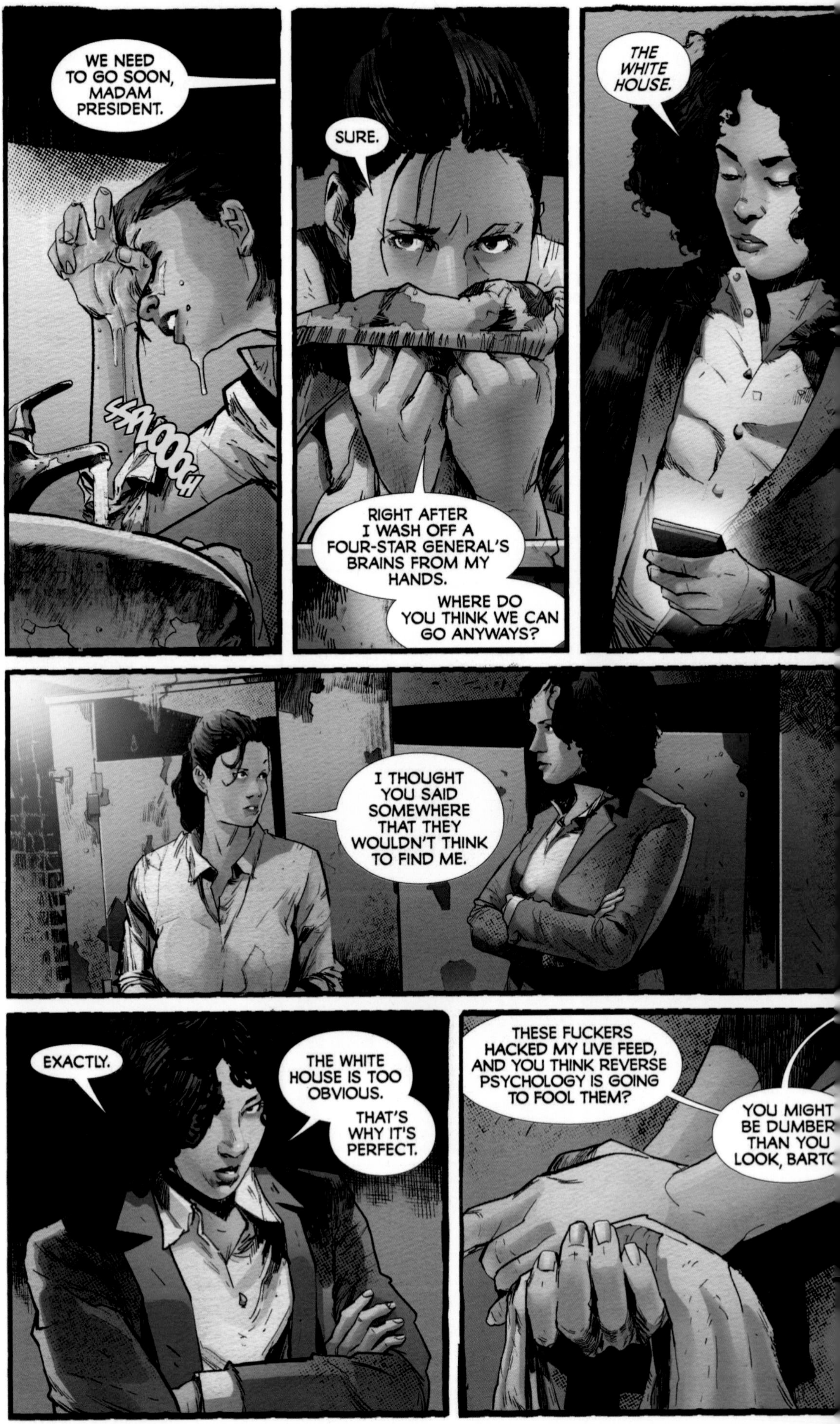
WE NEED TO GO SOON, MADAM PRESIDENT.
SSPLOOOCH
SURE.
RIGHT AFTER I WASH OFF A FOUR-STAR GENERAL'S BRAINS FROM MY HANDS.
WHERE DO YOU THINK WE CAN GO ANYWAYS?
THE WHITE HOUSE.
I THOUGHT YOU SAID SOMEWHERE THAT THEY WOULDN'T THINK TO FIND ME.
EXACTLY.
THE WHITE HOUSE IS TOO OBVIOUS.
THAT'S WHY IT'S PERFECT.
THESE FUCKERS HACKED MY LIVE FEED, AND YOU THINK REVERSE PSYCHOLOGY IS GOING TO FOOL THEM?
YOU MIGHT BE DUMBER THAN YOU LOOK, BARTO

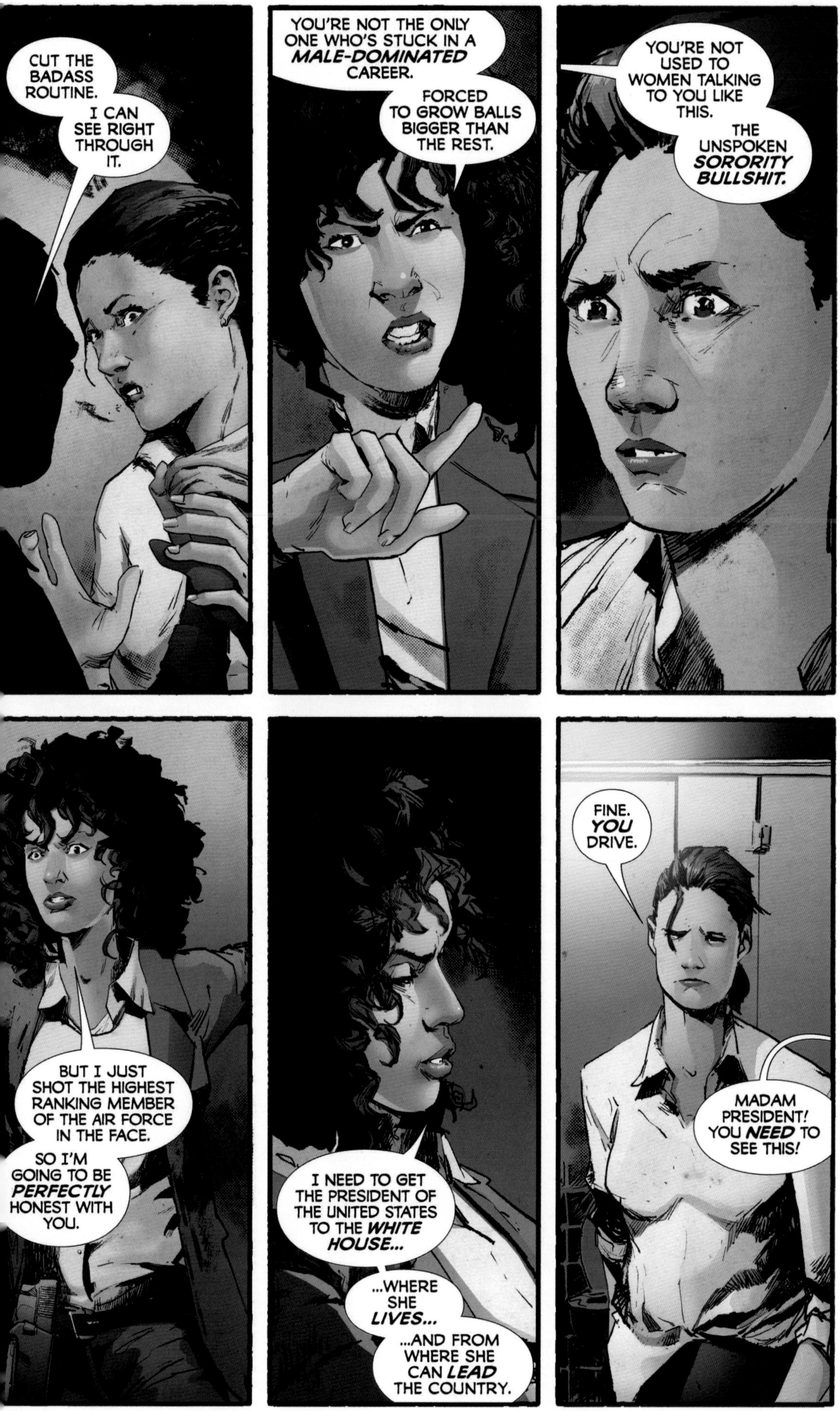
CUT THE BADASS ROUTINE.
I CAN SEE RIGHT THROUGH IT.
YOU'RE NOT THE ONLY ONE WHO'S STUCK IN A *MALE-DOMINATED* CAREER.
FORCED TO GROW BALLS BIGGER THAN THE REST.
YOU'RE NOT USED TO WOMEN TALKING TO YOU LIKE THIS.
THE UNSPOKEN *SORORITY BULLSHIT.*
BUT I JUST SHOT THE HIGHEST RANKING MEMBER OF THE AIR FORCE IN THE FACE.
SO I'M GOING TO BE *PERFECTLY* HONEST WITH YOU.
I NEED TO GET THE PRESIDENT OF THE UNITED STATES TO THE *WHITE HOUSE...*
...WHERE SHE *LIVES...*
...AND FROM WHERE SHE CAN *LEAD* THE COUNTRY.
FINE. *YOU* DRIVE.
MADAM PRESIDENT! YOU *NEED* TO SEE THIS!

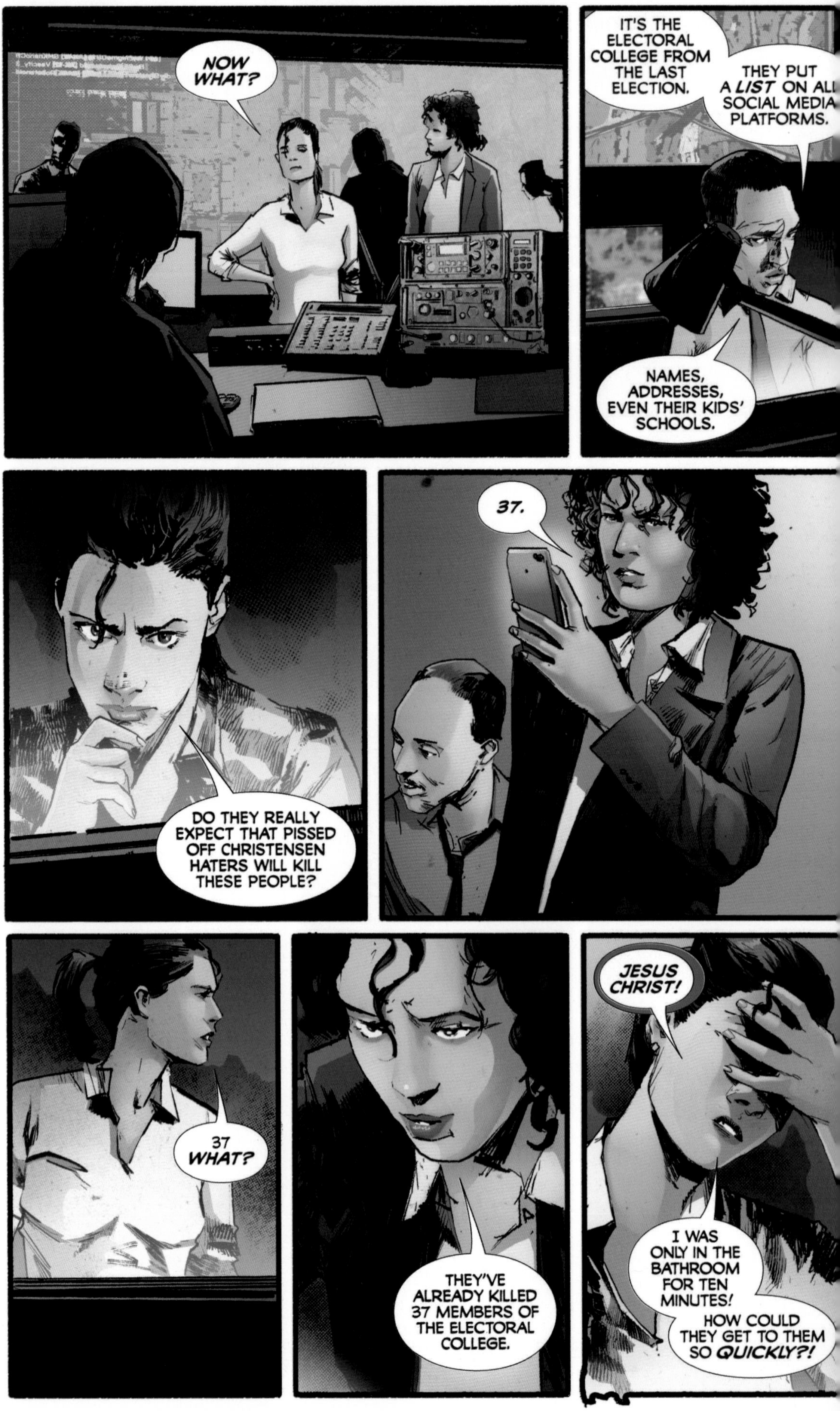
NOW WHAT?
IT'S THE ELECTORAL COLLEGE FROM THE LAST ELECTION.
THEY PUT A LIST ON ALL SOCIAL MEDIA PLATFORMS.
NAMES, ADDRESSES, EVEN THEIR KIDS' SCHOOLS.
DO THEY REALLY EXPECT THAT PISSED OFF CHRISTENSEN HATERS WILL KILL THESE PEOPLE?
37.
37 WHAT?
THEY'VE ALREADY KILLED 37 MEMBERS OF THE ELECTORAL COLLEGE.
JESUS CHRIST!
I WAS ONLY IN THE BATHROOM FOR TEN MINUTES!
HOW COULD THEY GET TO THEM SO QUICKLY?!

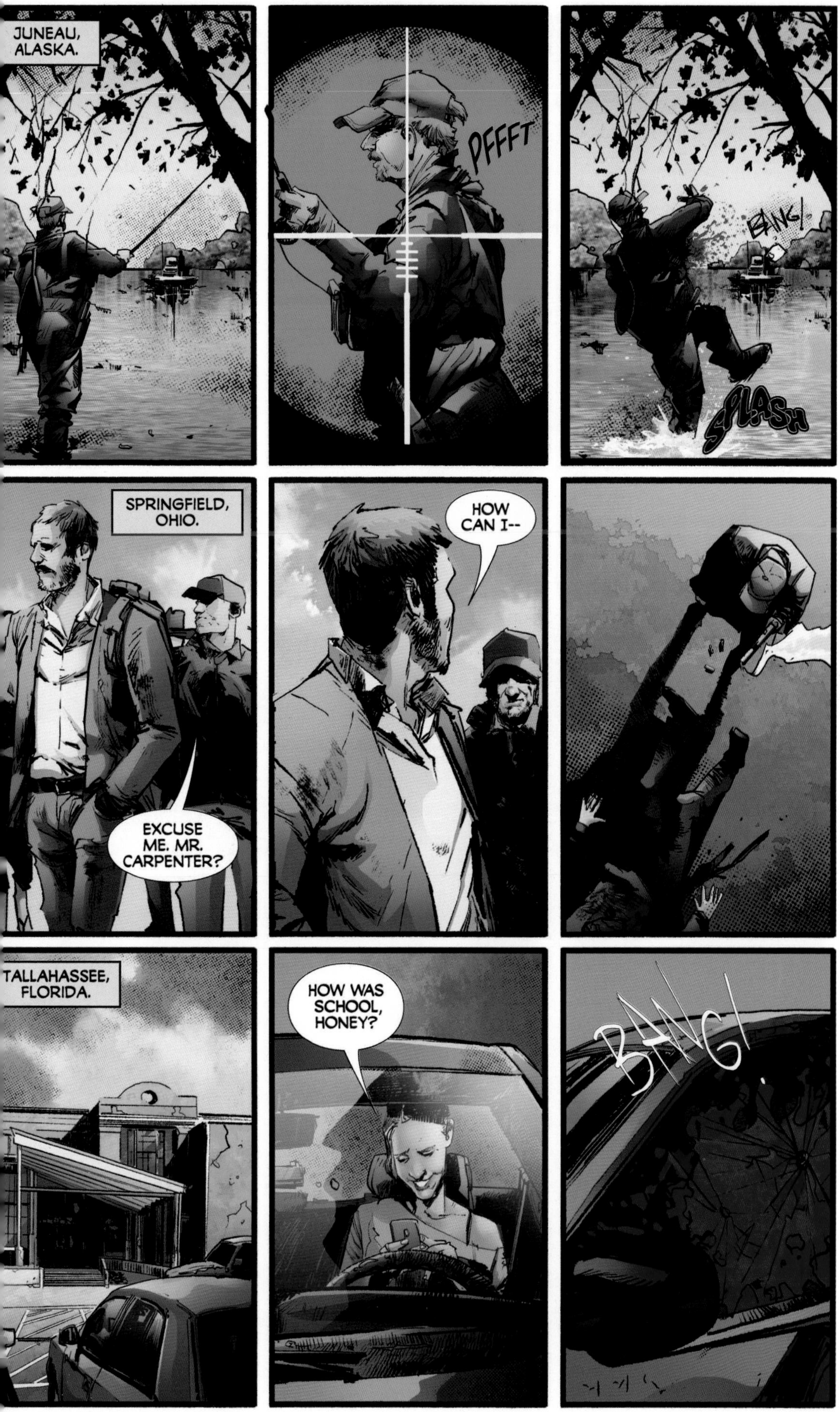
JUNEAU, ALASKA.
PFFFT
BANG!
SPLASH
SPRINGFIELD, OHIO.
EXCUSE ME. MR. CARPENTER?
HOW CAN I--
TALLAHASSEE, FLORIDA.
HOW WAS SCHOOL, HONEY?
BANG!

OKAY, MADAM PRESIDENT. LET'S GO.

WAIT! MATTHEW RODGERS.

HIS HOME IS ON THE WAY TO THE *WHITE HOUSE.*

MADAM PRESIDENT. WE DON'T HAVE TIME FOR A CARPOOL.

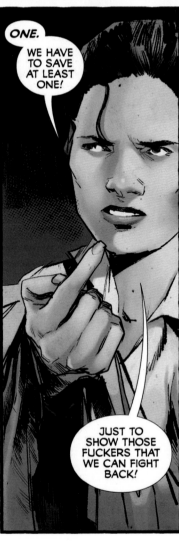

ONE.

WE HAVE TO SAVE AT LEAST ONE!

JUST TO SHOW THOSE FUCKERS THAT WE CAN FIGHT BACK!

THIS ASSHOLE BETTER BE WORTH IT.

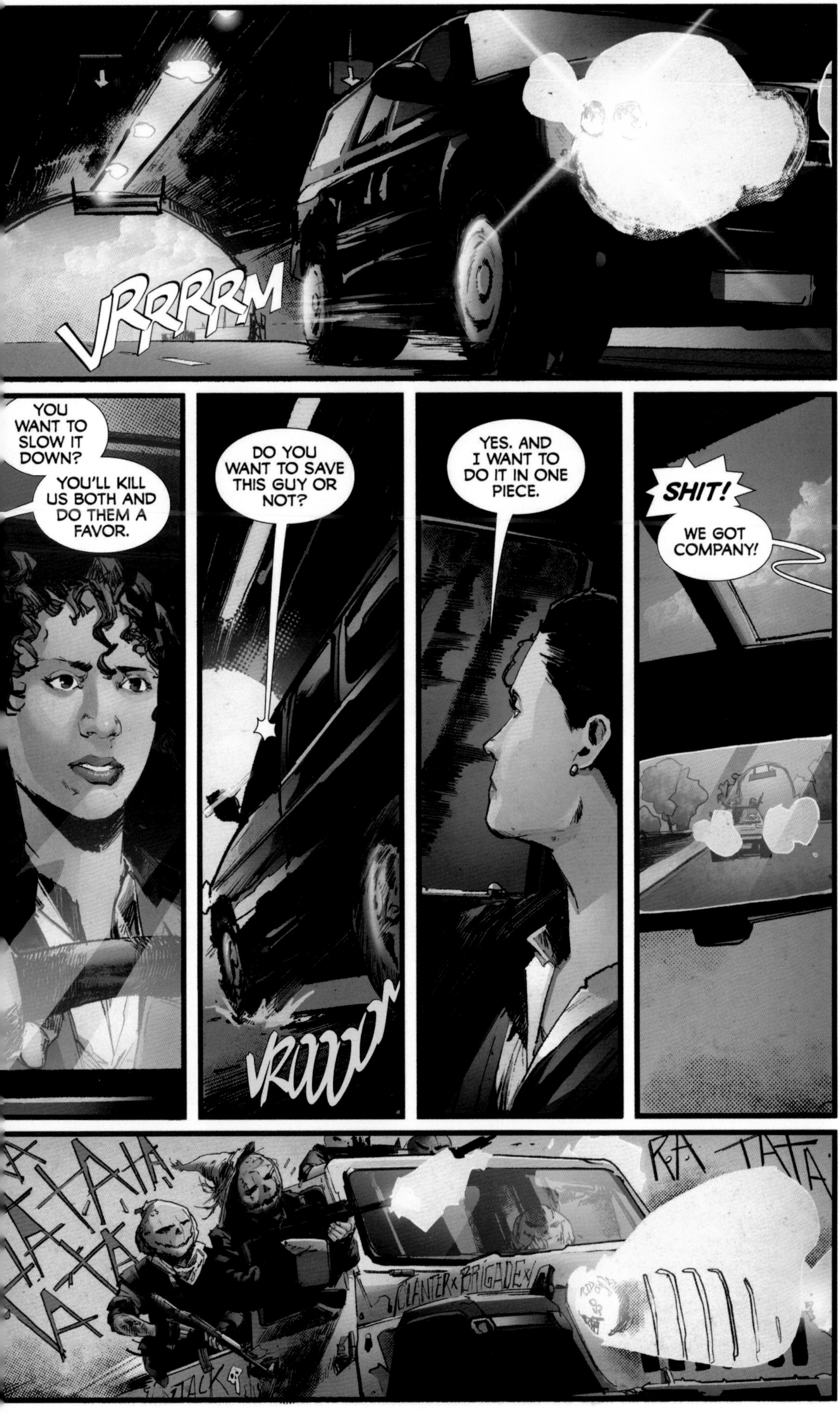
VRRRRM
YOU WANT TO SLOW IT DOWN?
YOU'LL KILL US BOTH AND DO THEM A FAVOR.
DO YOU WANT TO SAVE THIS GUY OR NOT?
VROOOOOM
YES. AND I WANT TO DO IT IN ONE PIECE.
SHIT!
WE GOT COMPANY!
RA TATA

KRAK

GODDAMN! THEY MUST HAVE BEEN WAITING FOR US TO LEAVE THE COMPOUND!

HOW MUCH *DAMAGE* CAN THIS CAR TAKE!?

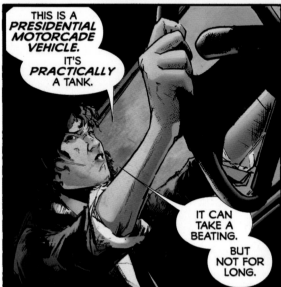

THIS IS A *PRESIDENTIAL MOTORCADE VEHICLE.* IT'S *PRACTICALLY* A TANK.

IT CAN TAKE A BEATING.

BUT NOT FOR LONG.

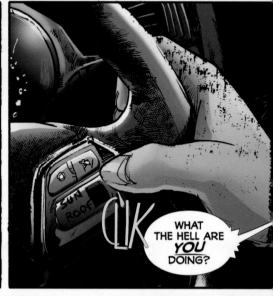

CLIK

WHAT THE HELL ARE *YOU* DOING?

CRUISE CONTROL IS ON. *GRAB* THE WHEEL.

HOLY SHIT!

PTING!

BANG! / RATATA RATATA

BANG!

KRAK

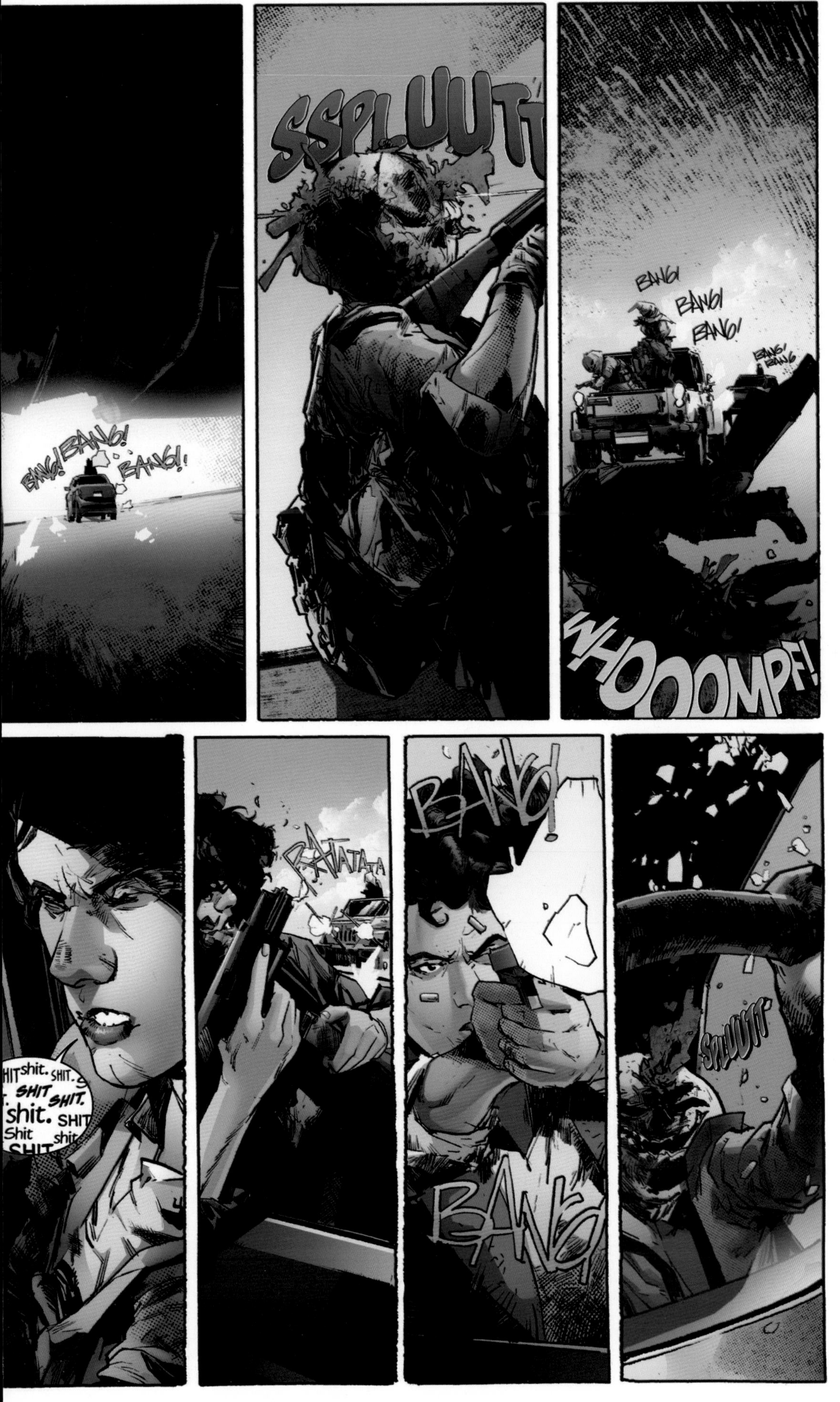
BANG! BANG! BANG!
SSPLUUTT
BANG! BANG! BANG! BANG! BANG!
WHOOOMPF!
shit. SHIT. SHIT SHIT. shit. SHIT Shit shit
RATATATATA
BANG!
BANG
SPLUUTT

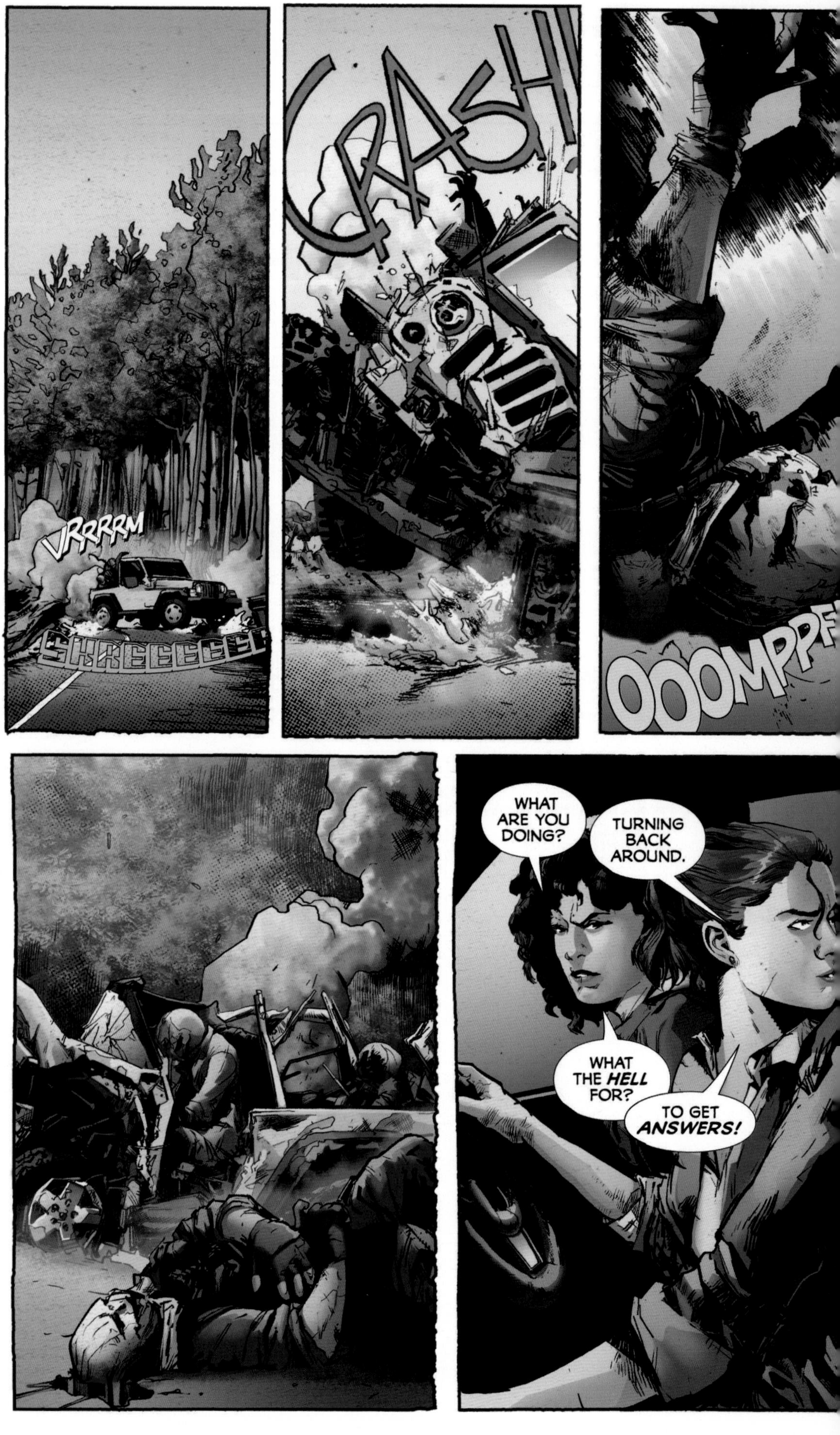
VRRRRM
SHREEEEEE
CRASH!
OOOMPPF
WHAT ARE YOU DOING?
TURNING BACK AROUND.
WHAT THE *HELL* FOR?
TO GET *ANSWERS!*

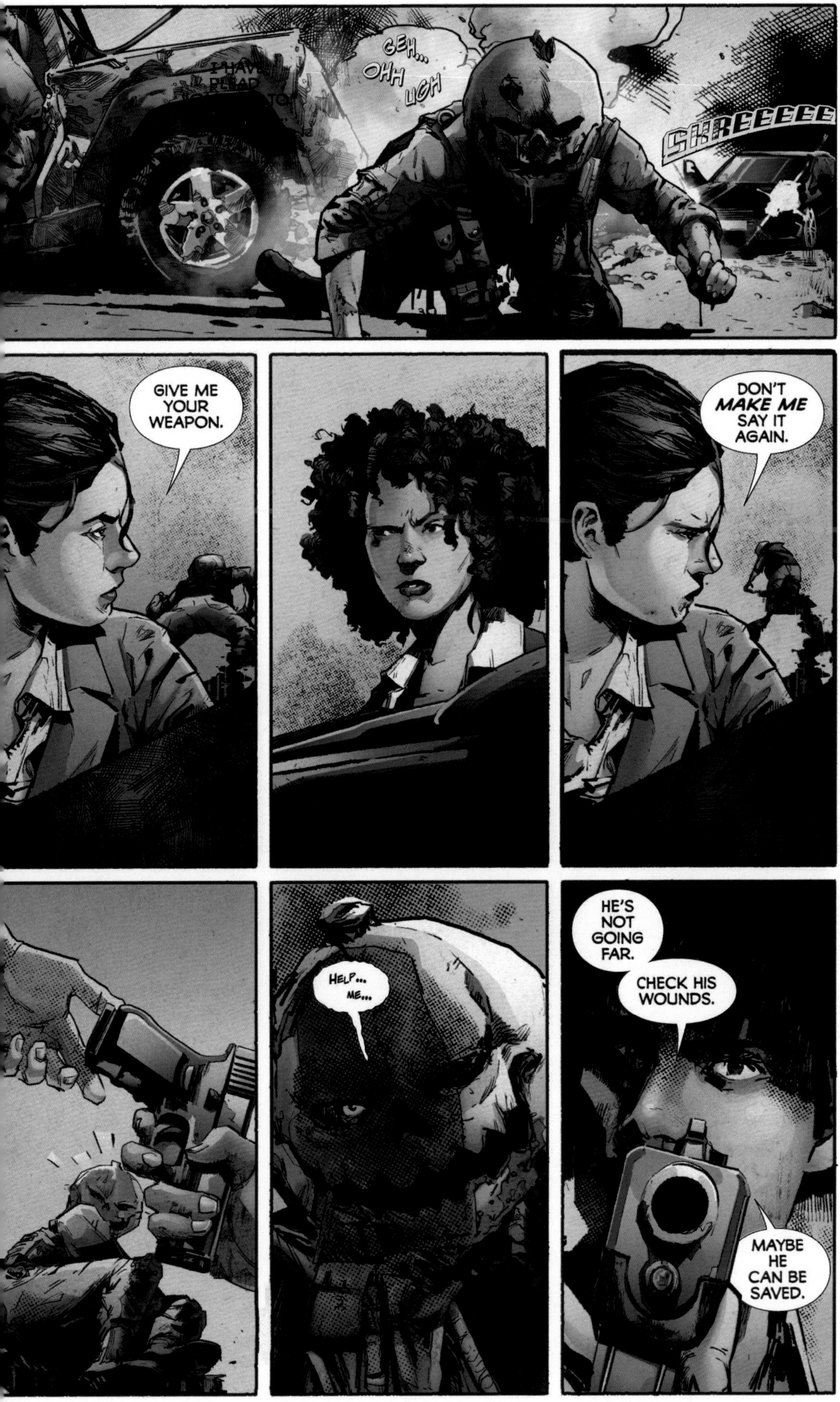
GEH... OHH UGH
SHREEEEEE
GIVE ME YOUR WEAPON.
DON'T *MAKE ME* SAY IT AGAIN.
HELP... ME...
HE'S NOT GOING FAR.
CHECK HIS WOUNDS.
MAYBE HE CAN BE SAVED.

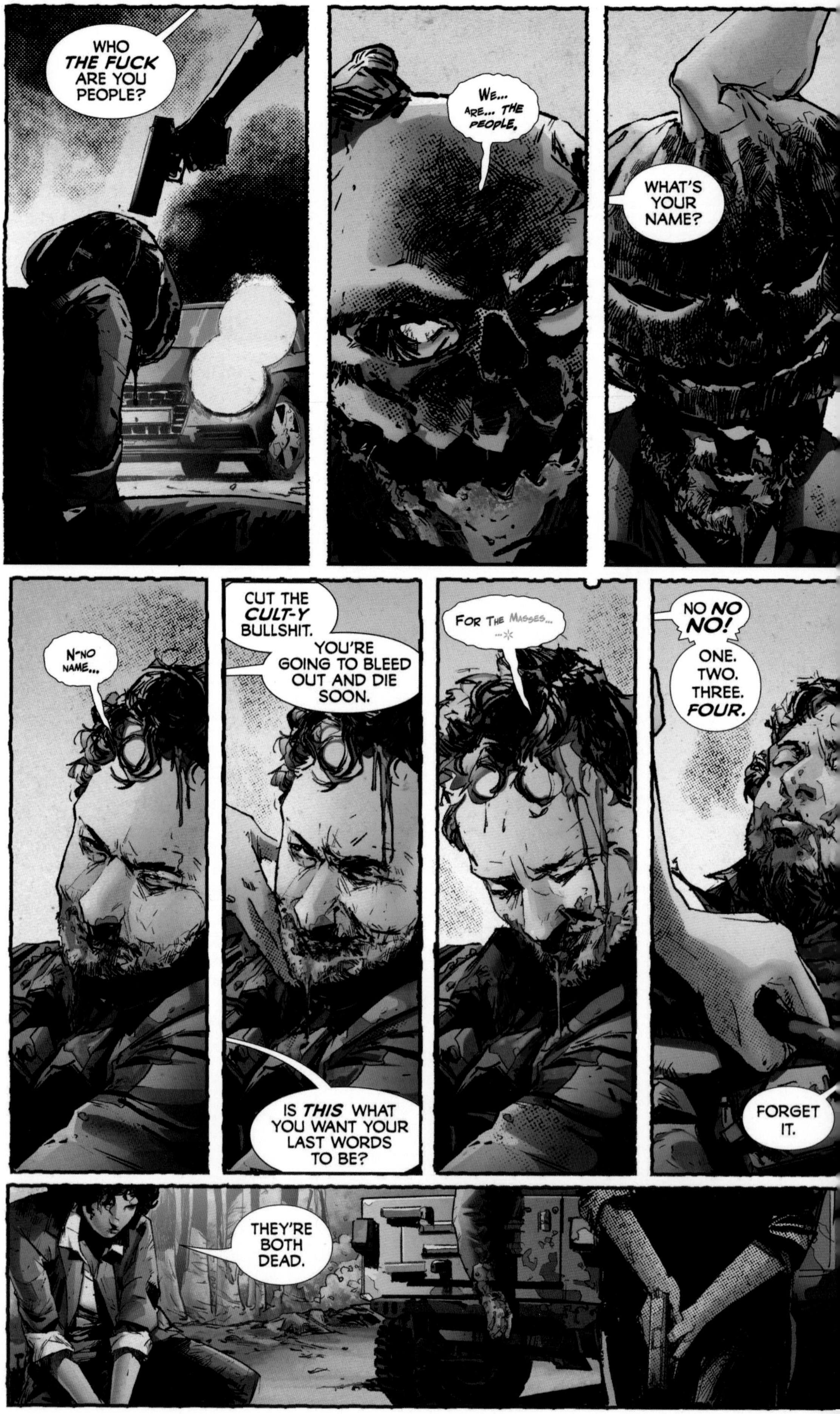
WHO THE FUCK ARE YOU PEOPLE?
WE... ARE... THE PEOPLE.
WHAT'S YOUR NAME?
N-NO NAME...
CUT THE CULT-Y BULLSHIT.
YOU'RE GOING TO BLEED OUT AND DIE SOON.
IS THIS WHAT YOU WANT YOUR LAST WORDS TO BE?
FOR THE MASSES...
NO NO NO!
ONE. TWO. THREE. FOUR.
FORGET IT.
THEY'RE BOTH DEAD.

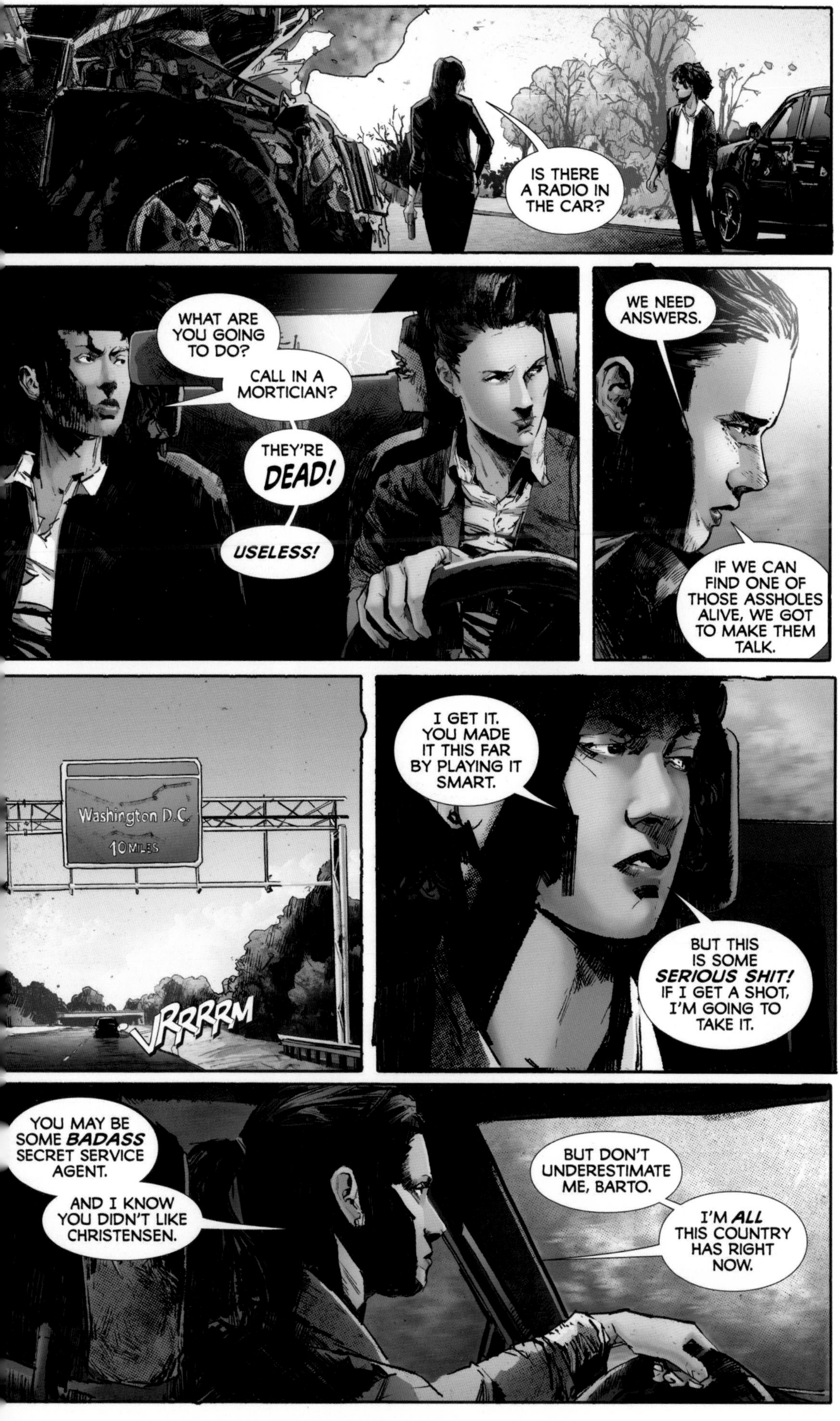
IS THERE A RADIO IN THE CAR?
WHAT ARE YOU GOING TO DO?
CALL IN A MORTICIAN?
THEY'RE *DEAD!*
USELESS!
WE NEED ANSWERS.
IF WE CAN FIND ONE OF THOSE ASSHOLES ALIVE, WE GOT TO MAKE THEM TALK.
Washington D.C.
10 MILES
VRRRRM
I GET IT. YOU MADE IT THIS FAR BY PLAYING IT SMART.
BUT THIS IS SOME *SERIOUS SHIT!* IF I GET A SHOT, I'M GOING TO TAKE IT.
YOU MAY BE SOME *BADASS* SECRET SERVICE AGENT.
AND I KNOW YOU DIDN'T LIKE CHRISTENSEN.
BUT DON'T UNDERESTIMATE ME, BARTO.
I'M *ALL* THIS COUNTRY HAS RIGHT NOW.

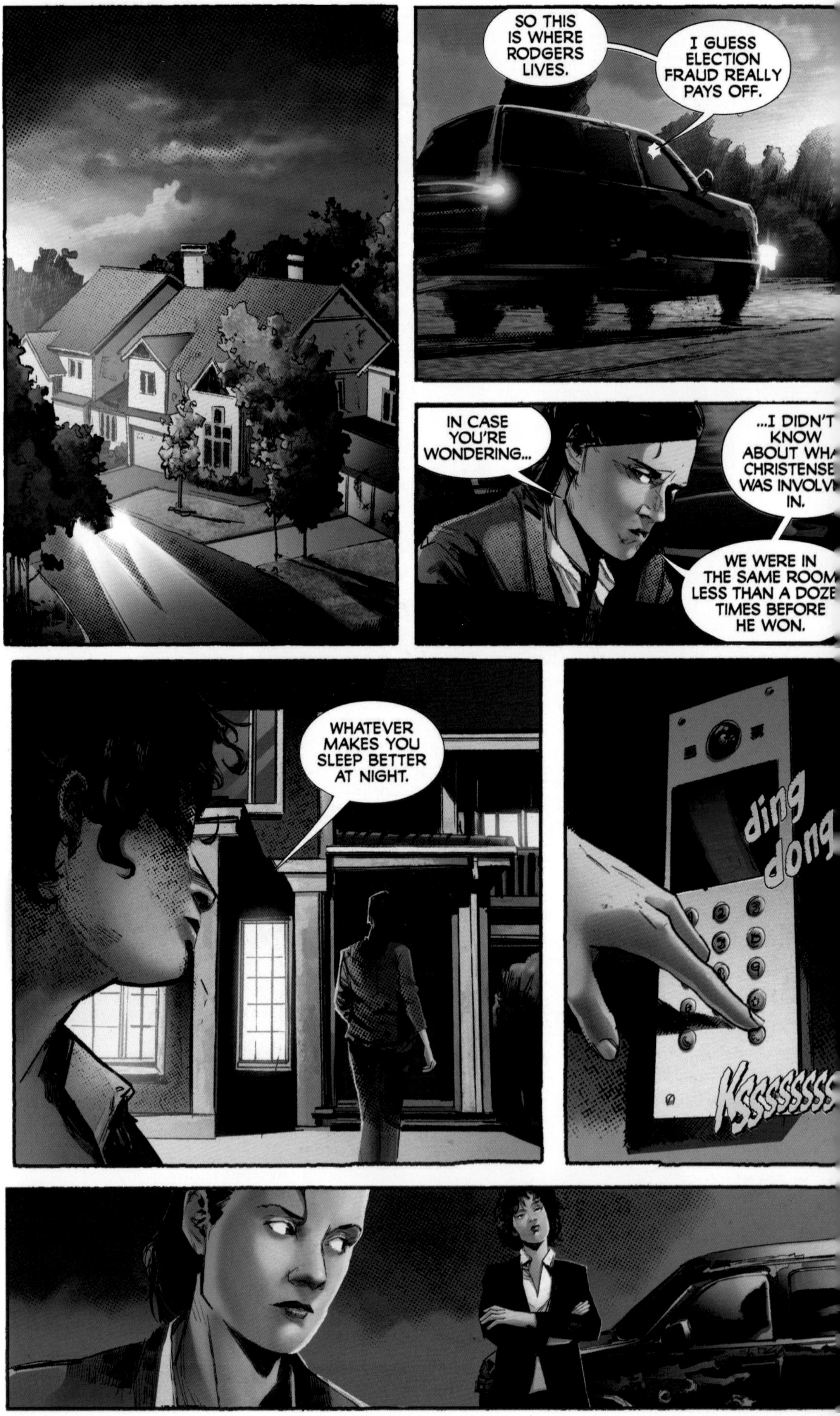

SO THIS IS WHERE RODGERS LIVES.
I GUESS ELECTION FRAUD REALLY PAYS OFF.
IN CASE YOU'RE WONDERING...
...I DIDN'T KNOW ABOUT WHA CHRISTENSE WAS INVOLV IN.
WE WERE IN THE SAME ROOM LESS THAN A DOZE TIMES BEFORE HE WON.
WHATEVER MAKES YOU SLEEP BETTER AT NIGHT.
ding dong
Ksssssss

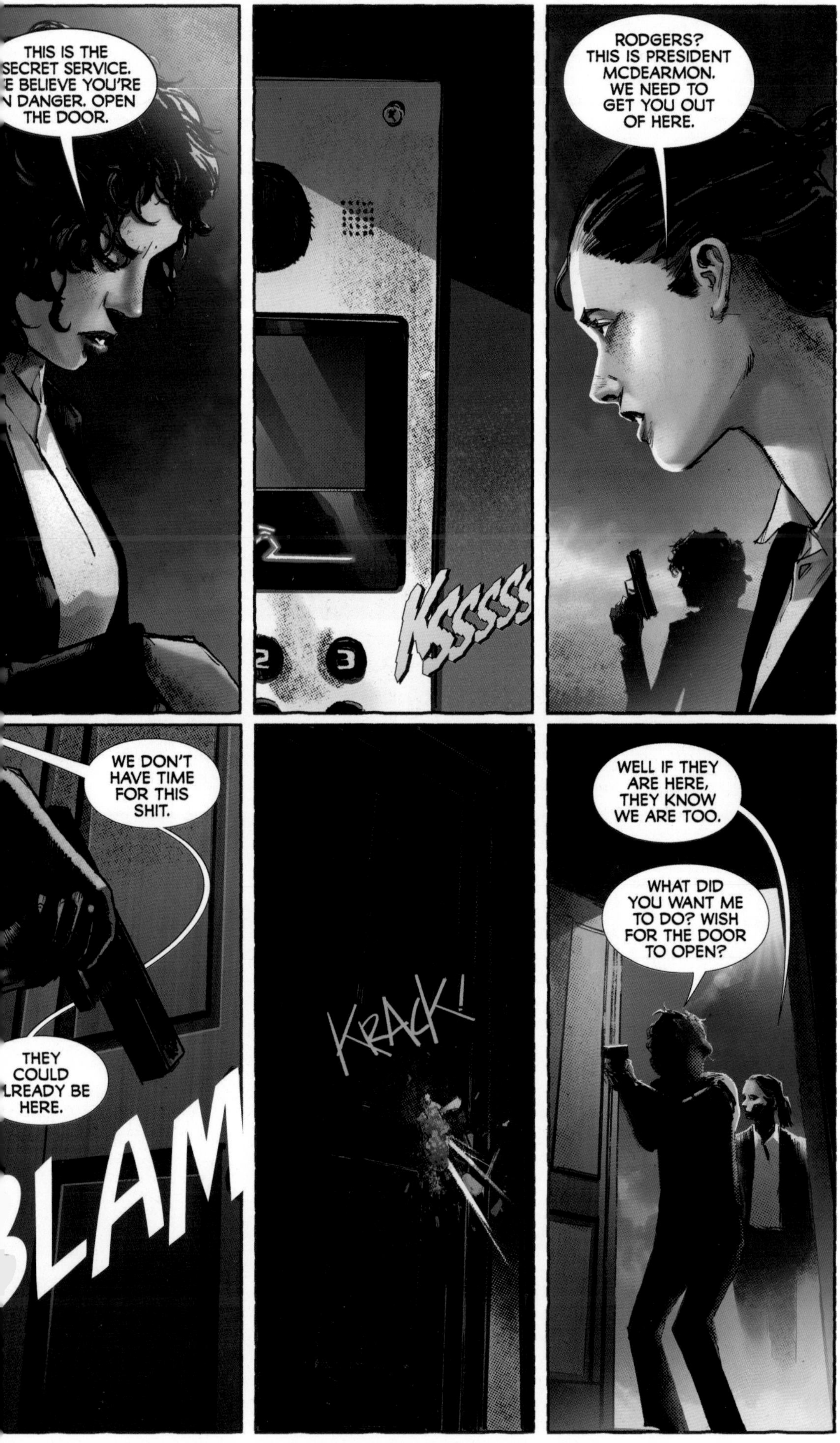
THIS IS THE SECRET SERVICE. E BELIEVE YOU'RE N DANGER. OPEN THE DOOR.
KSSSSS
RODGERS? THIS IS PRESIDENT MCDEARMON. WE NEED TO GET YOU OUT OF HERE.
WE DON'T HAVE TIME FOR THIS SHIT.
THEY COULD LREADY BE HERE.
BLAM
KRACK!
WELL IF THEY ARE HERE, THEY KNOW WE ARE TOO.
WHAT DID YOU WANT ME TO DO? WISH FOR THE DOOR TO OPEN?

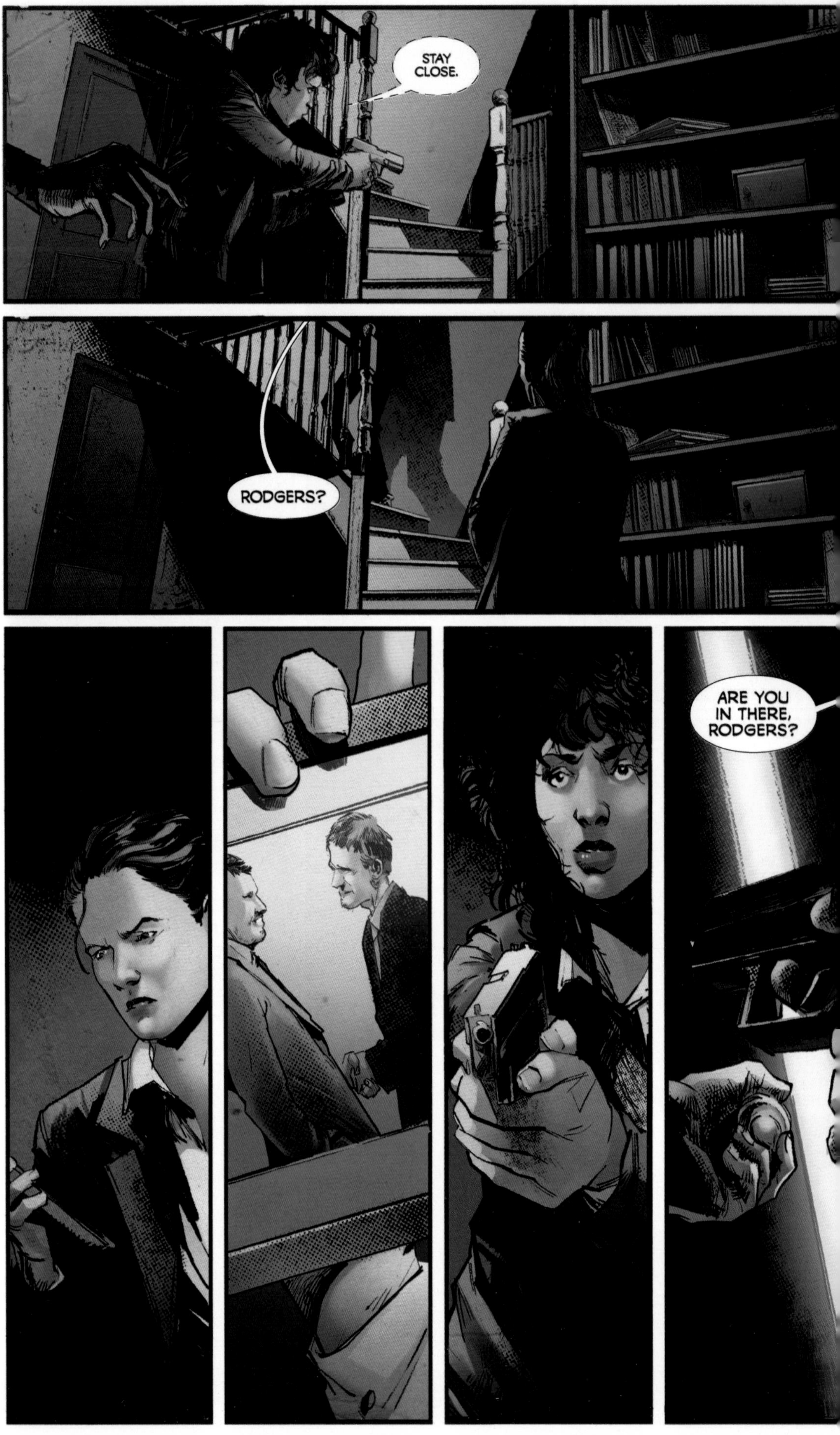
STAY CLOSE.
RODGERS?
ARE YOU IN THERE, RODGERS?

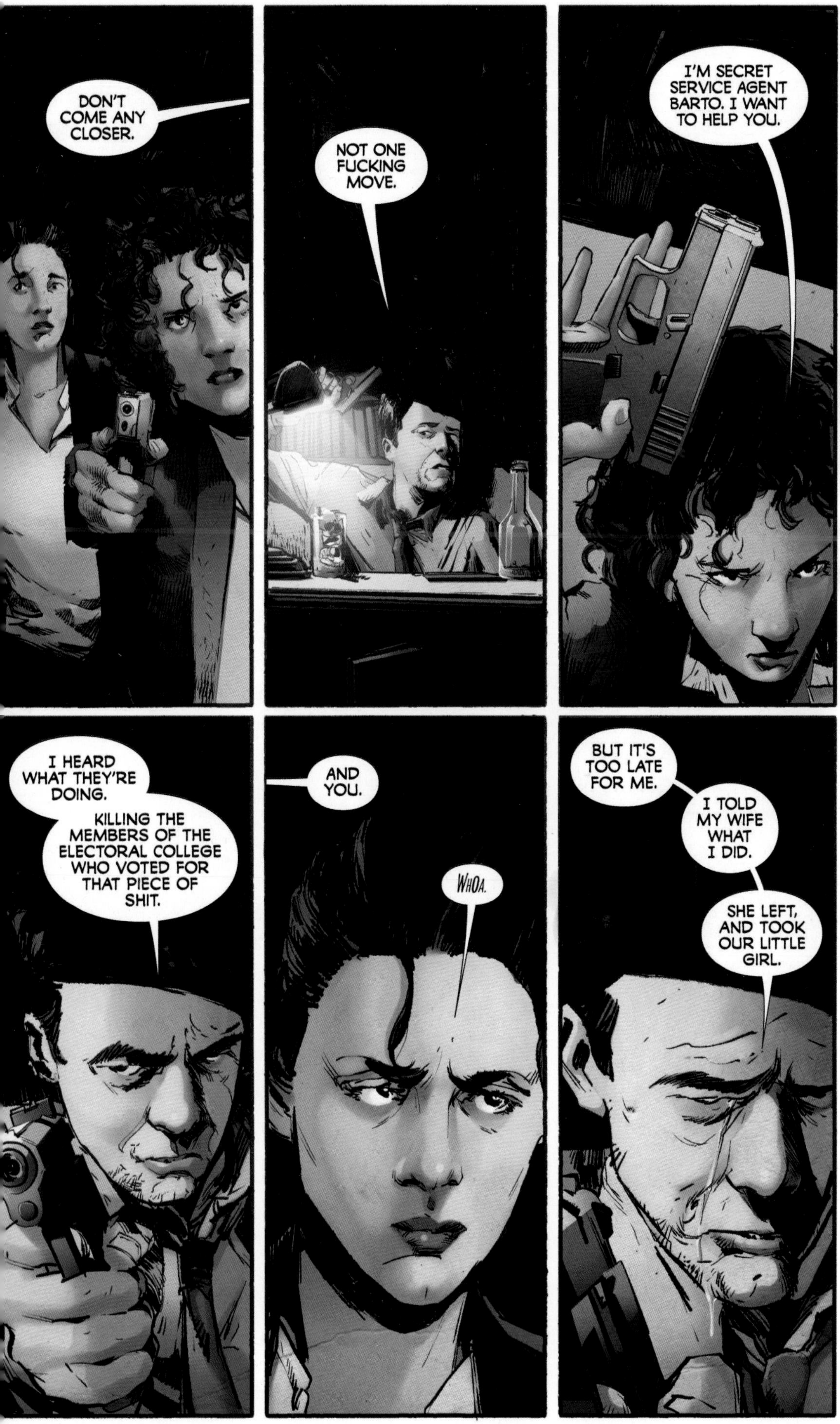
DON'T COME ANY CLOSER.
NOT ONE FUCKING MOVE.
I'M SECRET SERVICE AGENT BARTO. I WANT TO HELP YOU.
I HEARD WHAT THEY'RE DOING.
KILLING THE MEMBERS OF THE ELECTORAL COLLEGE WHO VOTED FOR THAT PIECE OF SHIT.
AND YOU.
WHOA.
BUT IT'S TOO LATE FOR ME.
I TOLD MY WIFE WHAT I DID.
SHE LEFT, AND TOOK OUR LITTLE GIRL.

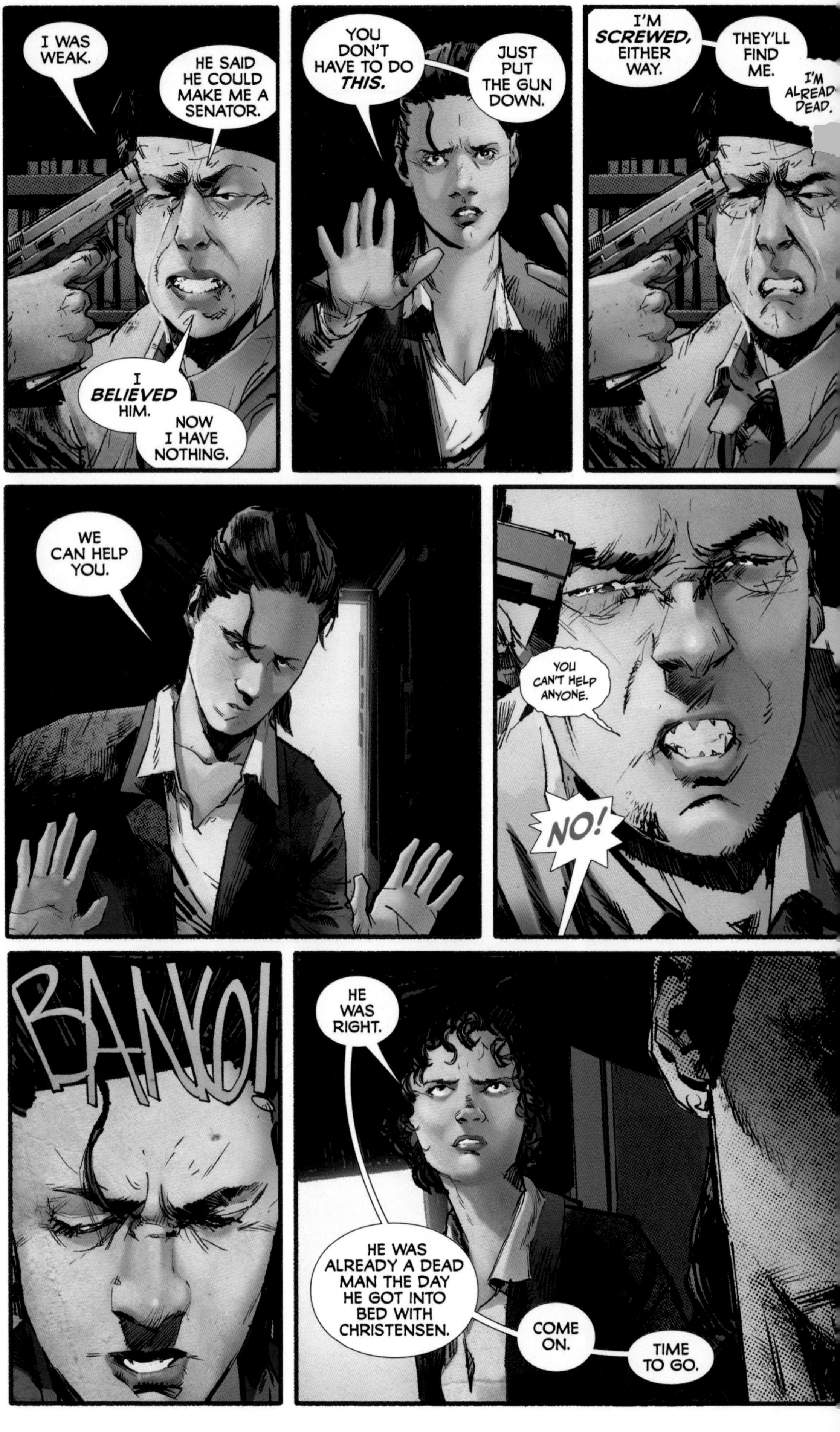
I WAS WEAK.
HE SAID HE COULD MAKE ME A SENATOR.
I BELIEVED HIM.
NOW I HAVE NOTHING.
YOU DON'T HAVE TO DO THIS.
JUST PUT THE GUN DOWN.
I'M SCREWED, EITHER WAY.
THEY'LL FIND ME.
I'M ALREAD DEAD.
WE CAN HELP YOU.
YOU CAN'T HELP ANYONE.
NO!
BANG!
HE WAS RIGHT.
HE WAS ALREADY A DEAD MAN THE DAY HE GOT INTO BED WITH CHRISTENSEN.
COME ON.
TIME TO GO.

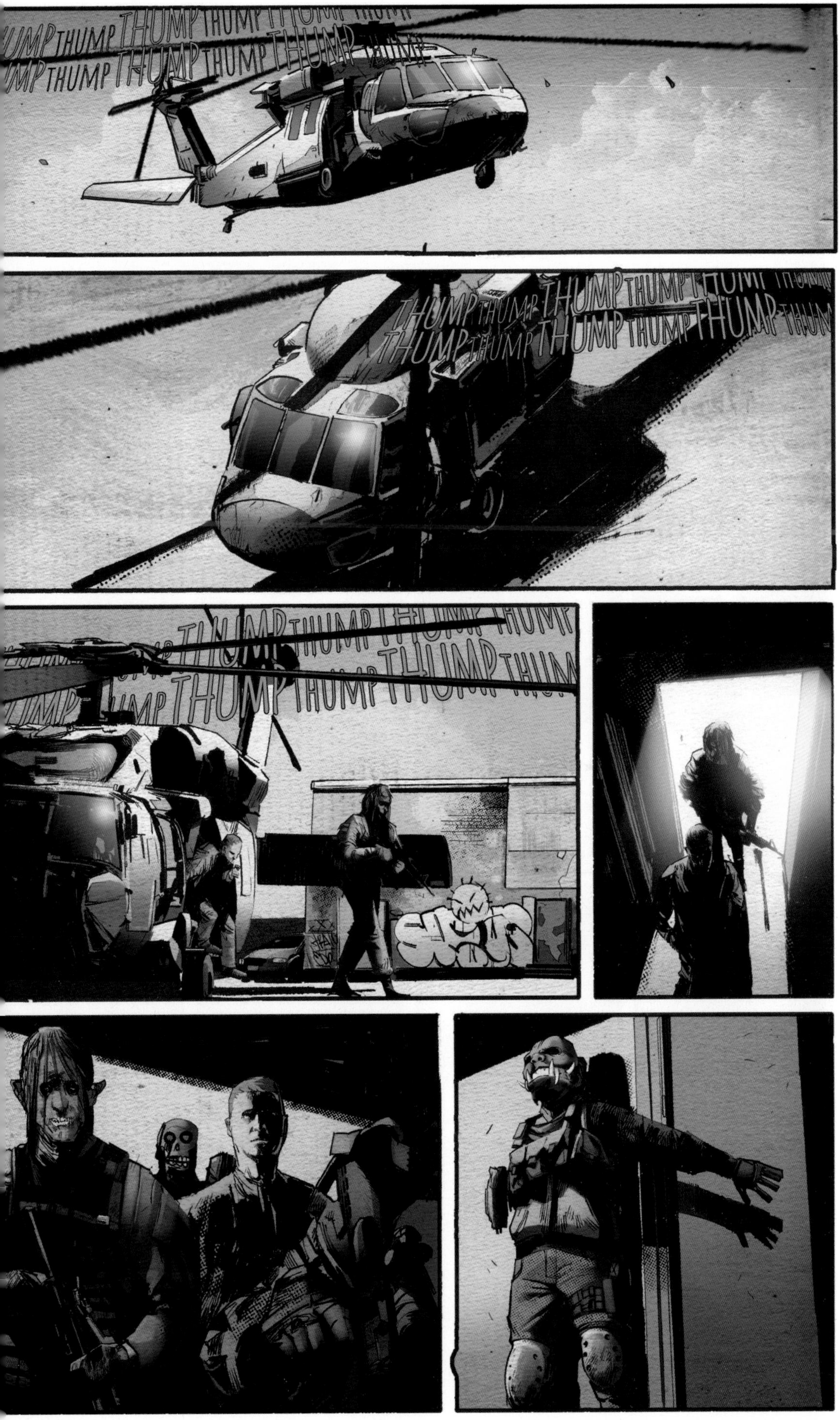
THUMP THUMP THUMP THUMP
THUMP THUMP THUMP THUMP
THUMP THUMP THUMP THUMP THUMP
THUMP THUMP THUMP THUMP THUMP
THUMP THUMP THUMP
THUMP THUMP THUMP

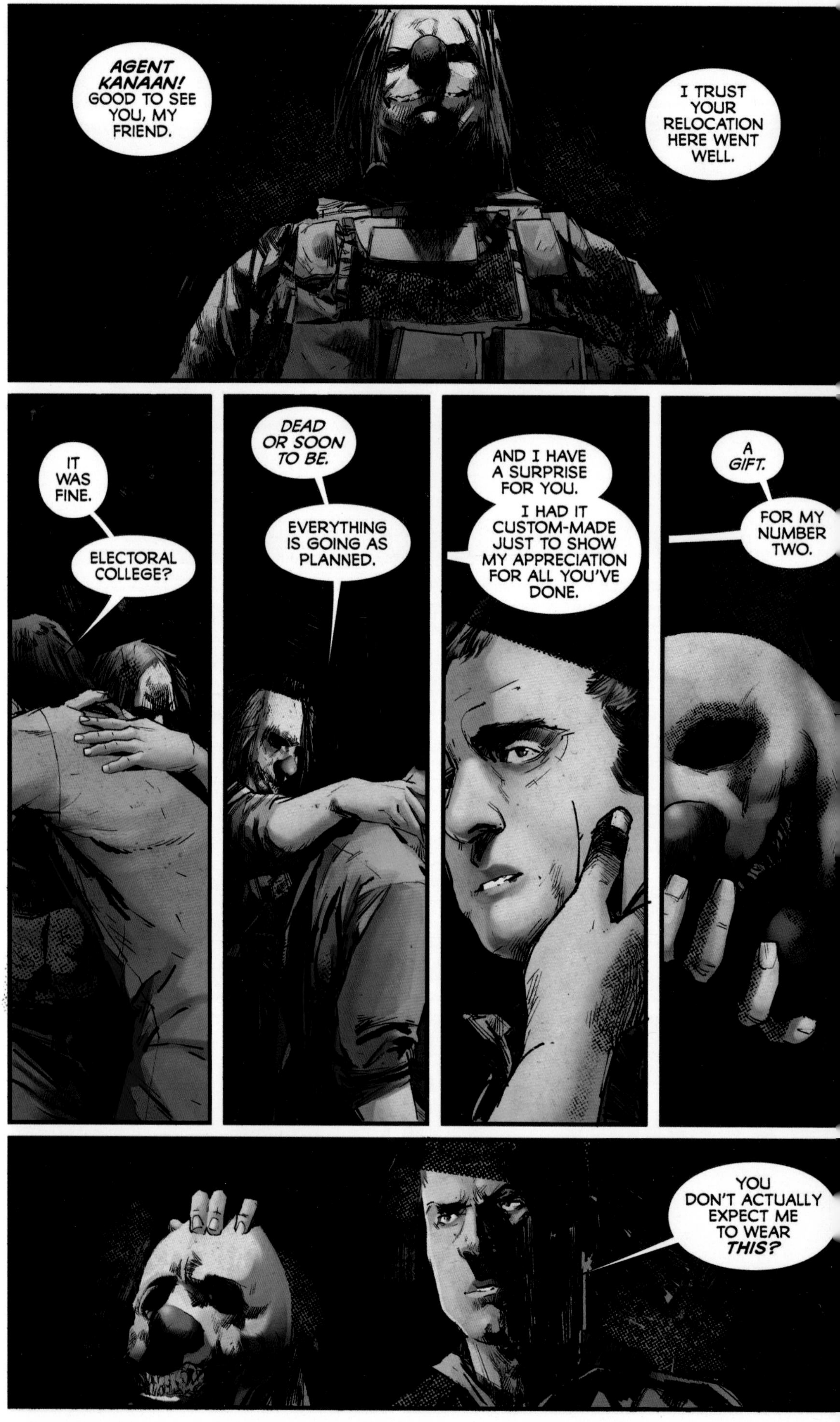
AGENT KANAAN! GOOD TO SEE YOU, MY FRIEND.
I TRUST YOUR RELOCATION HERE WENT WELL.
IT WAS FINE.
ELECTORAL COLLEGE?
DEAD OR SOON TO BE.
EVERYTHING IS GOING AS PLANNED.
AND I HAVE A SURPRISE FOR YOU.
I HAD IT CUSTOM-MADE JUST TO SHOW MY APPRECIATION FOR ALL YOU'VE DONE.
A GIFT.
FOR MY NUMBER TWO.
YOU DON'T ACTUALLY EXPECT ME TO WEAR THIS?

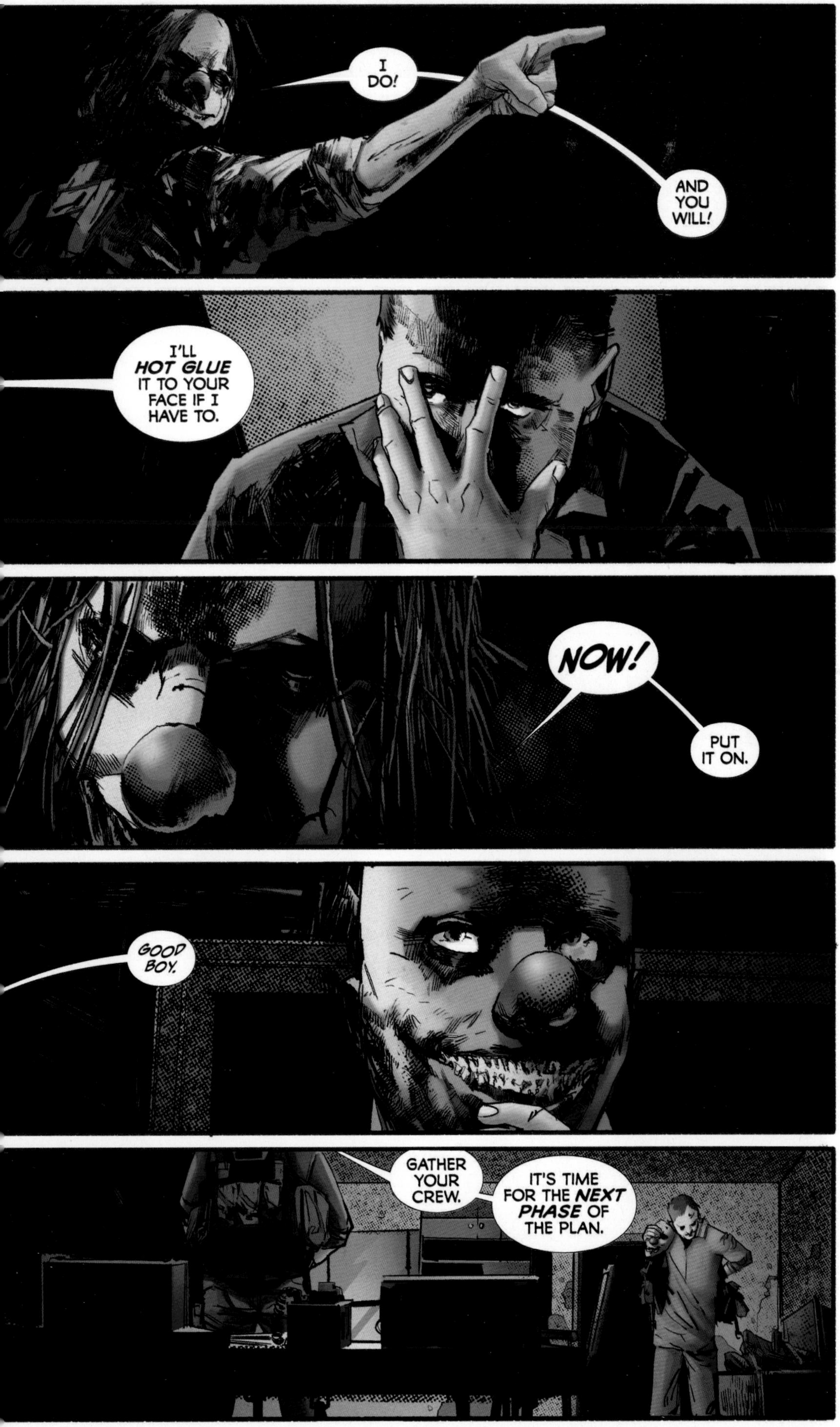

I DO!
AND YOU WILL!
I'LL HOT GLUE IT TO YOUR FACE IF I HAVE TO.
NOW!
PUT IT ON.
GOOD BOY.
GATHER YOUR CREW.
IT'S TIME FOR THE NEXT PHASE OF THE PLAN.

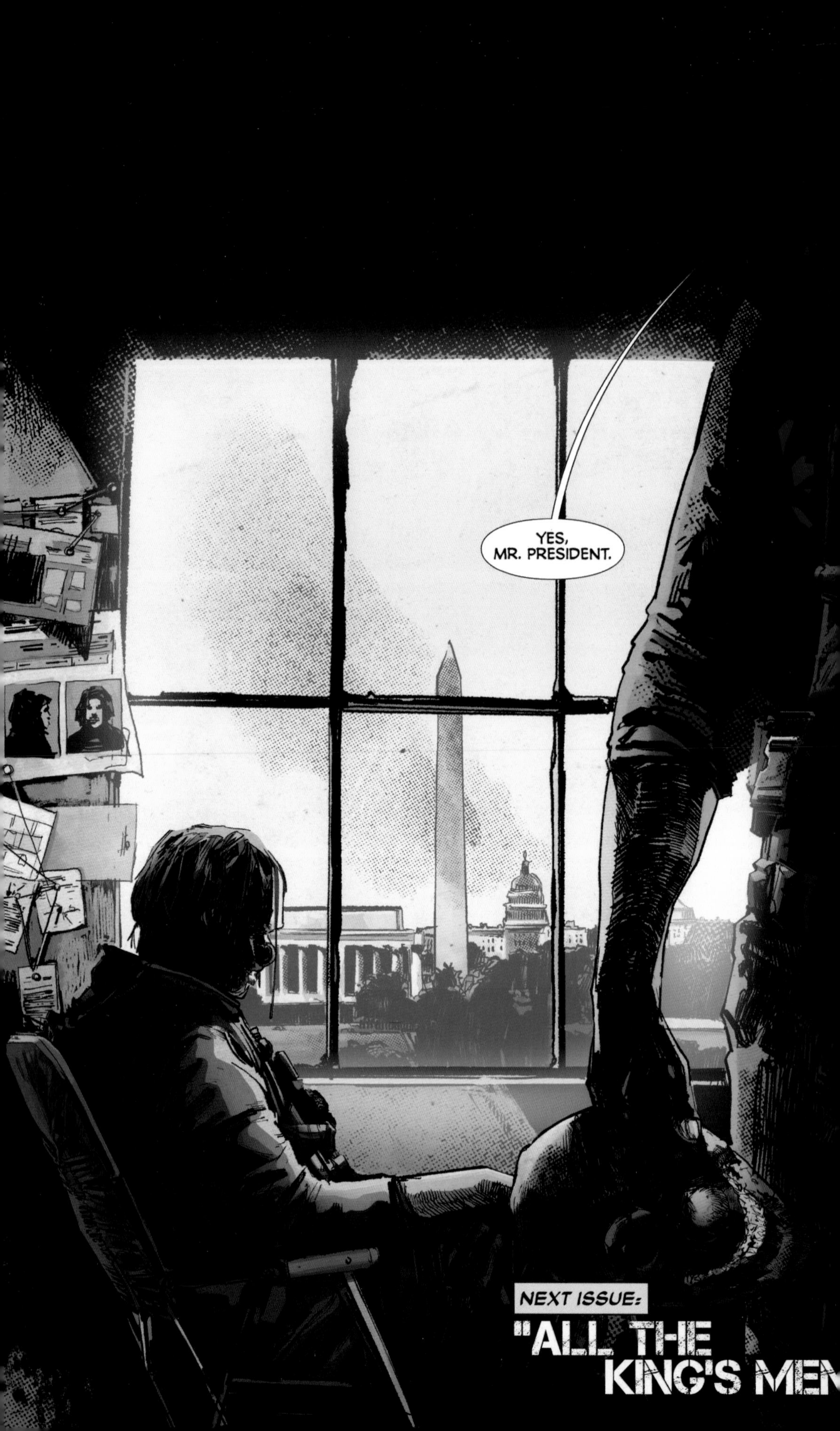
YES, MR. PRESIDENT.
NEXT ISSUE:
"ALL THE KING'S MEN

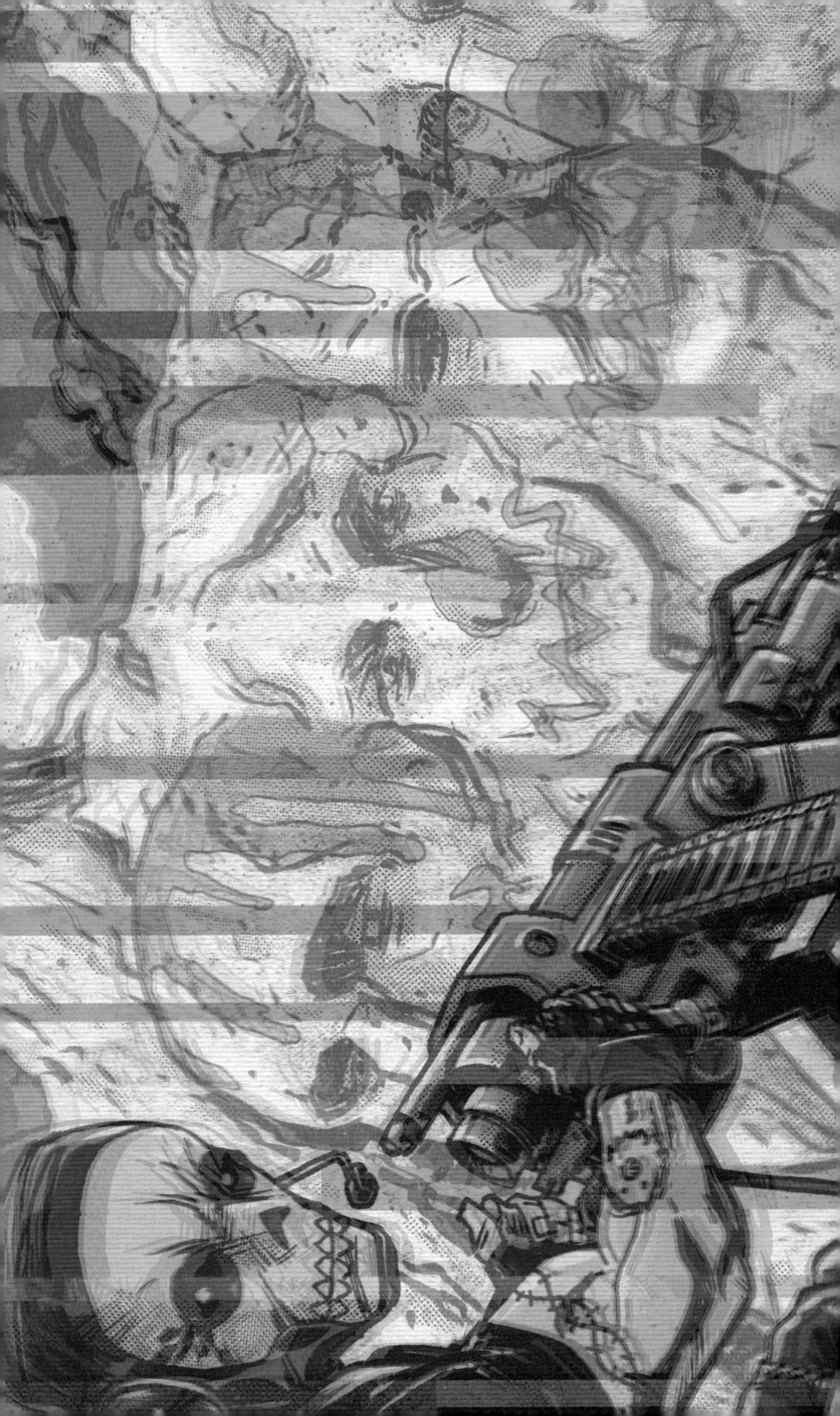

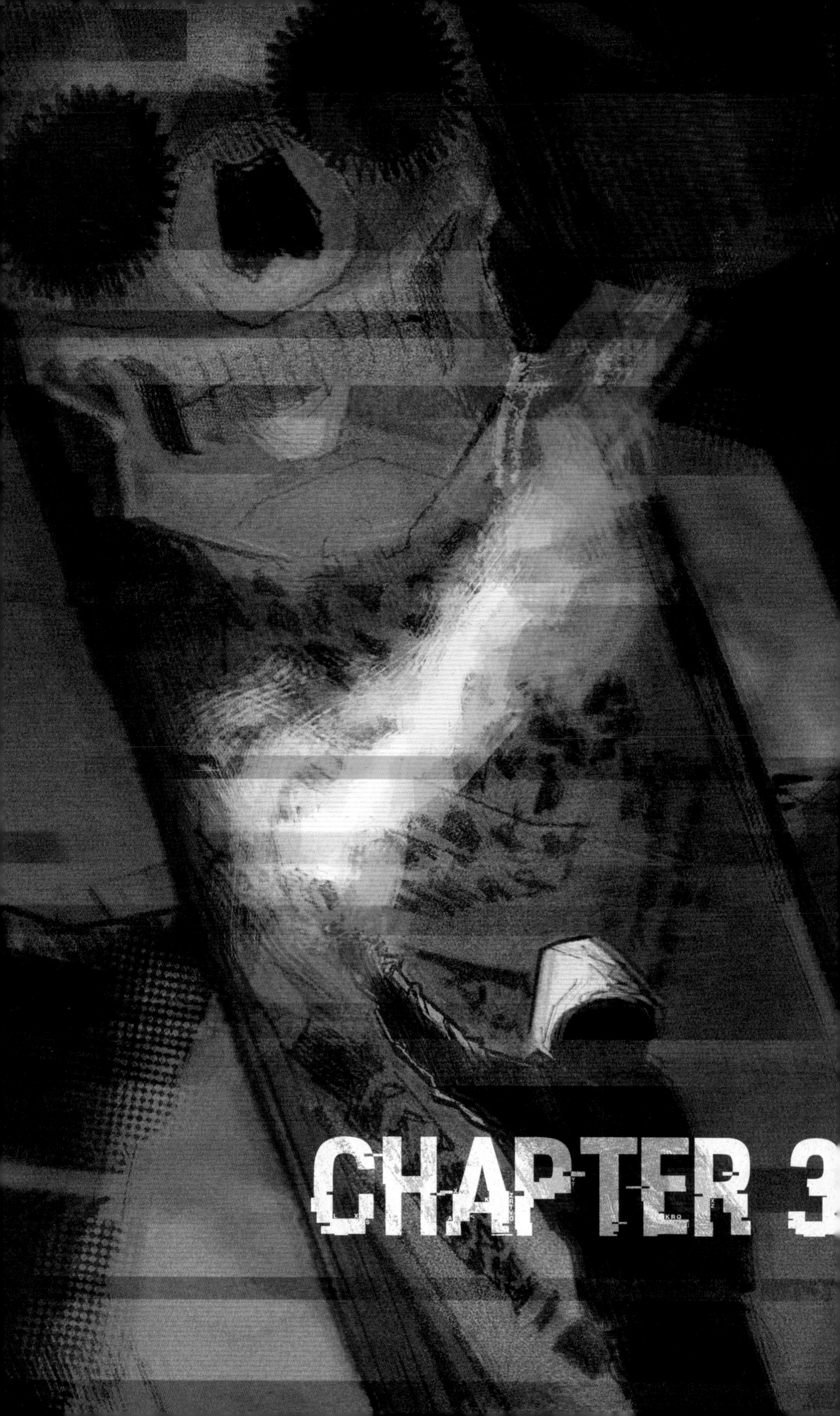
CHAPTER 3

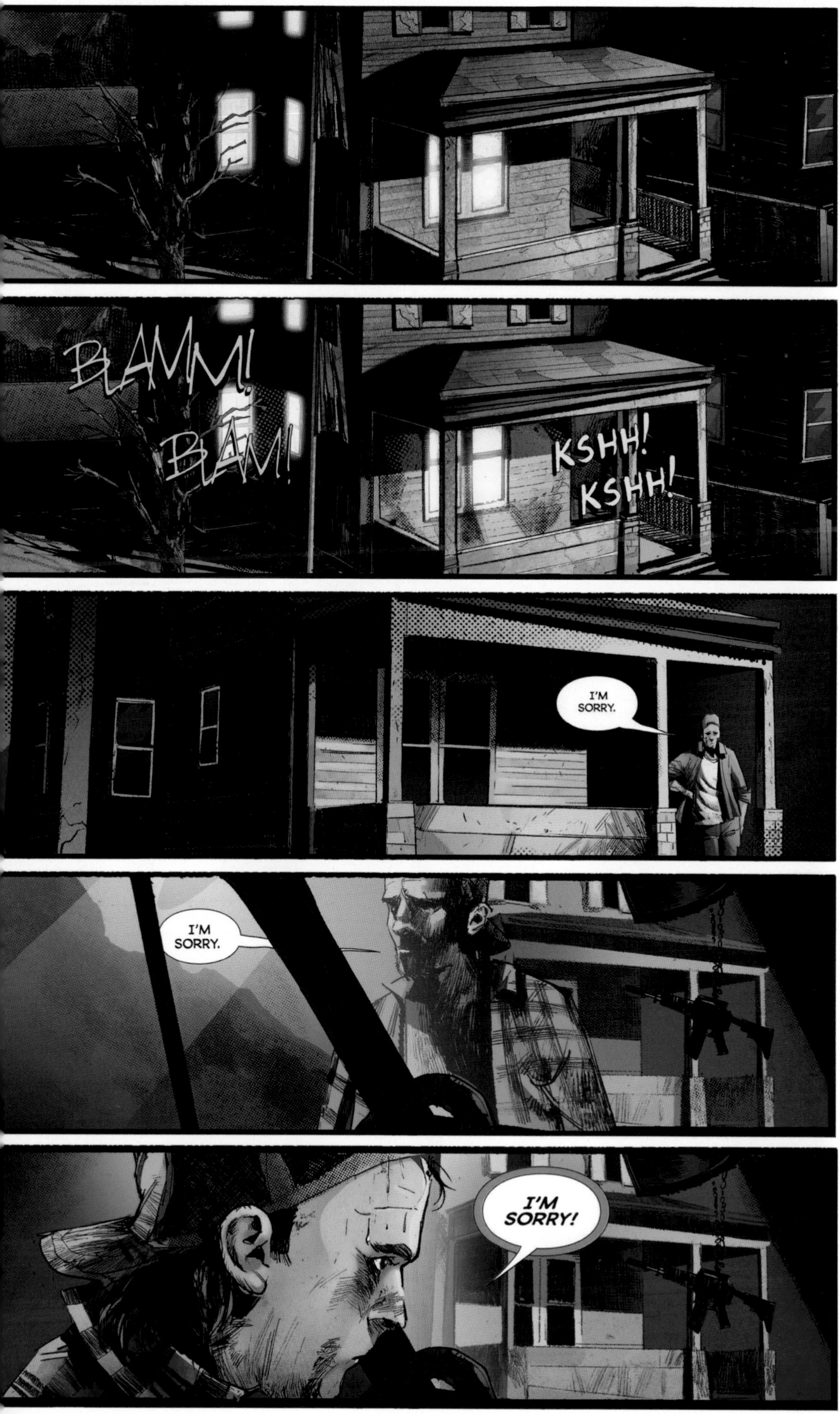
BLAMM!
BLAM!
KSHH!
KSHH!
I'M SORRY.
I'M SORRY.
I'M SORRY!

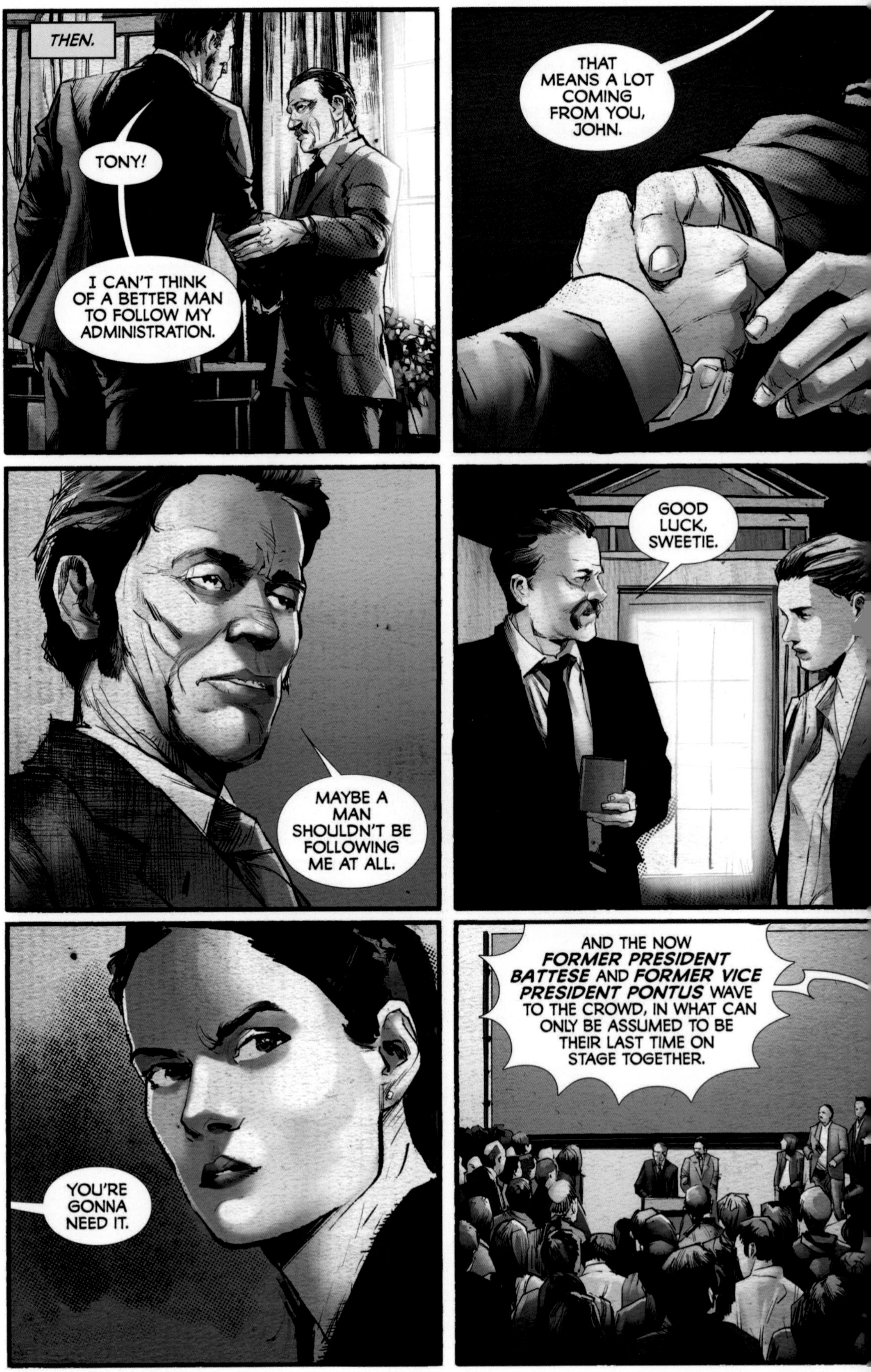
THEN.
TONY!
I CAN'T THINK OF A BETTER MAN TO FOLLOW MY ADMINISTRATION.
THAT MEANS A LOT COMING FROM YOU, JOHN.
MAYBE A MAN SHOULDN'T BE FOLLOWING ME AT ALL.
GOOD LUCK, SWEETIE.
YOU'RE GONNA NEED IT.
AND THE NOW FORMER PRESIDENT BATTESE AND FORMER VICE PRESIDENT PONTUS WAVE TO THE CROWD, IN WHAT CAN ONLY BE ASSUMED TO BE THEIR LAST TIME ON STAGE TOGETHER.

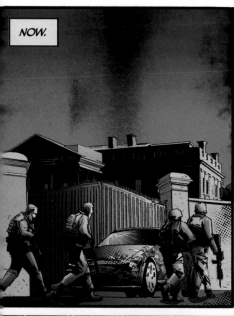

NOW.

WINDOW DOWN AND SHOW YOUR HANDS.

TOC TOC

MADAM VICE PRES--I MEAN, MADAM PRESIDENT.

I'M SO SORRY. I DIDN'T KNOW IT WAS YOU.

HEY, DIPSHIT!

OPEN THE GATE.

OPEN IT!

BZZZZ!

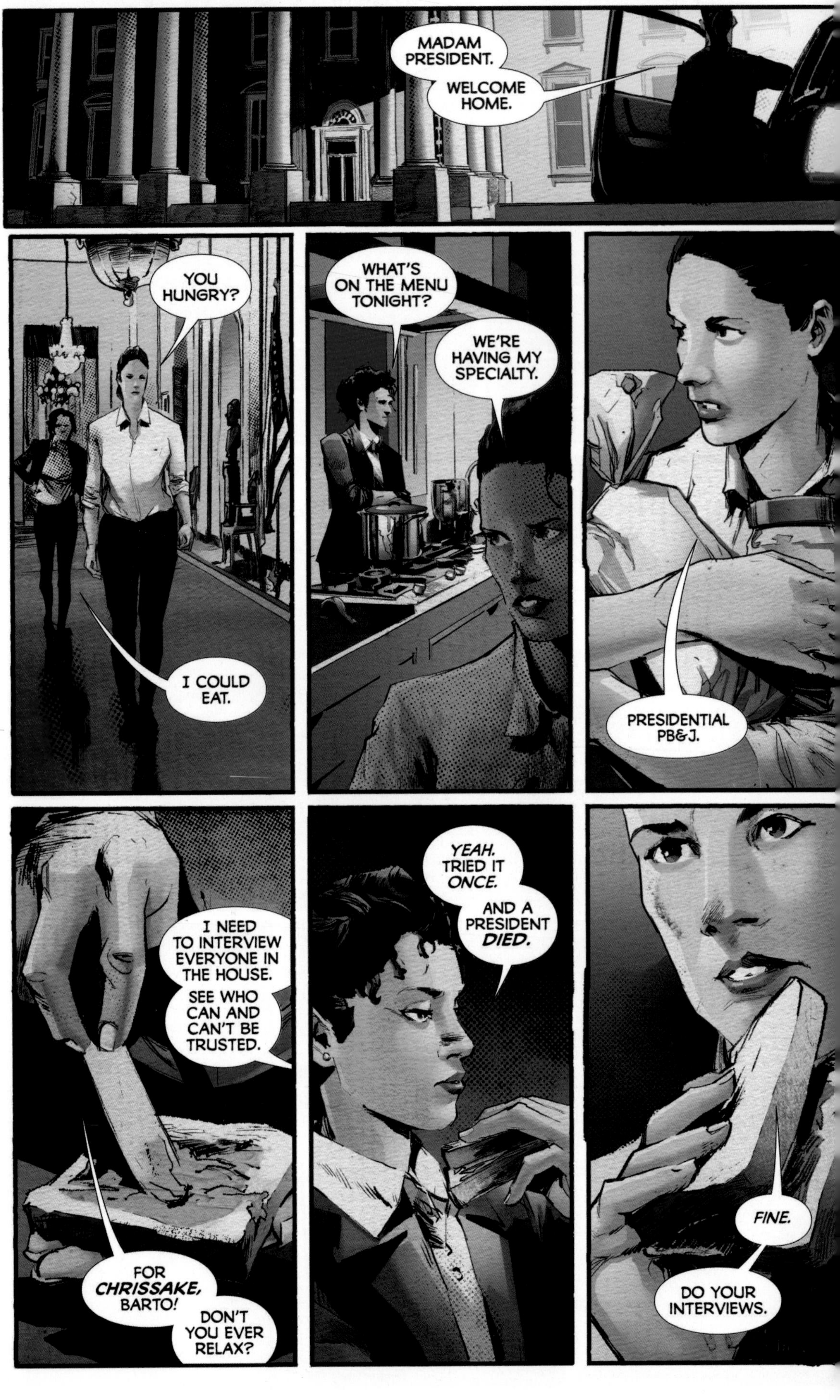
MADAM PRESIDENT.
WELCOME HOME.
YOU HUNGRY?
I COULD EAT.
WHAT'S ON THE MENU TONIGHT?
WE'RE HAVING MY SPECIALTY.
PRESIDENTIAL PB&J.
I NEED TO INTERVIEW EVERYONE IN THE HOUSE.
SEE WHO CAN AND CAN'T BE TRUSTED.
FOR *CHRISSAKE,* BARTO!
DON'T YOU EVER RELAX?
YEAH. TRIED IT *ONCE.*
AND A PRESIDENT *DIED.*
FINE.
DO YOUR INTERVIEWS.

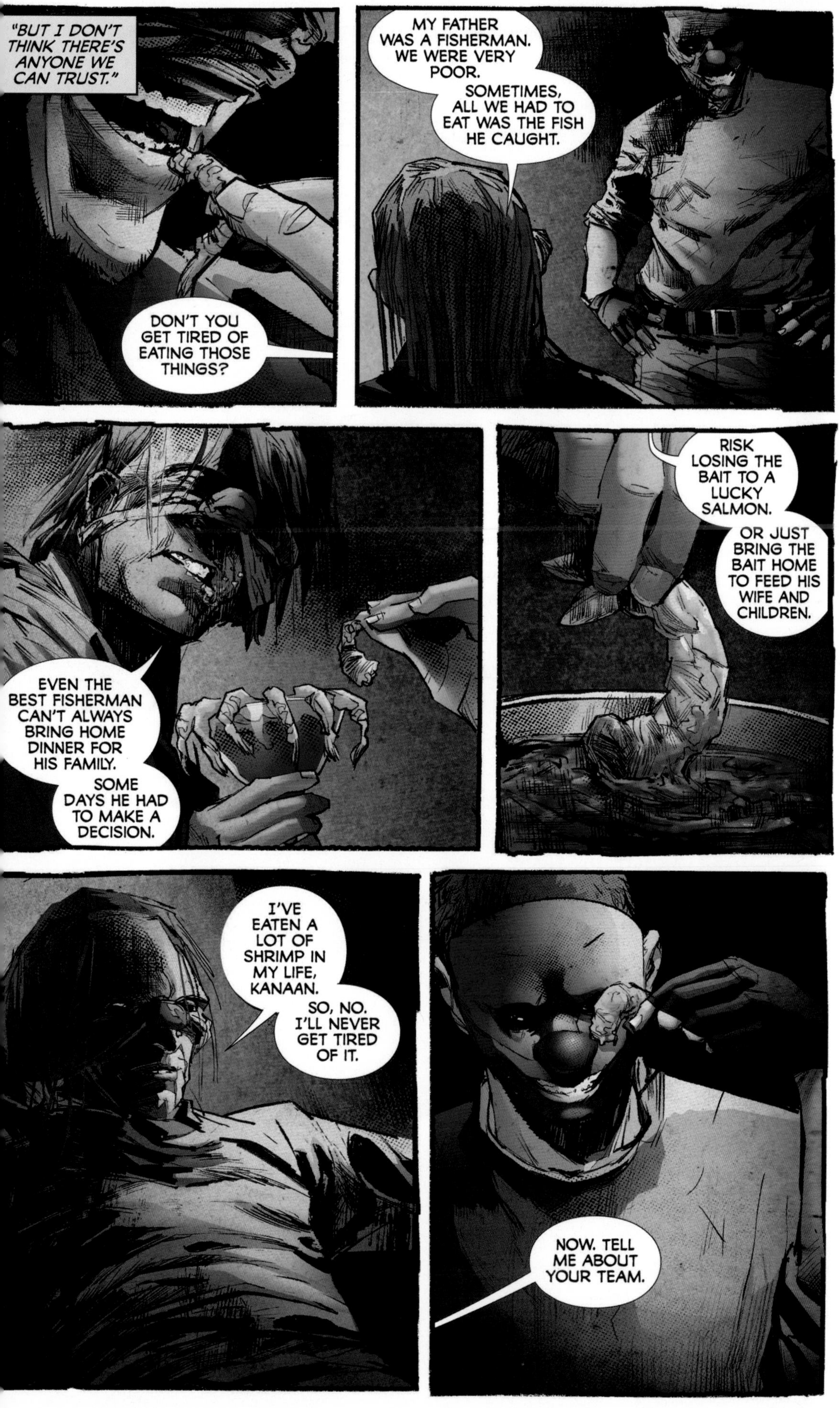
"BUT I DON'T THINK THERE'S ANYONE WE CAN TRUST."
DON'T YOU GET TIRED OF EATING THOSE THINGS?
MY FATHER WAS A FISHERMAN. WE WERE VERY POOR.
SOMETIMES, ALL WE HAD TO EAT WAS THE FISH HE CAUGHT.
EVEN THE BEST FISHERMAN CAN'T ALWAYS BRING HOME DINNER FOR HIS FAMILY.
SOME DAYS HE HAD TO MAKE A DECISION.
RISK LOSING THE BAIT TO A LUCKY SALMON.
OR JUST BRING THE BAIT HOME TO FEED HIS WIFE AND CHILDREN.
I'VE EATEN A LOT OF SHRIMP IN MY LIFE, KANAAN.
SO, NO. I'LL NEVER GET TIRED OF IT.
NOW. TELL ME ABOUT YOUR TEAM.

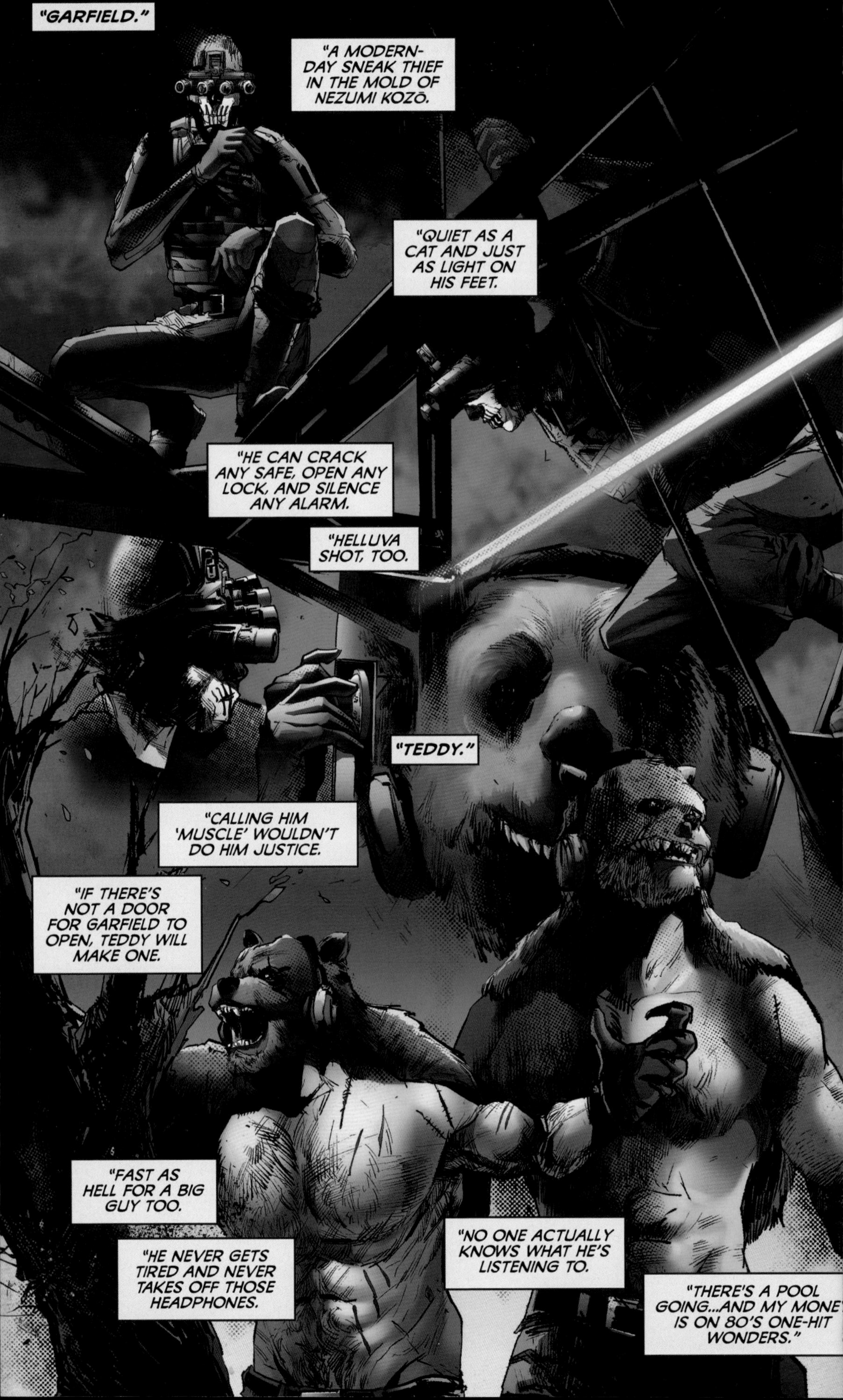
"GARFIELD."
"A MODERN-DAY SNEAK THIEF IN THE MOLD OF NEZUMI KOZŌ.
"QUIET AS A CAT AND JUST AS LIGHT ON HIS FEET.
"HE CAN CRACK ANY SAFE, OPEN ANY LOCK, AND SILENCE ANY ALARM.
"HELLUVA SHOT, TOO.
"TEDDY."
"CALLING HIM 'MUSCLE' WOULDN'T DO HIM JUSTICE.
"IF THERE'S NOT A DOOR FOR GARFIELD TO OPEN, TEDDY WILL MAKE ONE.
"FAST AS HELL FOR A BIG GUY TOO.
"HE NEVER GETS TIRED AND NEVER TAKES OFF THOSE HEADPHONES.
"NO ONE ACTUALLY KNOWS WHAT HE'S LISTENING TO.
"THERE'S A POOL GOING...AND MY MONE IS ON 80'S ONE-HIT WONDERS."

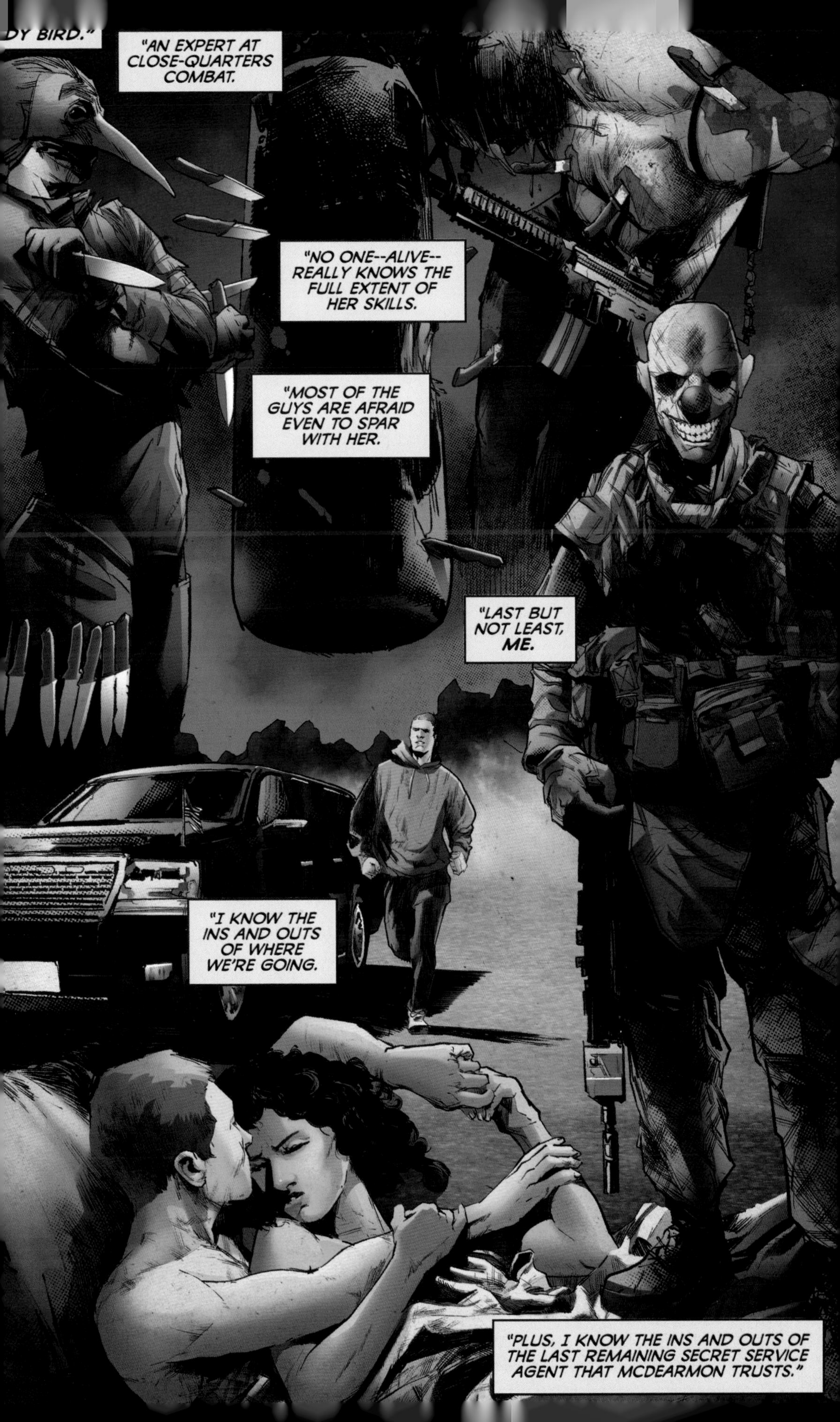
DY BIRD."
"AN EXPERT AT CLOSE-QUARTERS COMBAT.
"NO ONE--ALIVE--REALLY KNOWS THE FULL EXTENT OF HER SKILLS.
"MOST OF THE GUYS ARE AFRAID EVEN TO SPAR WITH HER.
"LAST BUT NOT LEAST, ME.
"I KNOW THE INS AND OUTS OF WHERE WE'RE GOING.
"PLUS, I KNOW THE INS AND OUTS OF THE LAST REMAINING SECRET SERVICE AGENT THAT MCDEARMON TRUSTS."

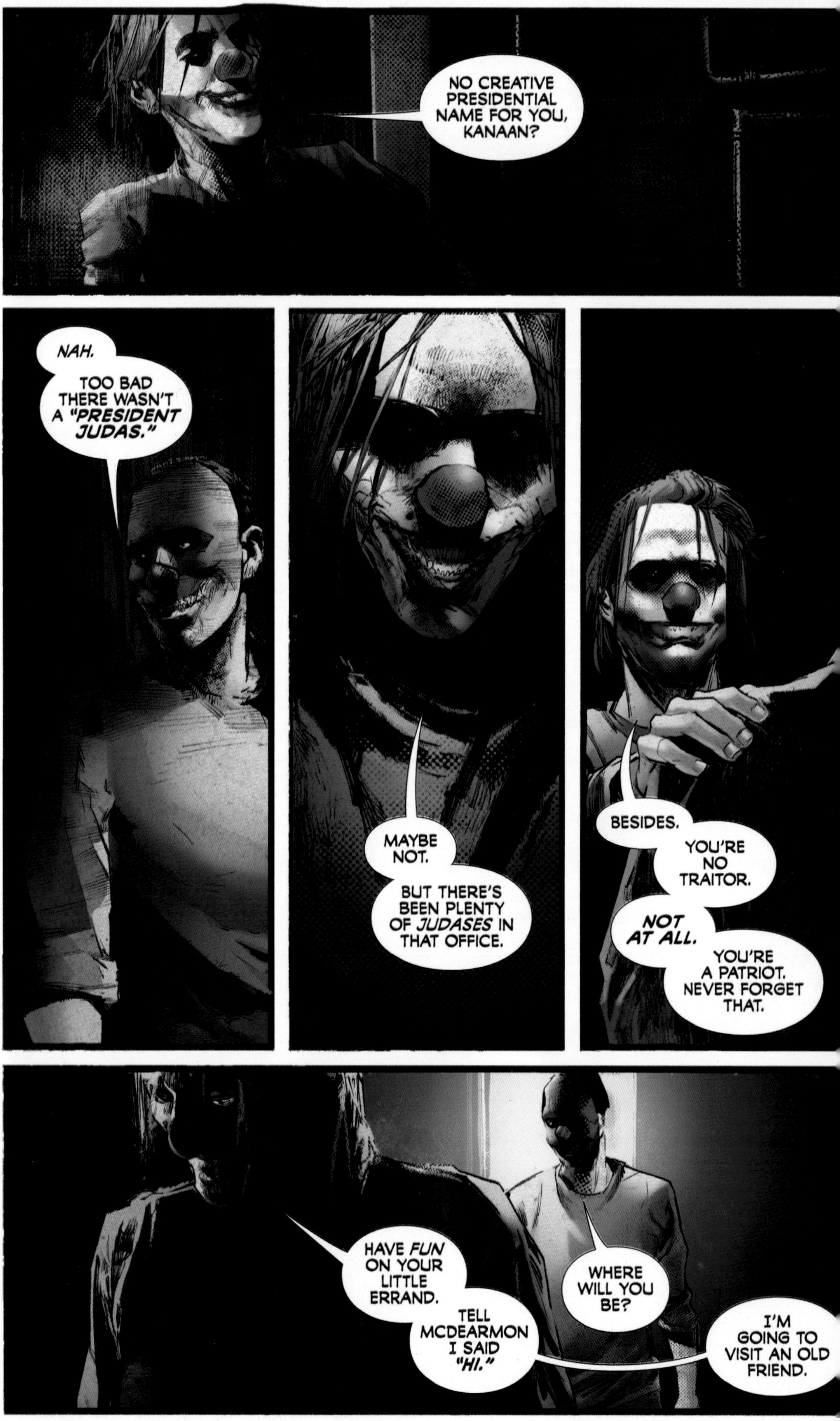
NO CREATIVE PRESIDENTIAL NAME FOR YOU, KANAAN?
NAH.
TOO BAD THERE WASN'T A "PRESIDENT JUDAS."
MAYBE NOT.
BUT THERE'S BEEN PLENTY OF JUDASES IN THAT OFFICE.
BESIDES.
YOU'RE NO TRAITOR.
NOT AT ALL.
YOU'RE A PATRIOT. NEVER FORGET THAT.
HAVE FUN ON YOUR LITTLE ERRAND.
TELL MCDEARMON I SAID "HI."
WHERE WILL YOU BE?
I'M GOING TO VISIT AN OLD FRIEND.

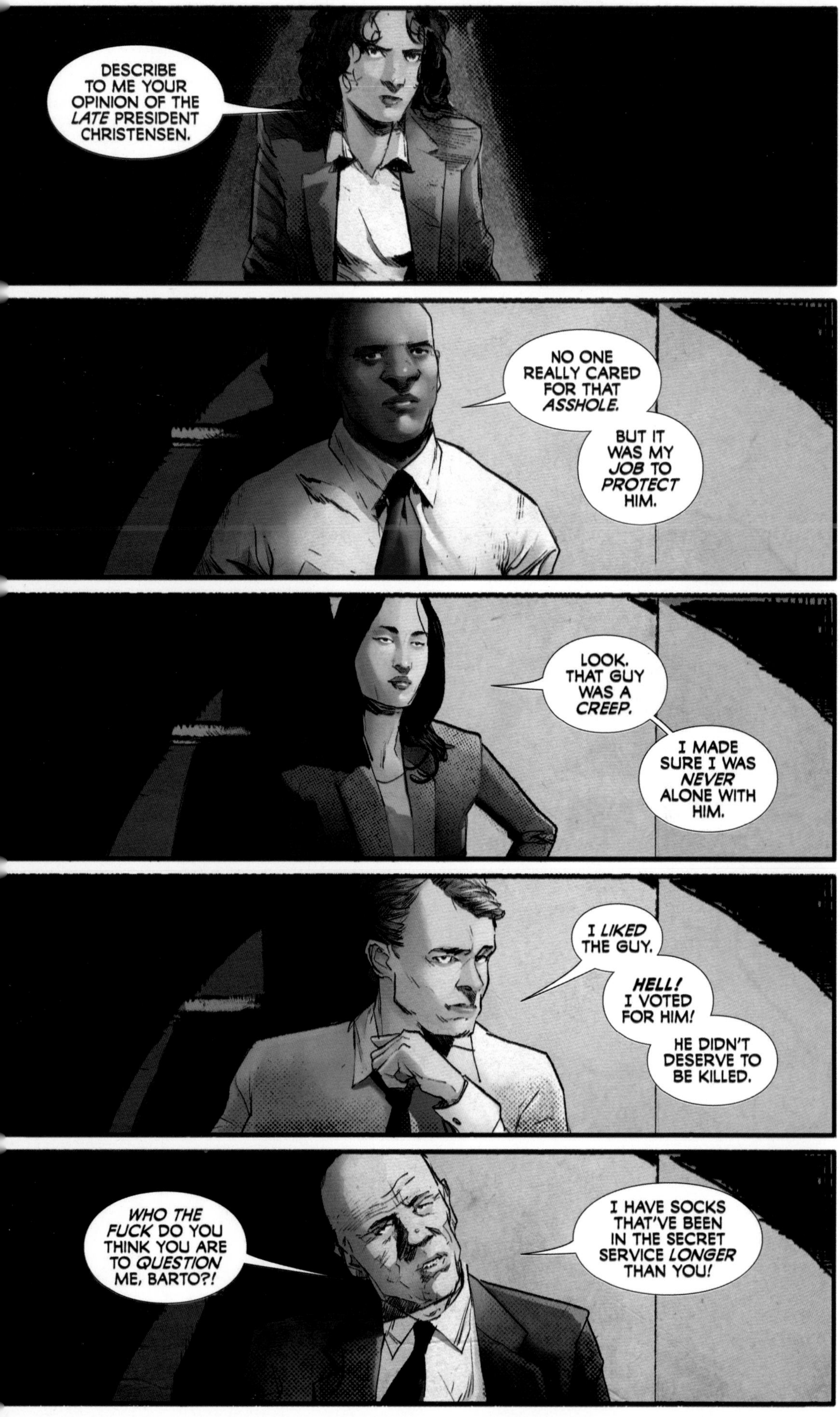
DESCRIBE TO ME YOUR OPINION OF THE *LATE* PRESIDENT CHRISTENSEN.
NO ONE REALLY CARED FOR THAT *ASSHOLE.*
BUT IT WAS MY *JOB* TO *PROTECT* HIM.
LOOK. THAT GUY WAS A *CREEP.*
I MADE SURE I WAS *NEVER* ALONE WITH HIM.
I *LIKED* THE GUY.
HELL! I VOTED FOR HIM!
HE DIDN'T DESERVE TO BE KILLED.
WHO THE FUCK DO YOU THINK YOU ARE TO *QUESTION* ME, BARTO?!
I HAVE SOCKS THAT'VE BEEN IN THE SECRET SERVICE *LONGER* THAN YOU!

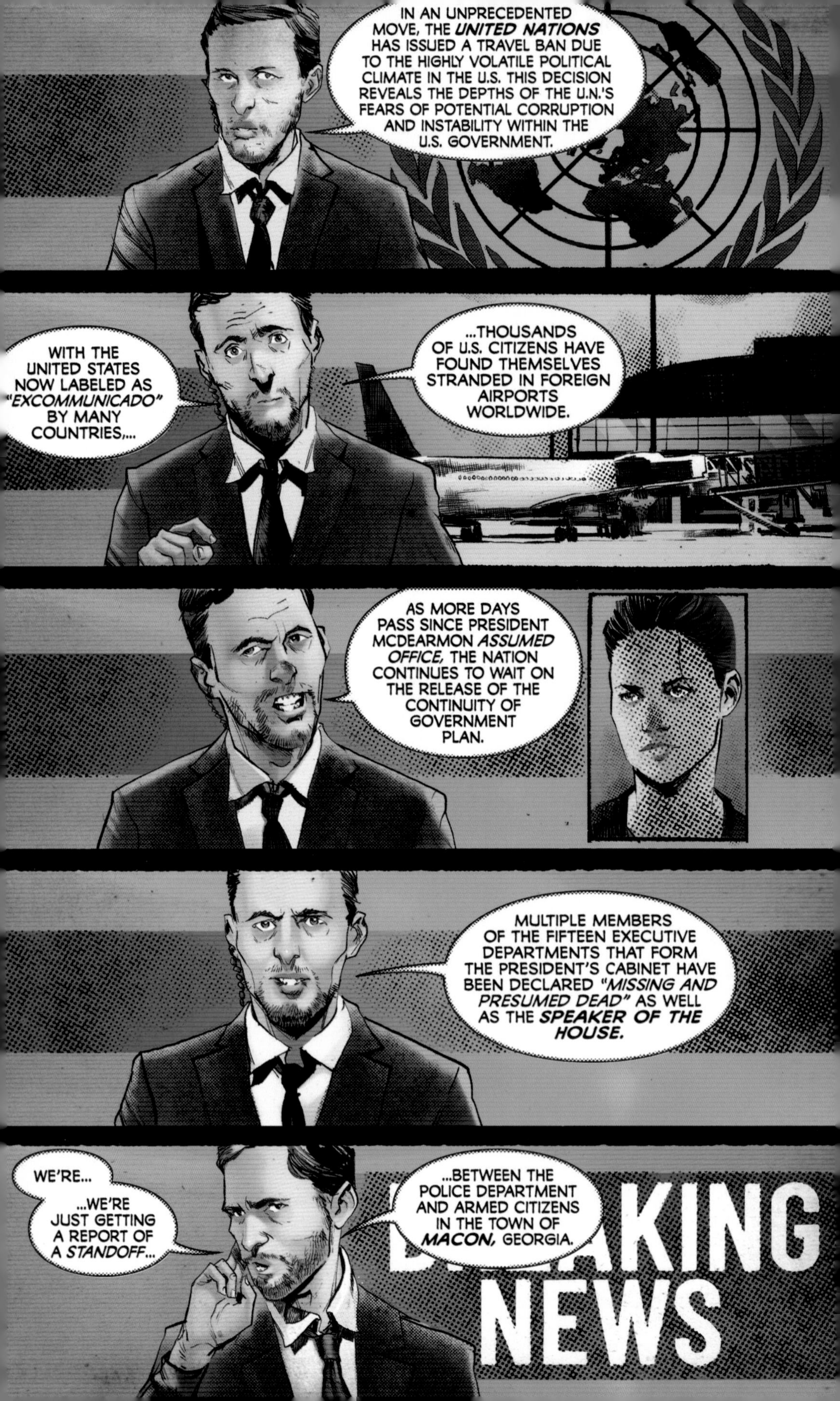

IN AN UNPRECEDENTED MOVE, THE UNITED NATIONS HAS ISSUED A TRAVEL BAN DUE TO THE HIGHLY VOLATILE POLITICAL CLIMATE IN THE U.S. THIS DECISION REVEALS THE DEPTHS OF THE U.N.'S FEARS OF POTENTIAL CORRUPTION AND INSTABILITY WITHIN THE U.S. GOVERNMENT.
WITH THE UNITED STATES NOW LABELED AS "EXCOMMUNICADO" BY MANY COUNTRIES,...
...THOUSANDS OF U.S. CITIZENS HAVE FOUND THEMSELVES STRANDED IN FOREIGN AIRPORTS WORLDWIDE.
AS MORE DAYS PASS SINCE PRESIDENT MCDEARMON ASSUMED OFFICE, THE NATION CONTINUES TO WAIT ON THE RELEASE OF THE CONTINUITY OF GOVERNMENT PLAN.
MULTIPLE MEMBERS OF THE FIFTEEN EXECUTIVE DEPARTMENTS THAT FORM THE PRESIDENT'S CABINET HAVE BEEN DECLARED "MISSING AND PRESUMED DEAD" AS WELL AS THE SPEAKER OF THE HOUSE.
WE'RE...
...WE'RE JUST GETTING A REPORT OF A STANDOFF...
...BETWEEN THE POLICE DEPARTMENT AND ARMED CITIZENS IN THE TOWN OF MACON, GEORGIA.
NEWS

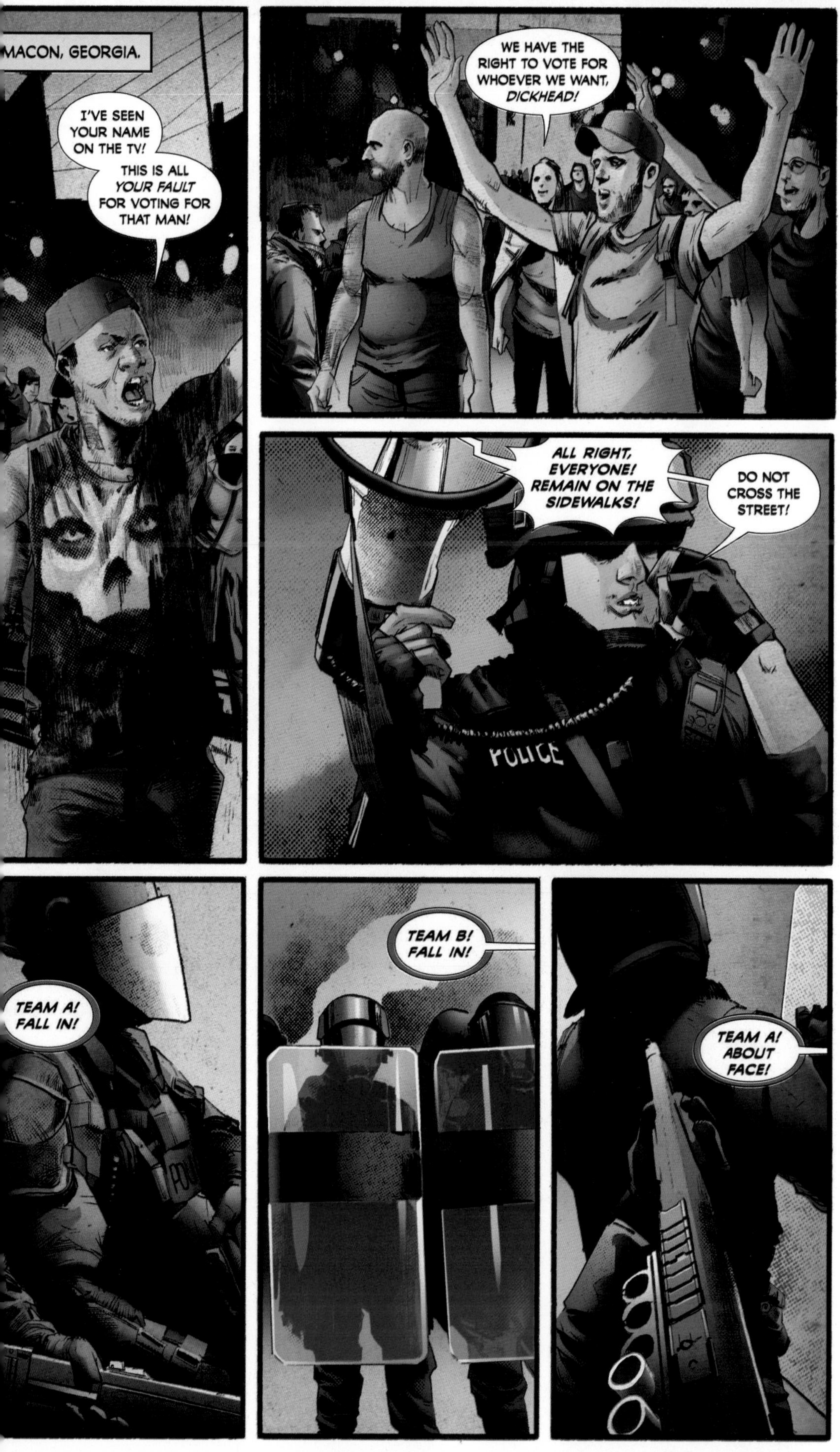
MACON, GEORGIA.
I'VE SEEN YOUR NAME ON THE TV!
THIS IS ALL *YOUR FAULT* FOR VOTING FOR THAT MAN!
WE HAVE THE RIGHT TO VOTE FOR WHOEVER WE WANT, *DICKHEAD!*
ALL RIGHT, EVERYONE! REMAIN ON THE SIDEWALKS!
DO NOT CROSS THE STREET!
POLICE
TEAM A! FALL IN!
TEAM B! FALL IN!
TEAM A! ABOUT FACE!

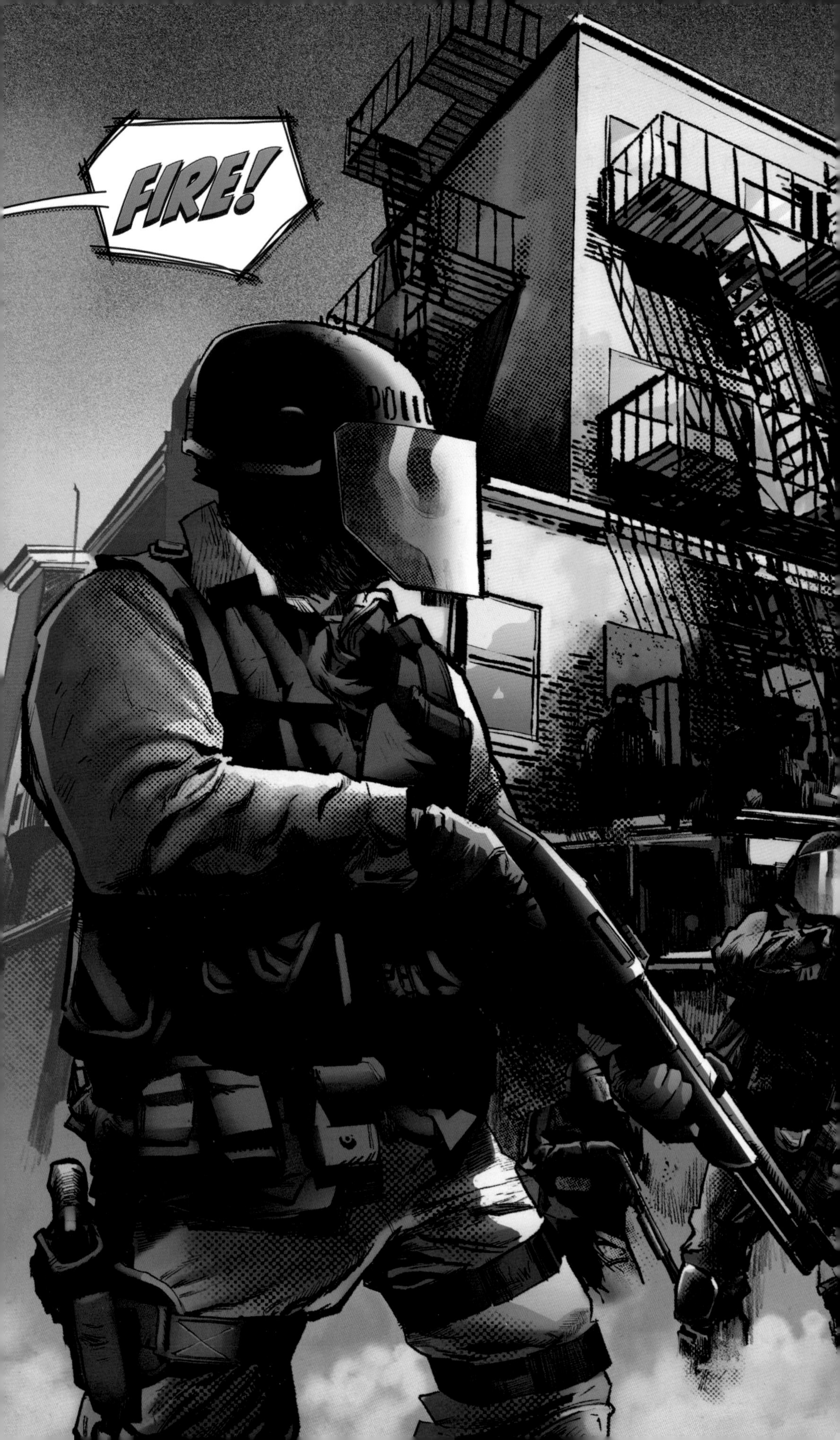
FIRE!

NO!
WHAT THE FUCK IS HAPPENING?!
MY GOD!!!
THEY CAN'T DO THIS!
DON'T!
IT'S THEM!
HEY!

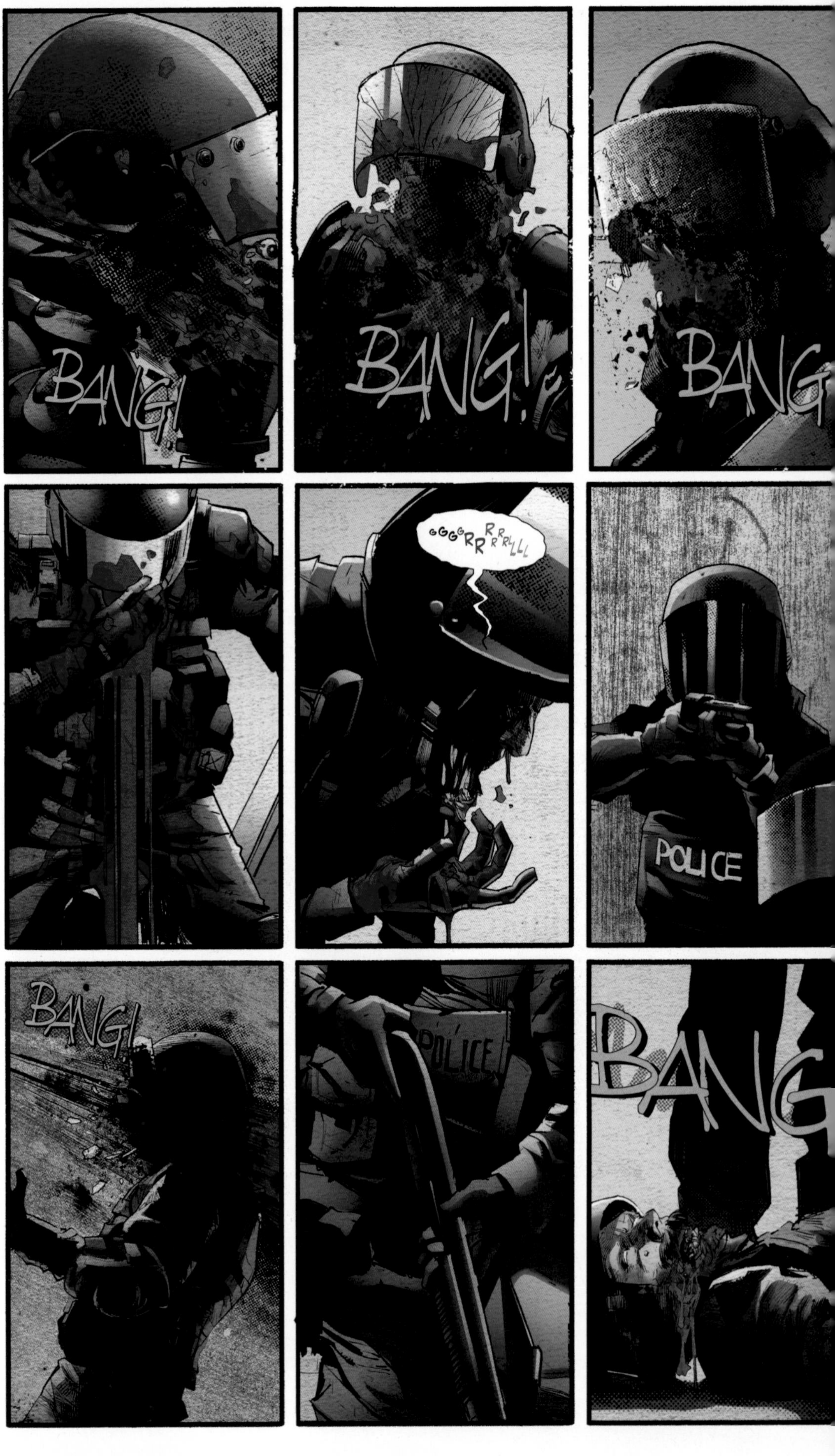
BANG!
BANG!
BANG
GGGGRRRRRRLLLL
POLICE
BANG!
POLICE
BANG

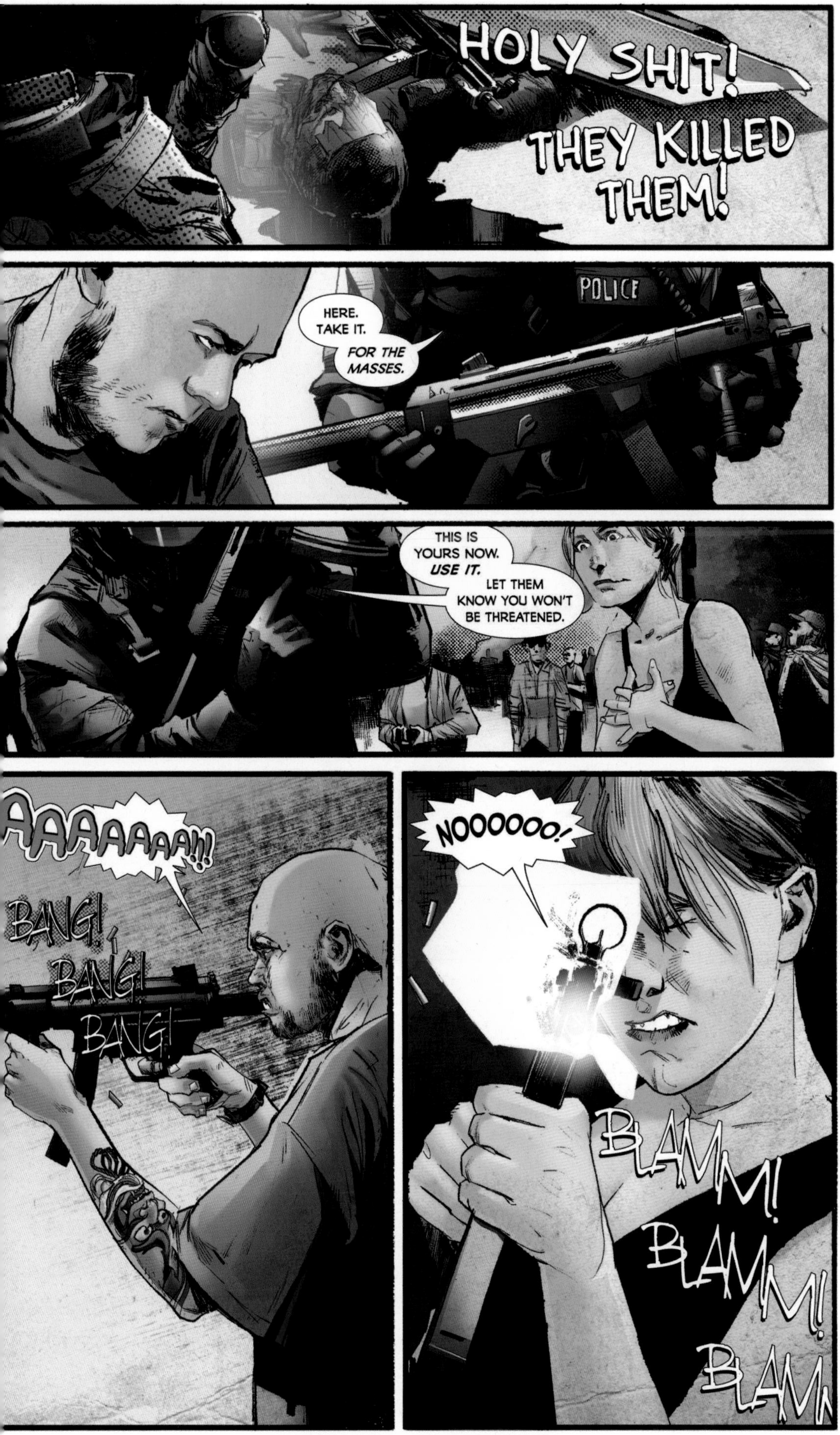

HOLY SHIT!
THEY KILLED THEM!
POLICE
HERE. TAKE IT. FOR THE MASSES.
THIS IS YOURS NOW. USE IT. LET THEM KNOW YOU WON'T BE THREATENED.
AAAAAAAA!!!
BANG! BANG! BANG!
NOOOOOO!
BLAMM! BLAMM! BLAM

CATOCTIN MOUNTAIN, MARYLAND.

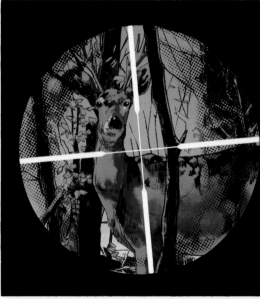

SONOVA.

THUMP THUMP THUMP THUMP
THUMP THUMP THUMP THUMP

GODDAMN IT!

THUMP THUMP THUMP THUMP THUMP
THUMP

THUMP THUMP THUMP THUMP THUMP THUMP THUMP THUMP THUMP THUMP THUMP THUMP

KEEP IT RUNNING.

THIS WON'T TAKE *LONG.*

I WAS WONDERING WHO'D COME FIRST.

THE CAVALRY OR *YOU.*

JOHN. I *AM* THE CAVALRY.

NO SECURITY DETAIL.

I RESPECT THAT.

I FIGURED, IF SOMEONE REALLY WANTED ME DEAD, THEN NOTHING WOULD *STOP* THEM.

YOU'RE RIGHT ABOUT THAT, MY FRIEND.

I SEE YOU GOT MY *GIFT.* HAVEN'T OPENED IT YET?

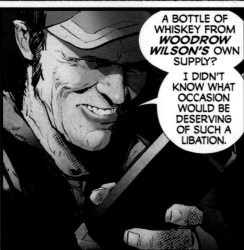

A BOTTLE OF WHISKEY FROM *WOODROW WILSON'S* OWN SUPPLY?

I DIDN'T KNOW WHAT OCCASION WOULD BE DESERVING OF SUCH A LIBATION.

NOW.

NOW'S THE TIME, JOHN.

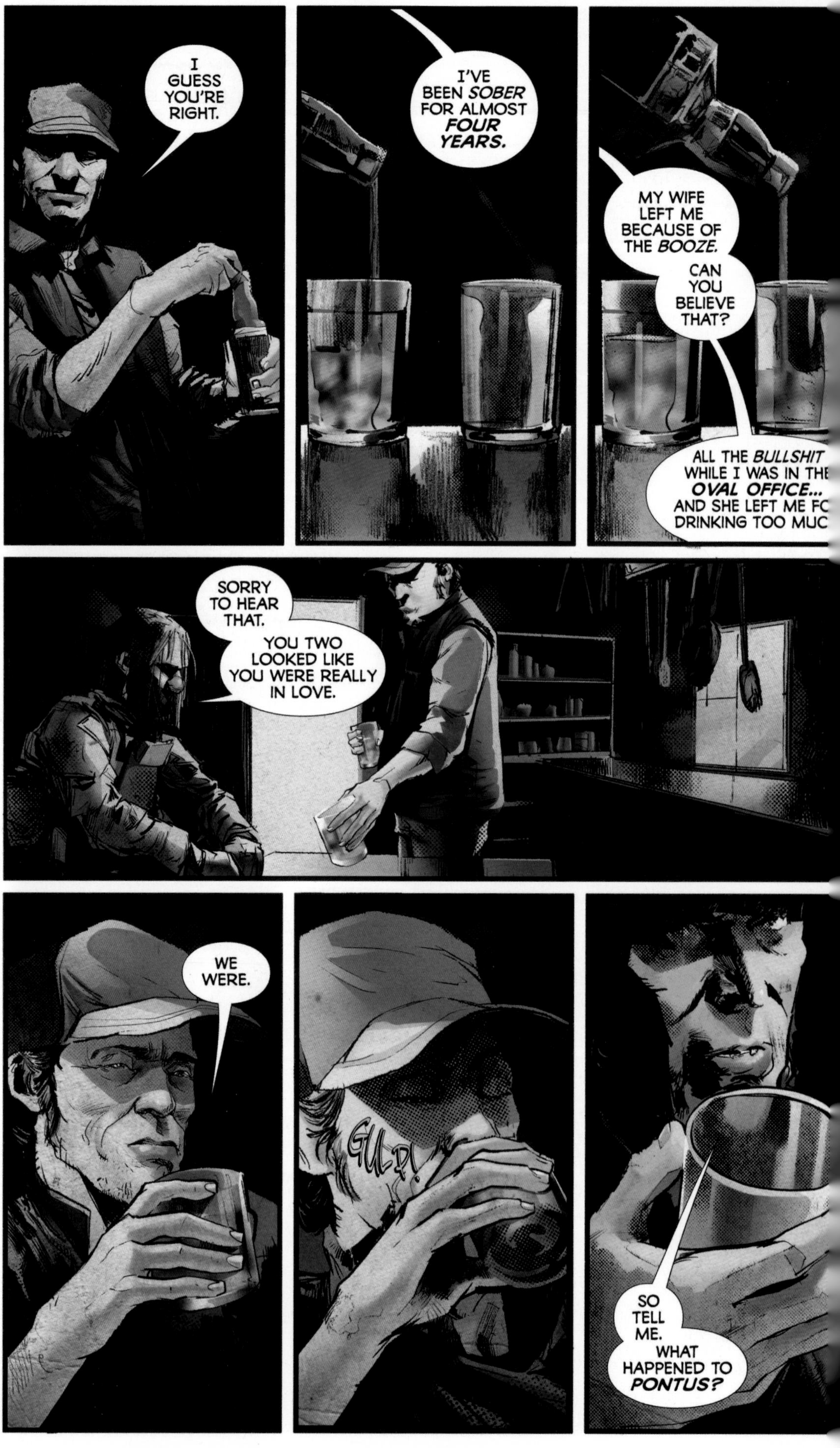
I GUESS YOU'RE RIGHT.
I'VE BEEN *SOBER* FOR ALMOST *FOUR YEARS.*
MY WIFE LEFT ME BECAUSE OF THE *BOOZE.*
CAN YOU BELIEVE THAT?
ALL THE *BULLSHIT* WHILE I WAS IN THE *OVAL OFFICE...* AND SHE LEFT ME FO DRINKING TOO MUC
SORRY TO HEAR THAT.
YOU TWO LOOKED LIKE YOU WERE REALLY IN LOVE.
WE WERE.
GULP!
SO TELL ME.
WHAT HAPPENED TO *PONTUS?*

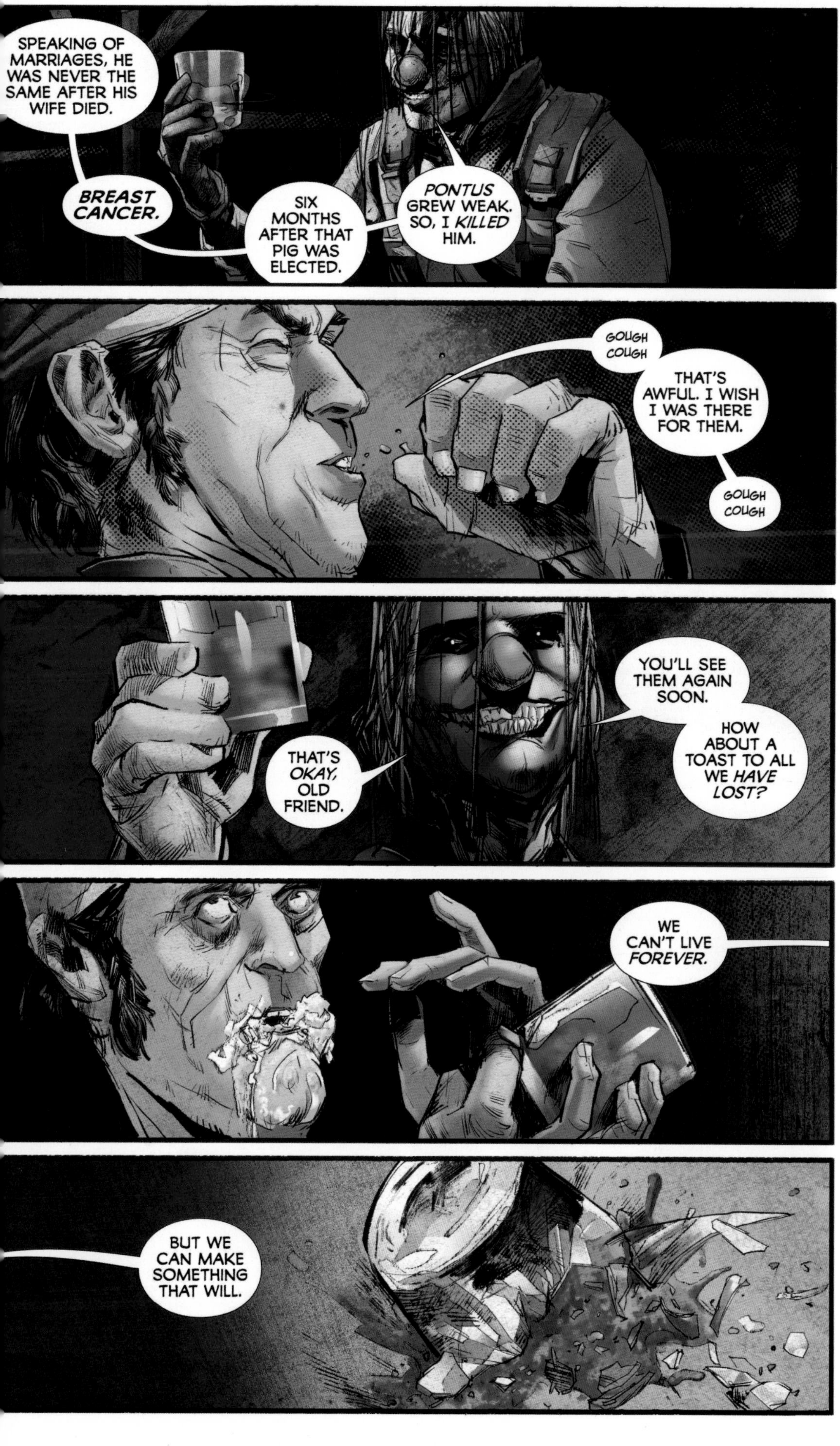
SPEAKING OF MARRIAGES, HE WAS NEVER THE SAME AFTER HIS WIFE DIED.
BREAST CANCER.
SIX MONTHS AFTER THAT PIG WAS ELECTED.
PONTUS GREW WEAK. SO, I KILLED HIM.
GOUGH COUGH
THAT'S AWFUL. I WISH I WAS THERE FOR THEM.
GOUGH COUGH
THAT'S OKAY, OLD FRIEND.
YOU'LL SEE THEM AGAIN SOON.
HOW ABOUT A TOAST TO ALL WE HAVE LOST?
WE CAN'T LIVE FOREVER.
BUT WE CAN MAKE SOMETHING THAT WILL.

HOW'D IT GO?

ANYONE LEFT ON OUR SIDE?

I WENT TO THE ACADEMY WITH MANY OF THEM.

A WEEK AGO, I'D HAVE GIVEN MY LIFE FOR ANY OF THEM.

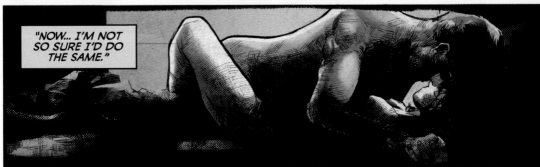

"NOW... I'M NOT SO SURE I'D DO THE SAME."

ARE YOU TELLING ME THERE'S NO ONE WE CAN TRUST?

WE NEED TO PLAY IT SAFE.

NO ONE IN THE WHITE HOUSE BUT YOU AND ME.

IF THE AGENTS WANT TO PROTECT YOU, THEY CAN DO IT FROM OUTSIDE THE FENCE.

IT'D TAKE A TANK TO GET IN HERE ANYWAYS.

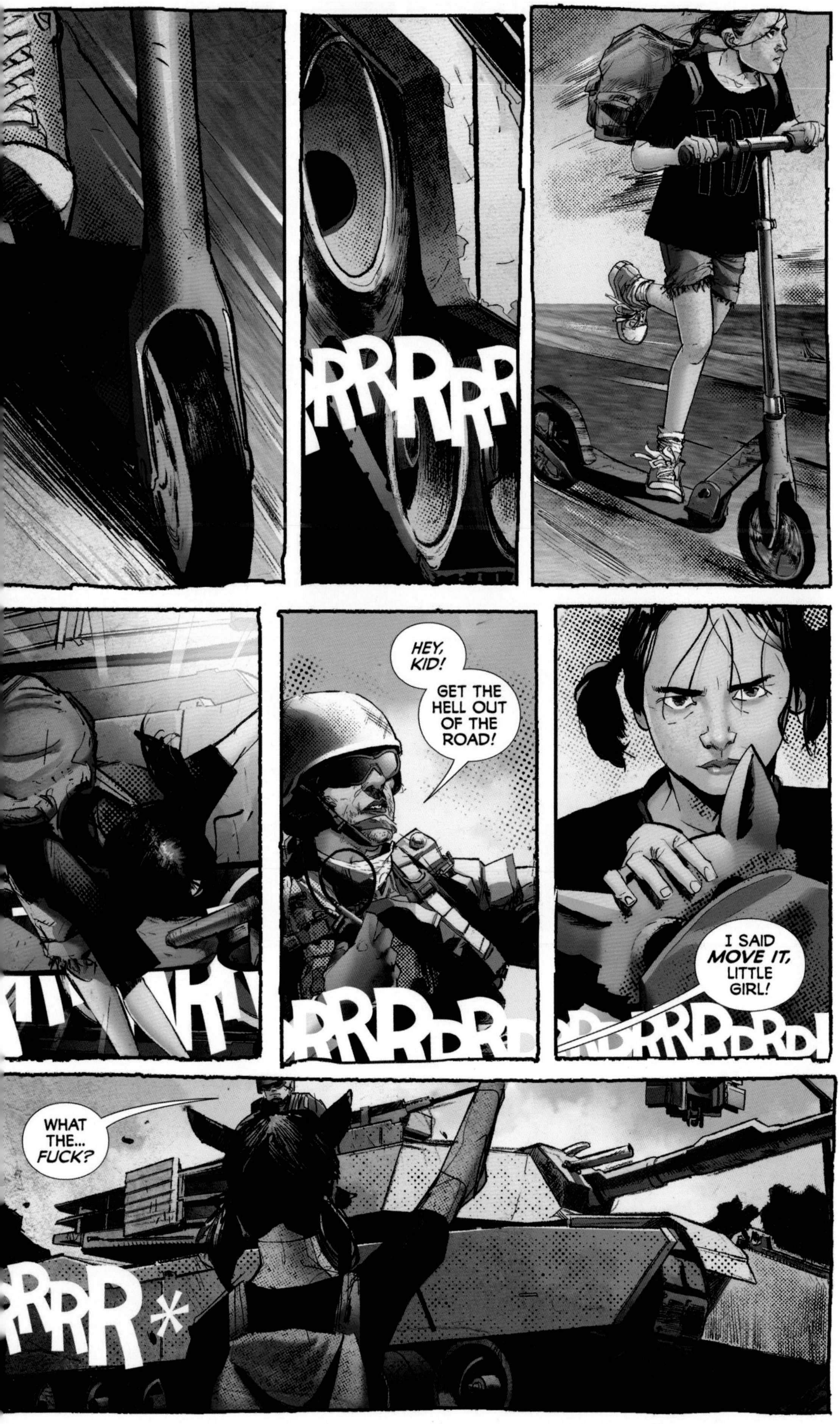
HEY, KID!
GET THE HELL OUT OF THE ROAD!
I SAID MOVE IT, LITTLE GIRL!
WHAT THE... FUCK?

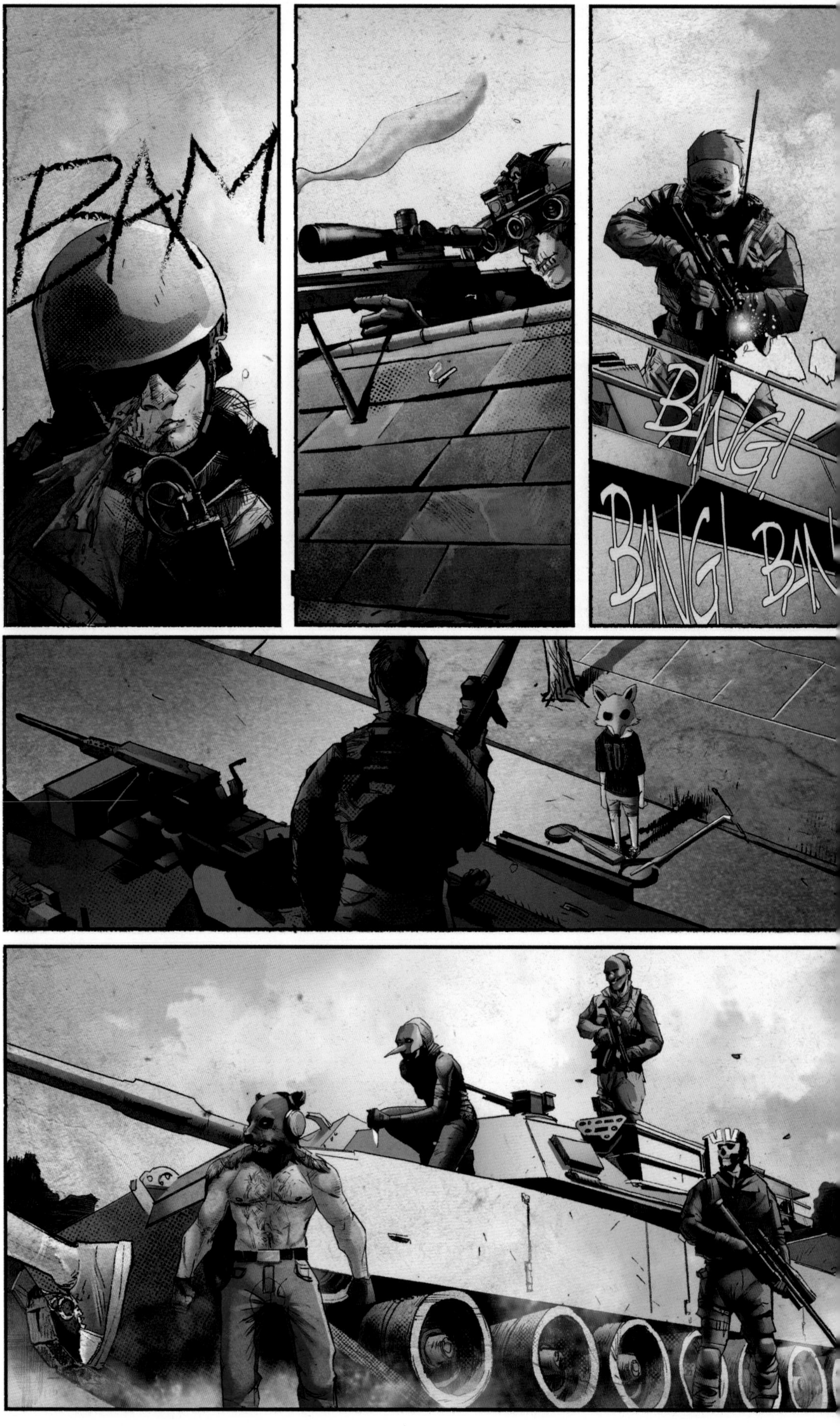
BAM
BANG!
BANG! BAN

SNFF
SNFF

I'M SORRY, SON.

I *FAILED* YOU.

I COULDN'T DO IT.

I COULDN'T KILL THEM.

PLEASE *FORGIVE* ME.

PLEASE, FORGIVE ME.

CHHK
CHHK

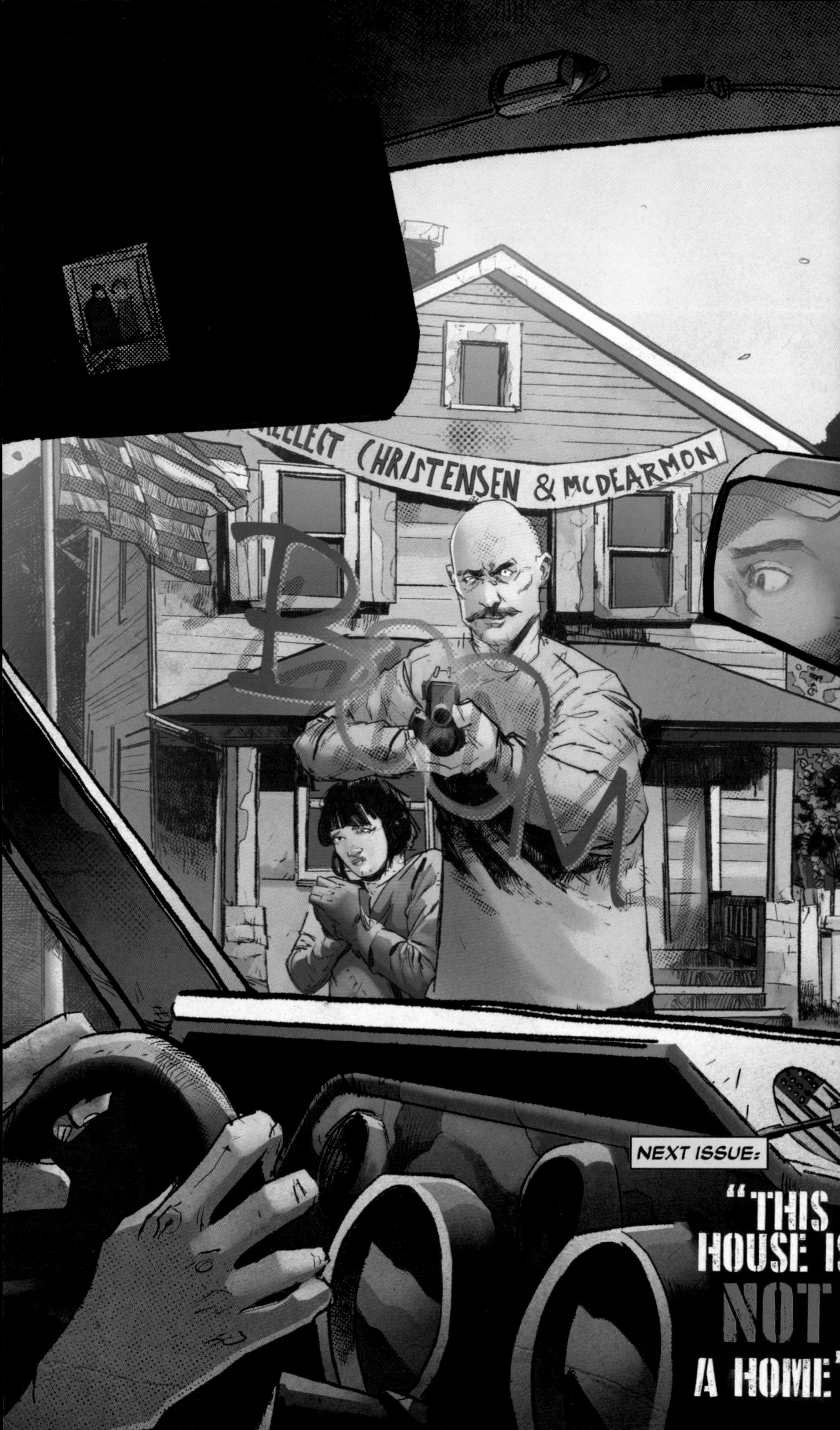

ELECT CHRISTENSEN & MCDEARMON
BOOM
NEXT ISSUE:
"THIS HOUSE IS NOT A HOME"

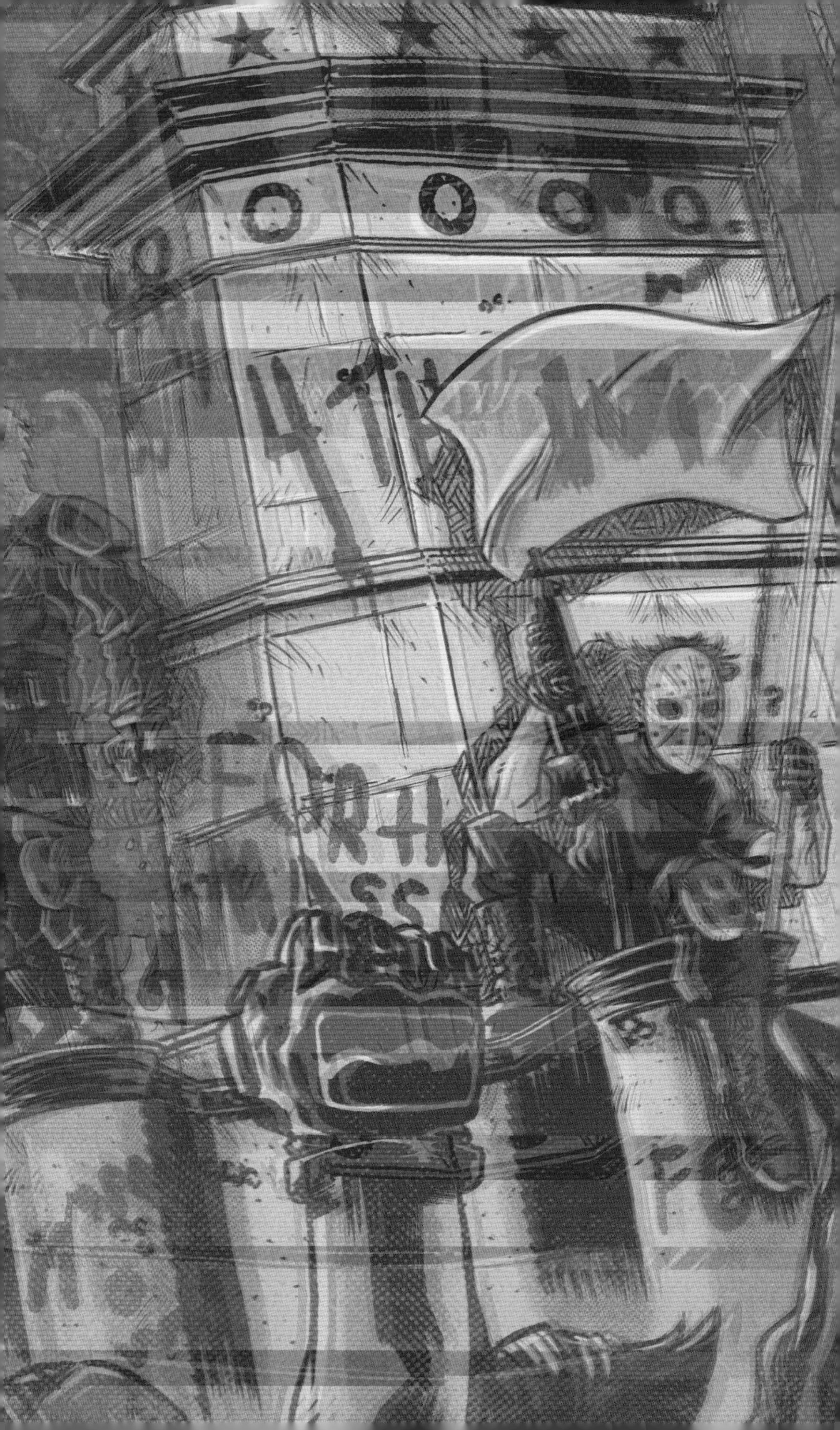

CHAPTER 4

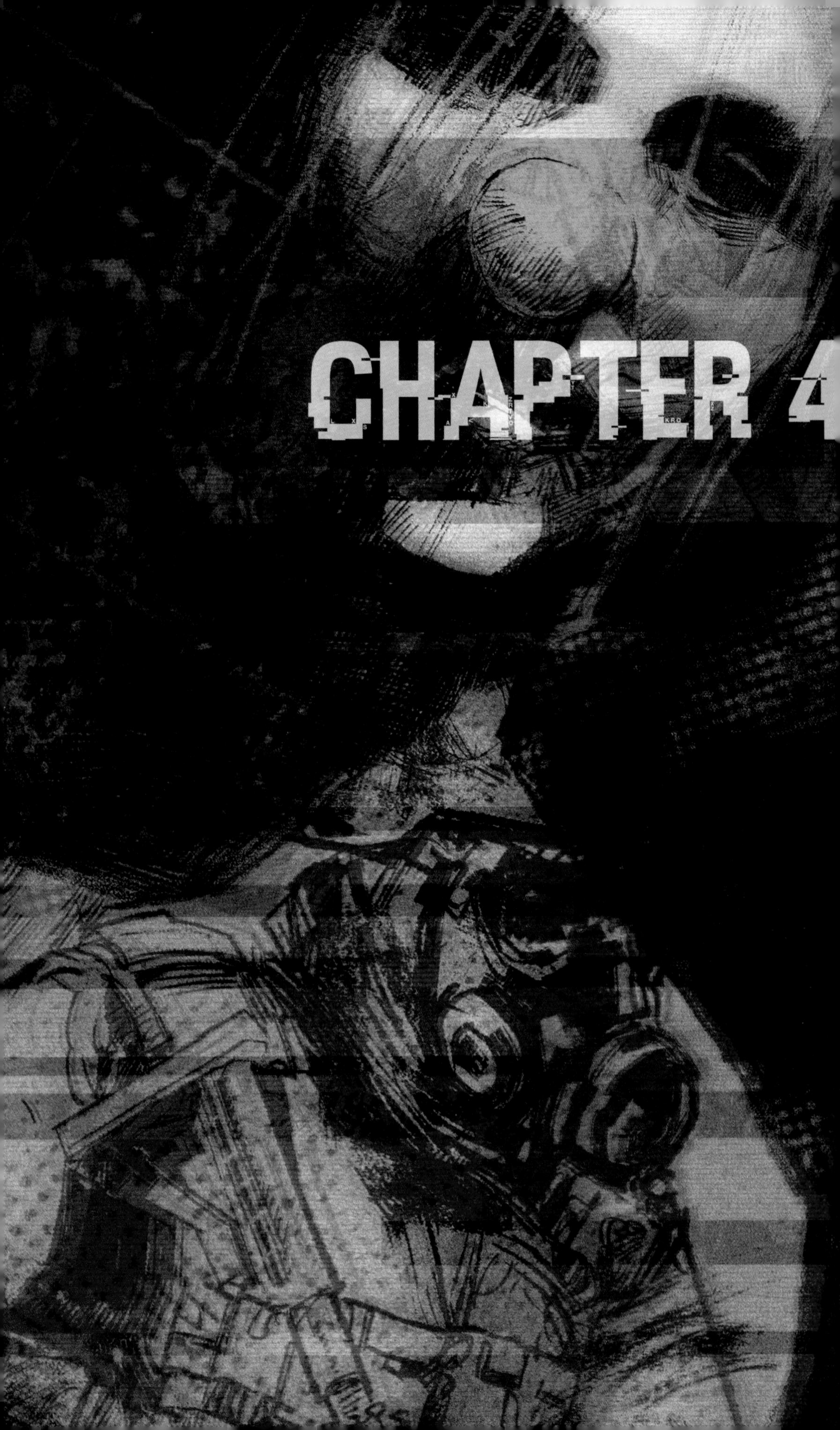

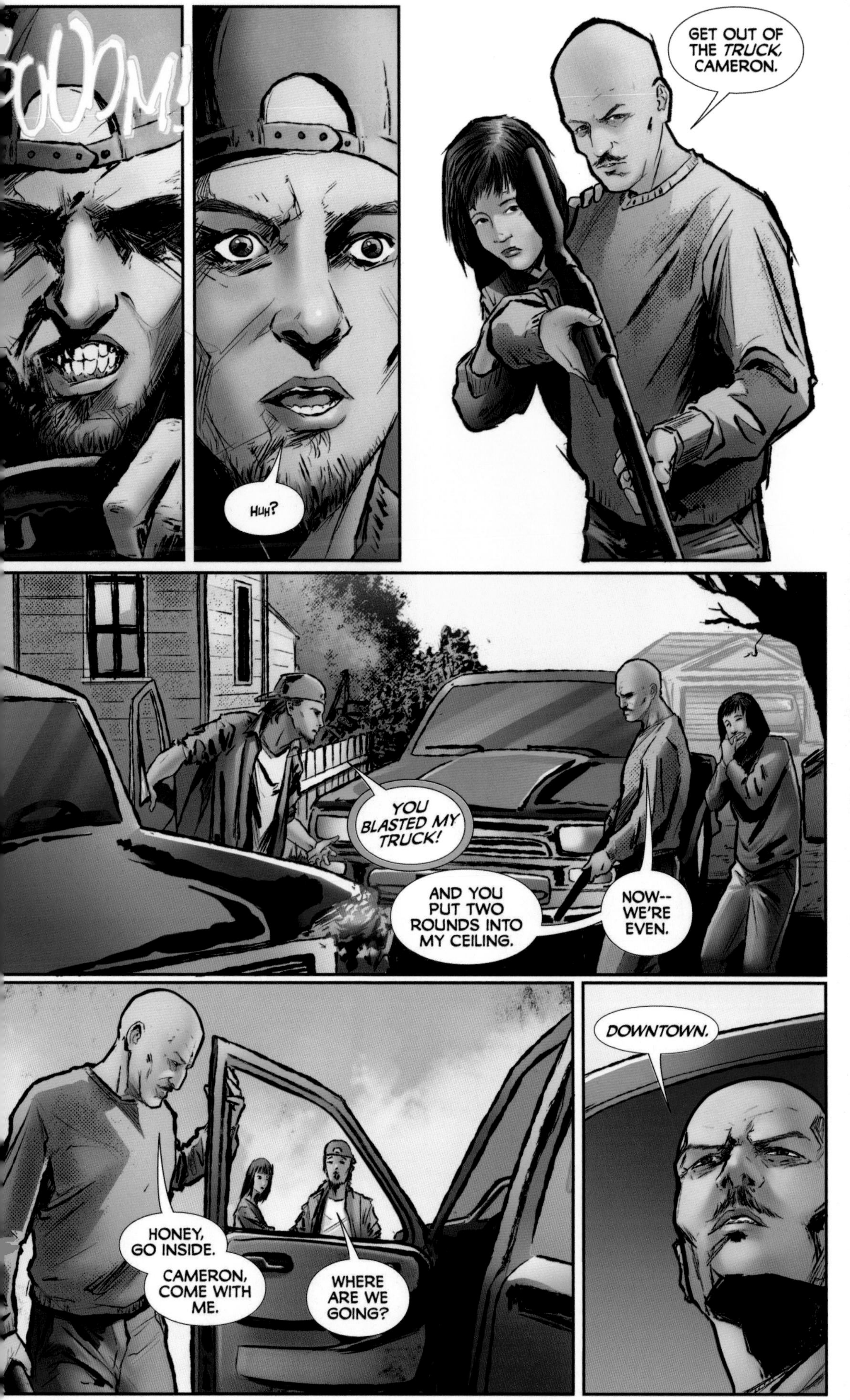
BOOOM!
HUH?
GET OUT OF THE *TRUCK,* CAMERON.
YOU BLASTED MY TRUCK!
AND YOU PUT TWO ROUNDS INTO MY CEILING.
NOW-- WE'RE EVEN.
HONEY, GO INSIDE.
CAMERON, COME WITH ME.
WHERE ARE WE GOING?
DOWNTOWN.

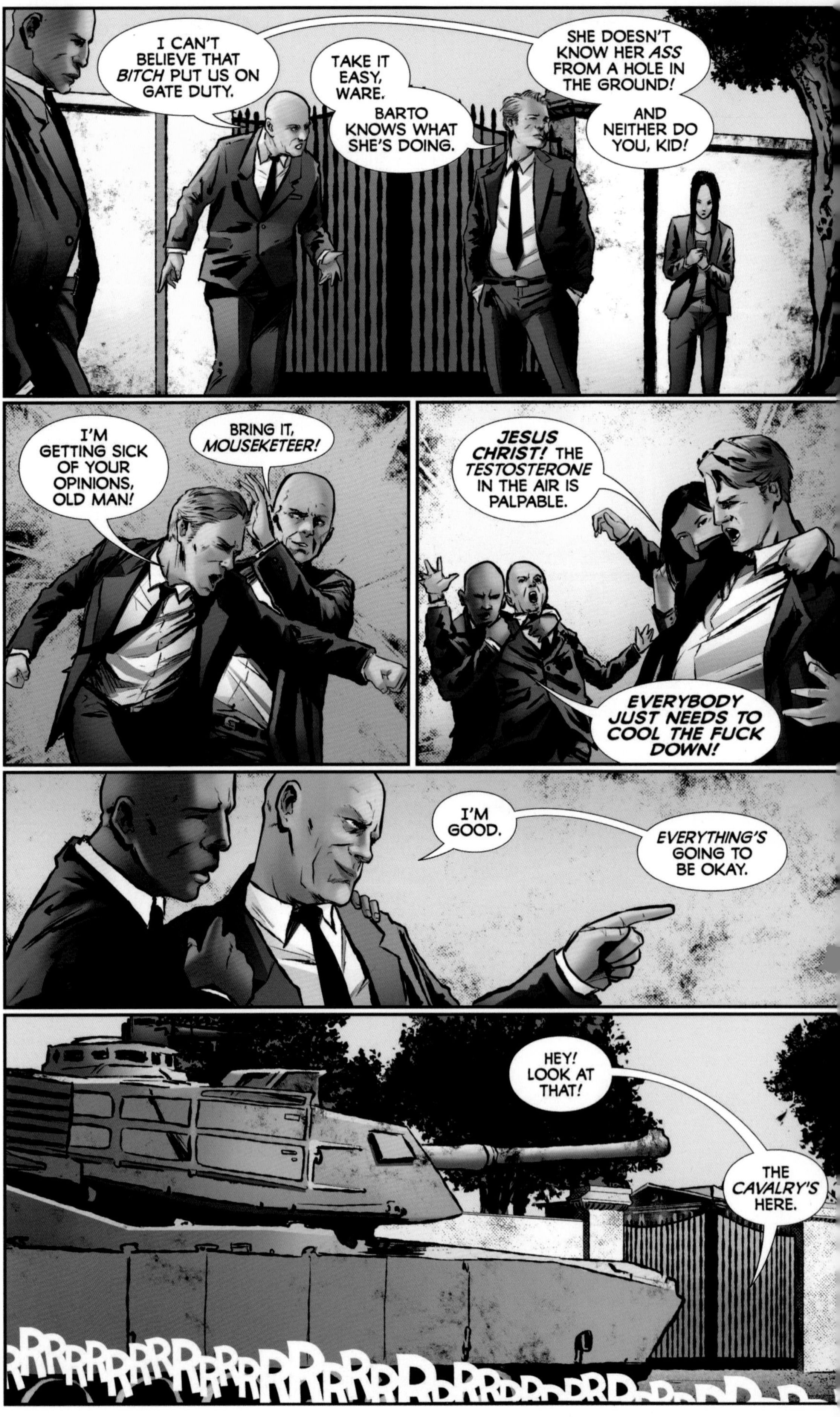
I CAN'T BELIEVE THAT BITCH PUT US ON GATE DUTY.
SHE DOESN'T KNOW HER ASS FROM A HOLE IN THE GROUND!
TAKE IT EASY, WARE.
BARTO KNOWS WHAT SHE'S DOING.
AND NEITHER DO YOU, KID!
I'M GETTING SICK OF YOUR OPINIONS, OLD MAN!
BRING IT, MOUSEKETEER!
JESUS CHRIST! THE TESTOSTERONE IN THE AIR IS PALPABLE.
EVERYBODY JUST NEEDS TO COOL THE FUCK DOWN!
I'M GOOD.
EVERYTHING'S GOING TO BE OKAY.
HEY! LOOK AT THAT!
THE CAVALRY'S HERE.
RRRRRRRRRRRRRRRRRRRRRRRRRRRRRR

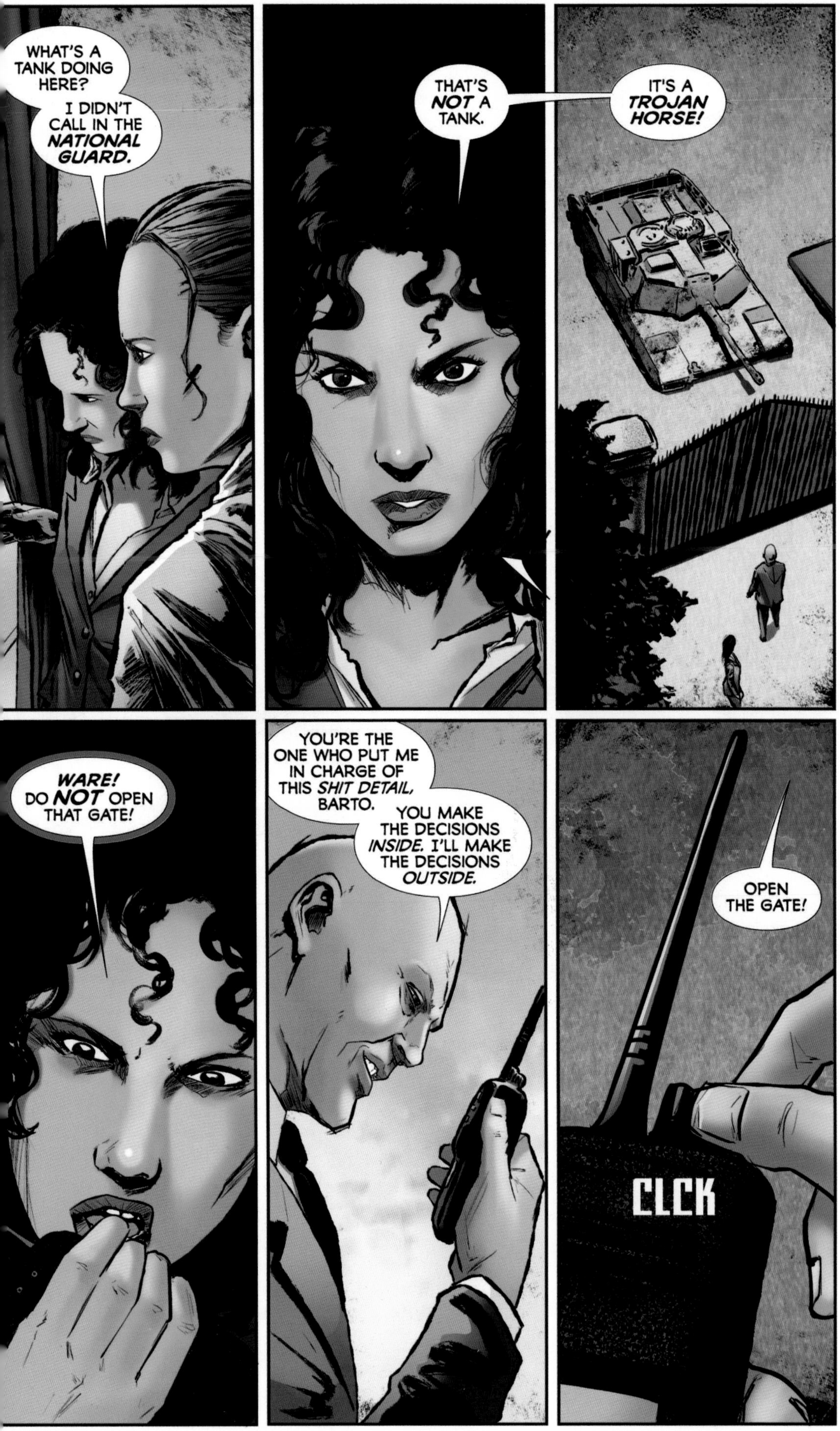
WHAT'S A TANK DOING HERE?
I DIDN'T CALL IN THE *NATIONAL GUARD.*
THAT'S *NOT* A TANK.
IT'S A *TROJAN HORSE!*
WARE! DO ***NOT*** OPEN THAT GATE!
YOU'RE THE ONE WHO PUT ME IN CHARGE OF THIS *SHIT DETAIL,* BARTO.
YOU MAKE THE DECISIONS *INSIDE.* I'LL MAKE THE DECISIONS *OUTSIDE.*
OPEN THE GATE!
CLCK

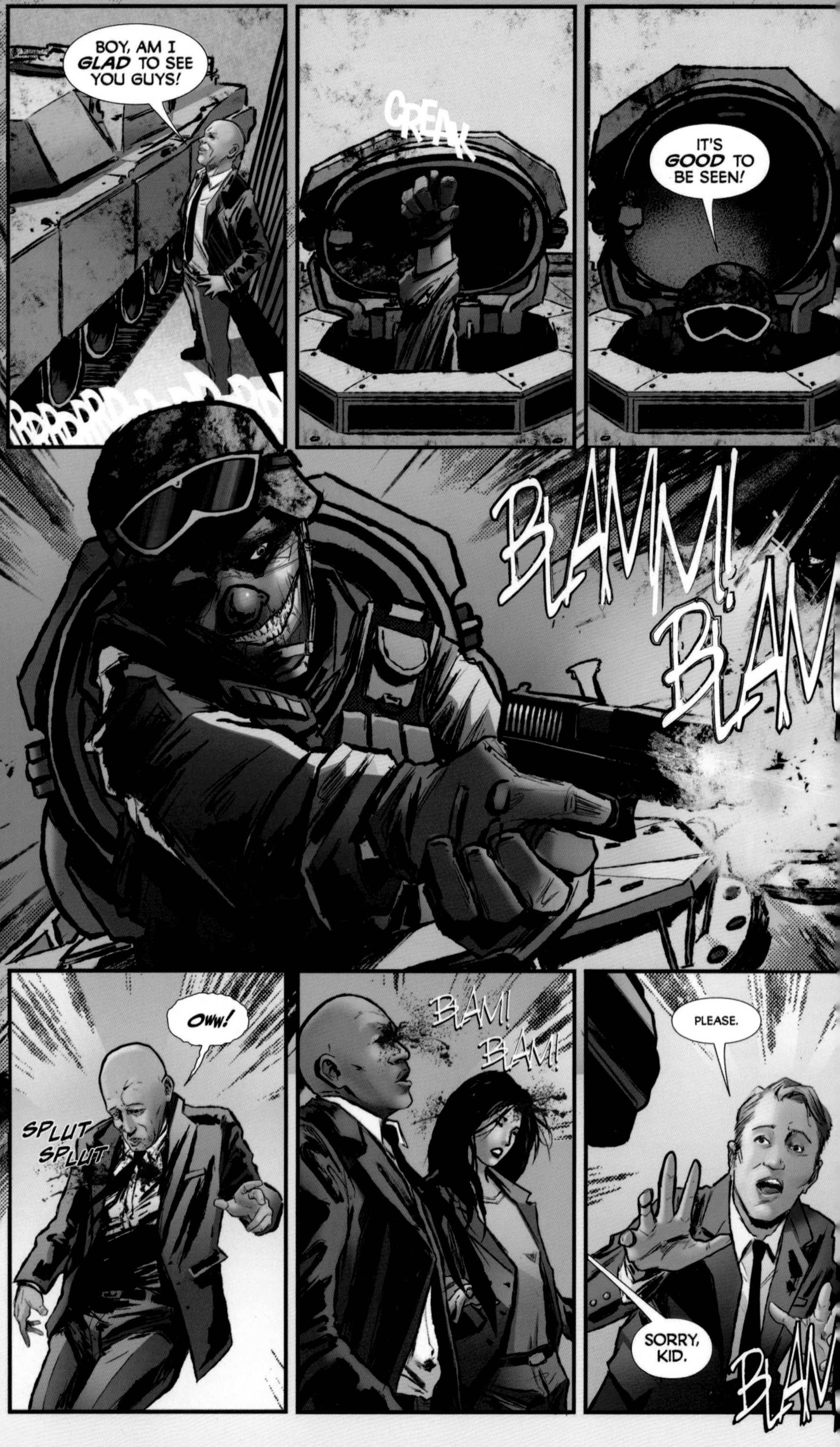
BOY, AM I GLAD TO SEE YOU GUYS!
RRRRRRRRRRRRRRR
CREAK
IT'S GOOD TO BE SEEN!
BLAMM!
BLAM
OWW!
SPLUT
SPLUT
BLAM!
BLAM!
PLEASE.
SORRY, KID.
BLAM

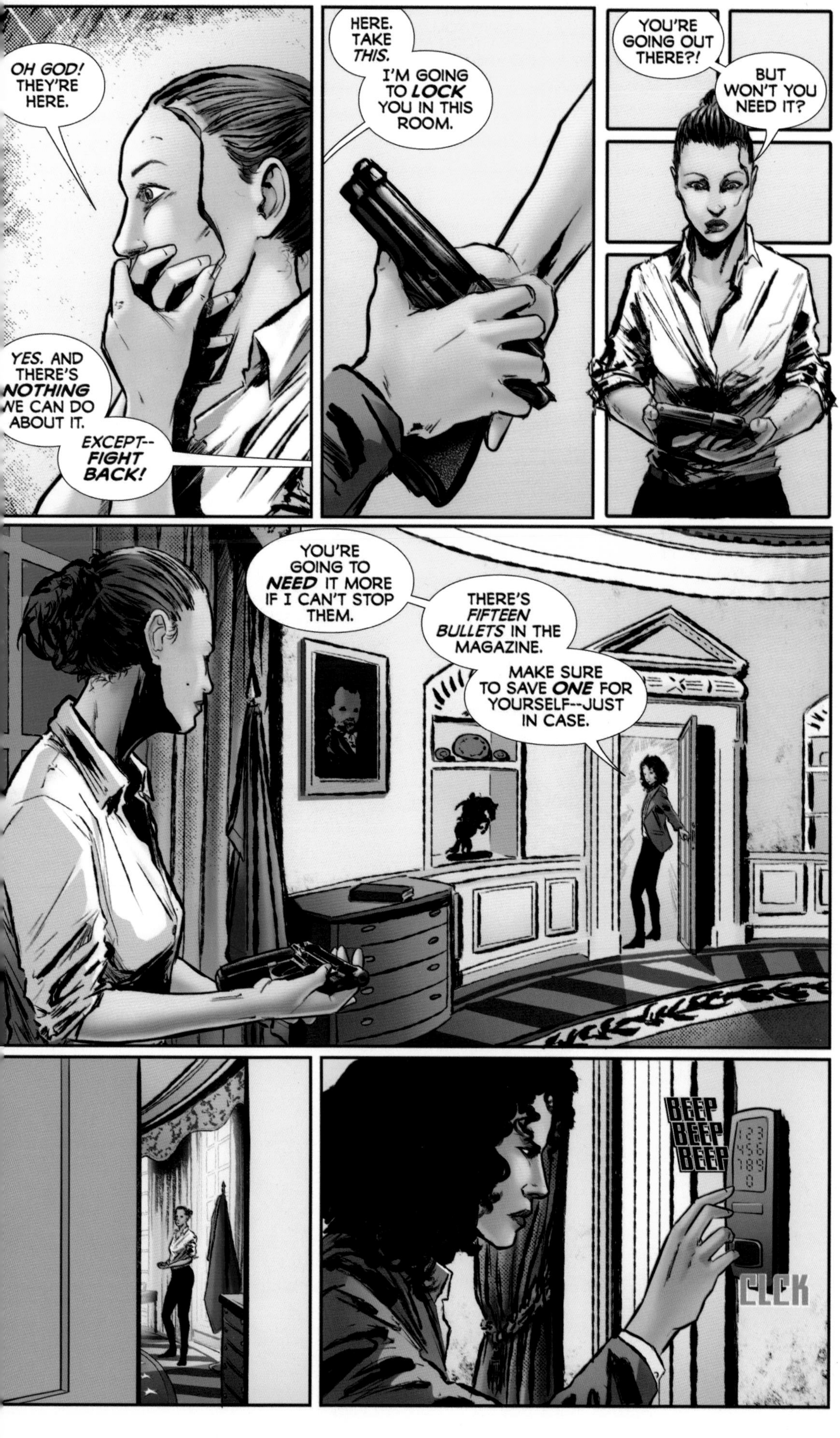
OH GOD! THEY'RE HERE.
YES. AND THERE'S NOTHING WE CAN DO ABOUT IT.
EXCEPT-- FIGHT BACK!
HERE. TAKE THIS.
I'M GOING TO LOCK YOU IN THIS ROOM.
YOU'RE GOING OUT THERE?!
BUT WON'T YOU NEED IT?
YOU'RE GOING TO NEED IT MORE IF I CAN'T STOP THEM.
THERE'S FIFTEEN BULLETS IN THE MAGAZINE.
MAKE SURE TO SAVE ONE FOR YOURSELF--JUST IN CASE.
BEEP BEEP BEEP
CLICK

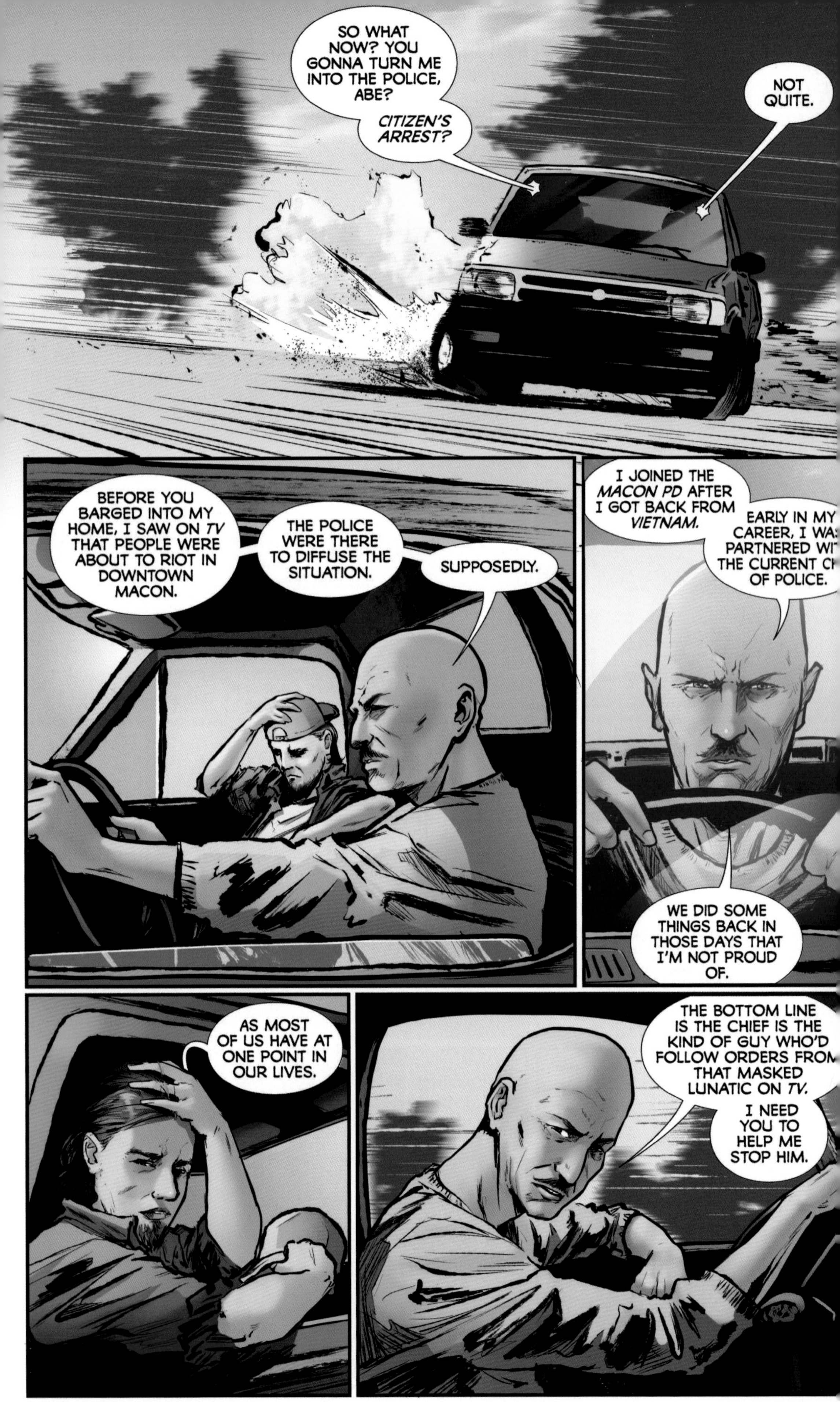
SO WHAT NOW? YOU GONNA TURN ME INTO THE POLICE, ABE?
CITIZEN'S ARREST?
NOT QUITE.
BEFORE YOU BARGED INTO MY HOME, I SAW ON *TV* THAT PEOPLE WERE ABOUT TO RIOT IN DOWNTOWN MACON.
THE POLICE WERE THERE TO DIFFUSE THE SITUATION.
SUPPOSEDLY.
I JOINED THE *MACON PD* AFTER I GOT BACK FROM *VIETNAM.*
EARLY IN MY CAREER, I WA
WE DID SOME THINGS BACK IN THOSE DAYS THAT I'M NOT PROUD OF.
AS MOST OF US HAVE AT ONE POINT IN OUR LIVES.
THE BOTTOM LINE IS THE CHIEF IS THE KIND OF GUY WHO'D
THAT MASKED LUNATIC ON *TV.*
I NEED YOU TO HELP ME STOP HIM.

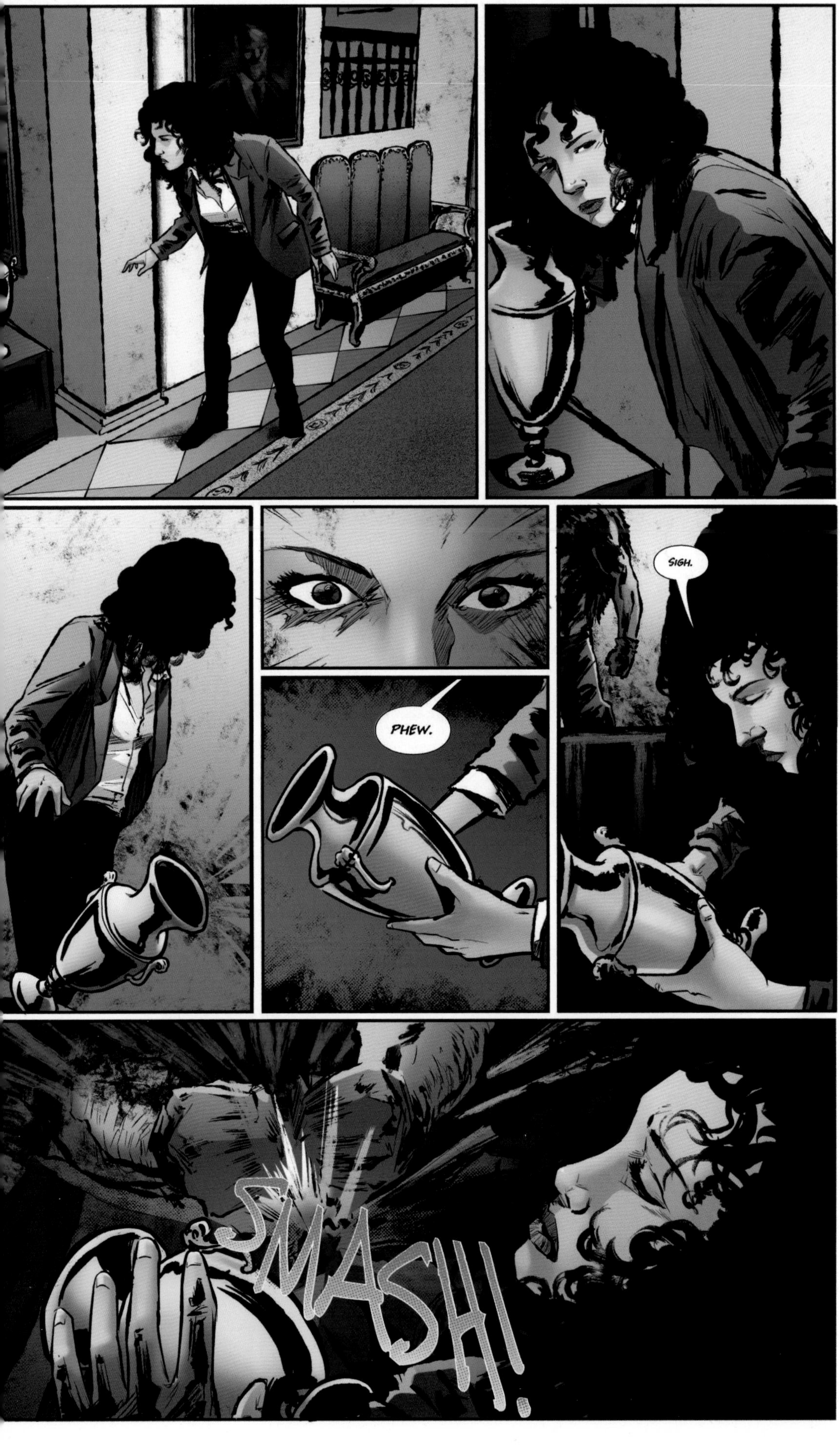
PHEW.
SIGH.
SMASH!

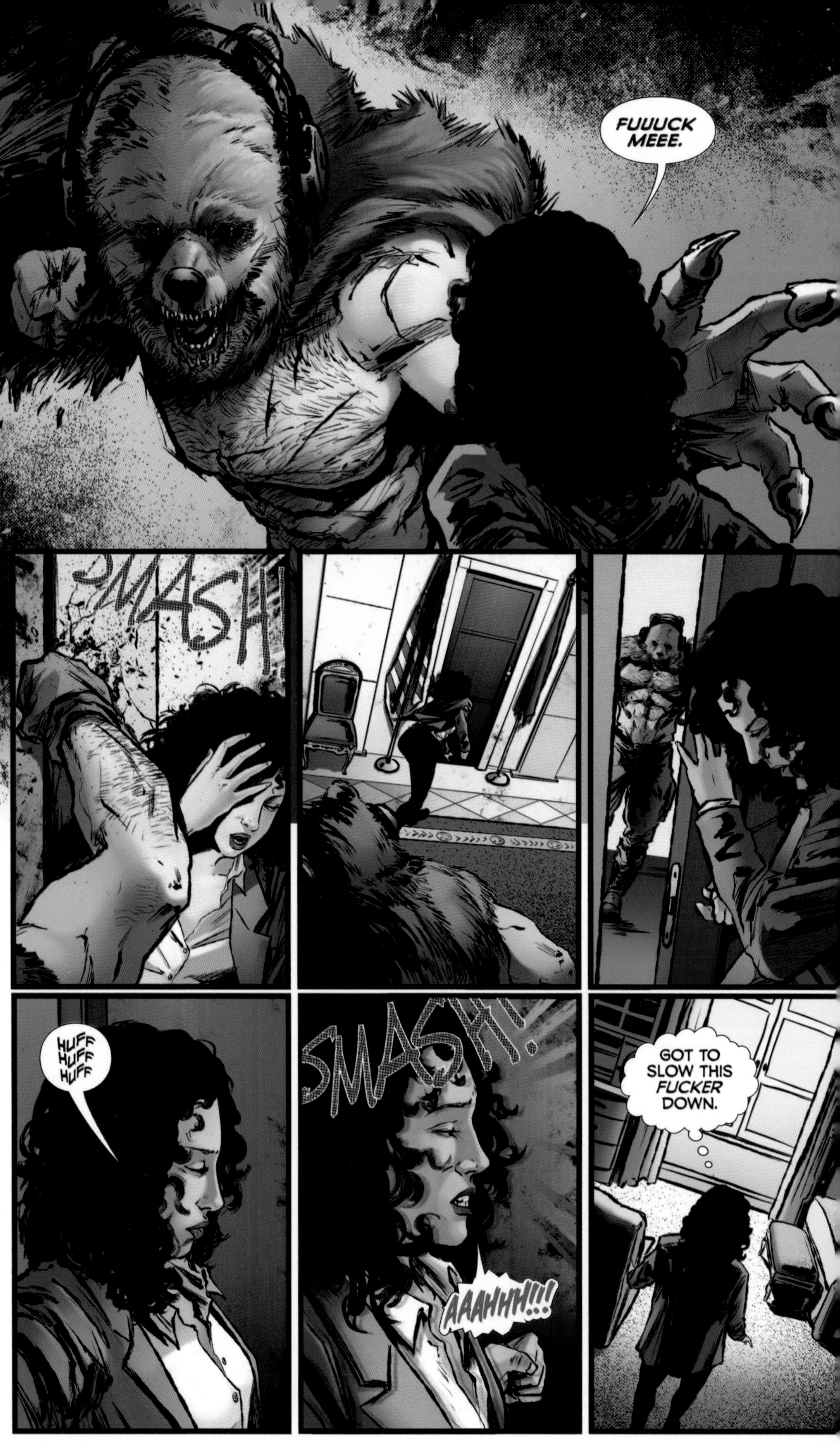
FUUUCK MEEE.
SMASH!
HUFF HUFF HUFF
SMASH!
AAAHHH!!!
GOT TO SLOW THIS FUCKER DOWN.

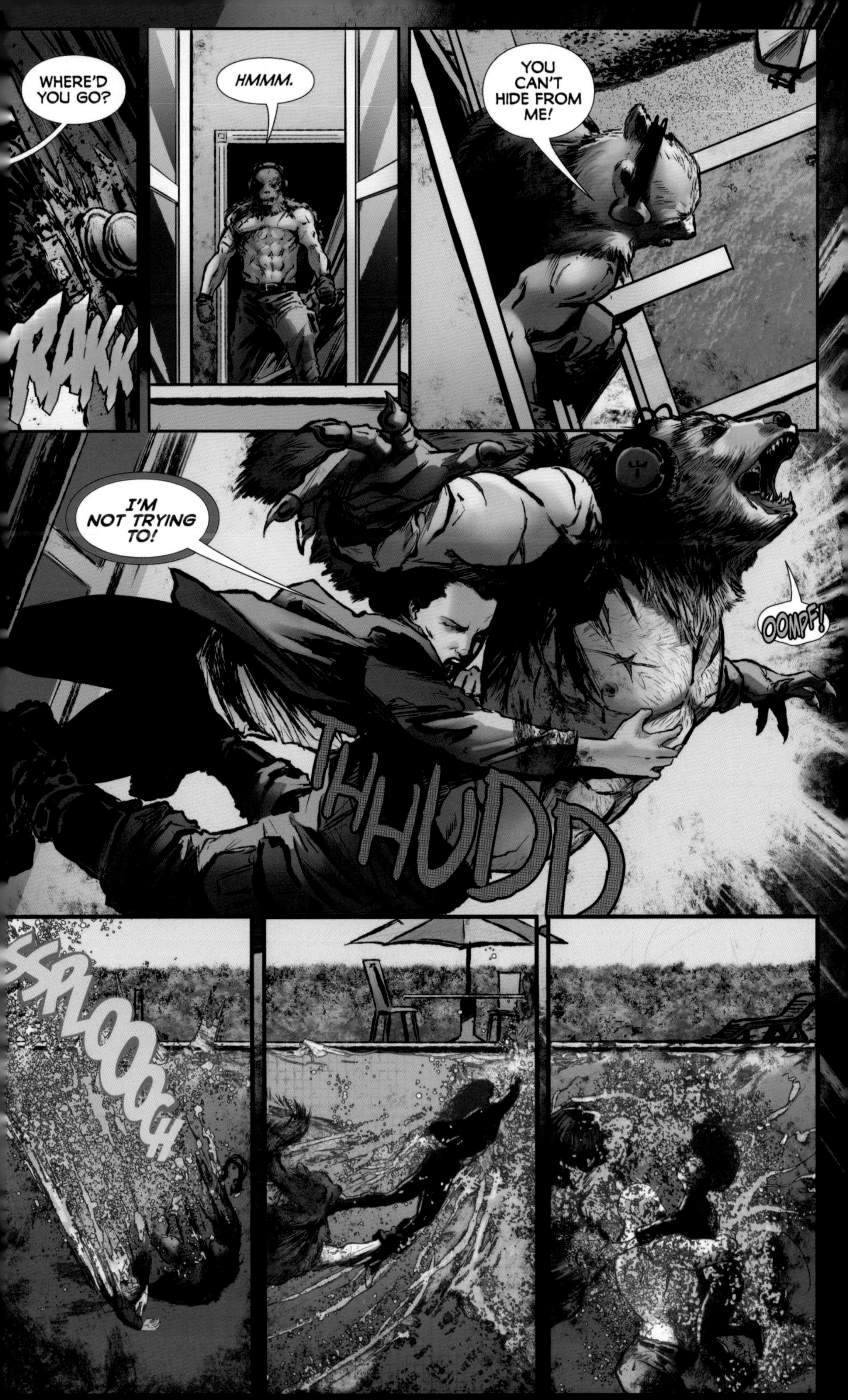
WHERE'D YOU GO?
KRAKK
HMMM.
YOU CAN'T HIDE FROM ME!
I'M NOT TRYING TO!
OOMPF!
THHUDD
SPLOOOSH

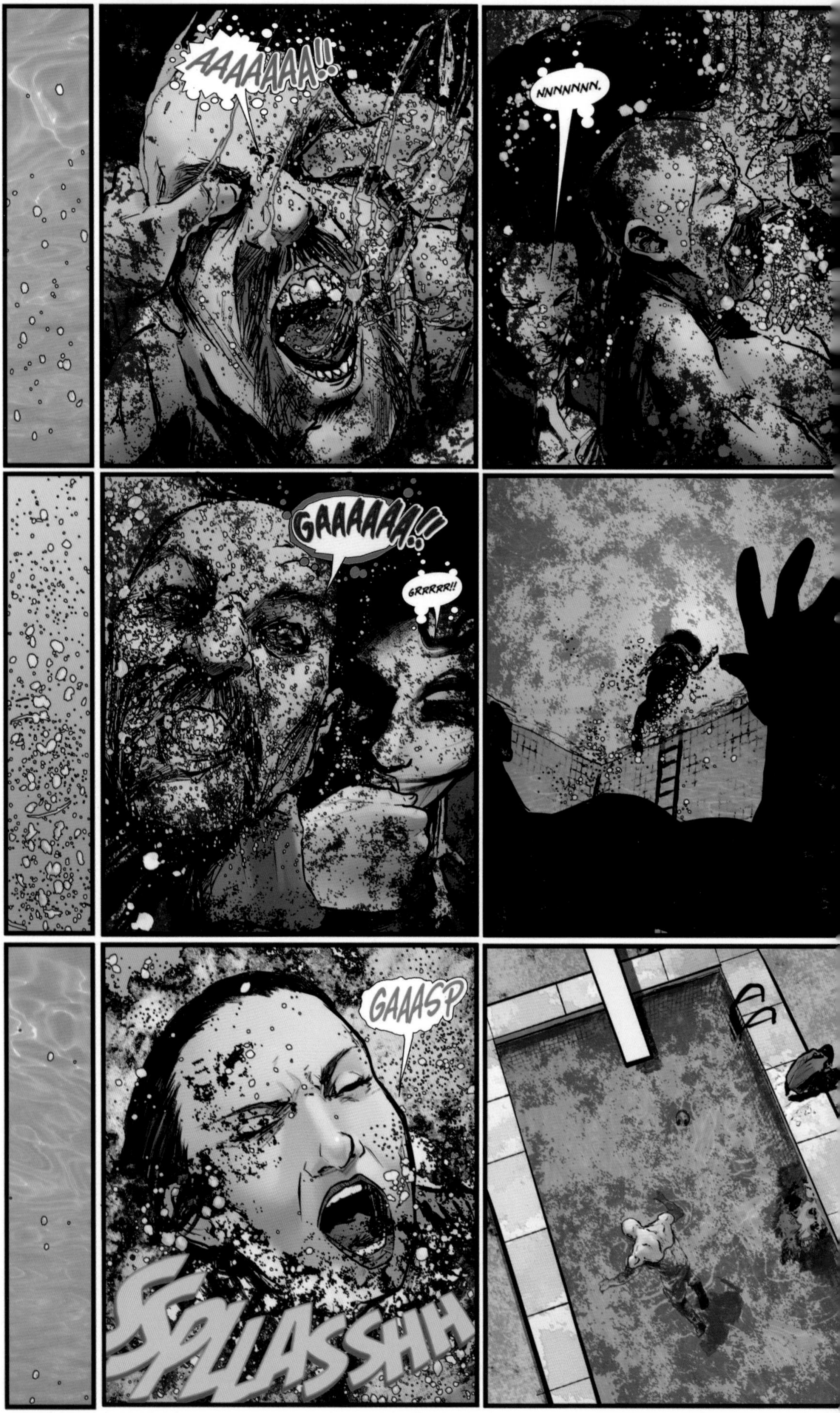
AAAAAAA!!
NNNNNNN.
GAAAAAA!!
GRRRRR!!
GAAASP
SPLASSHH

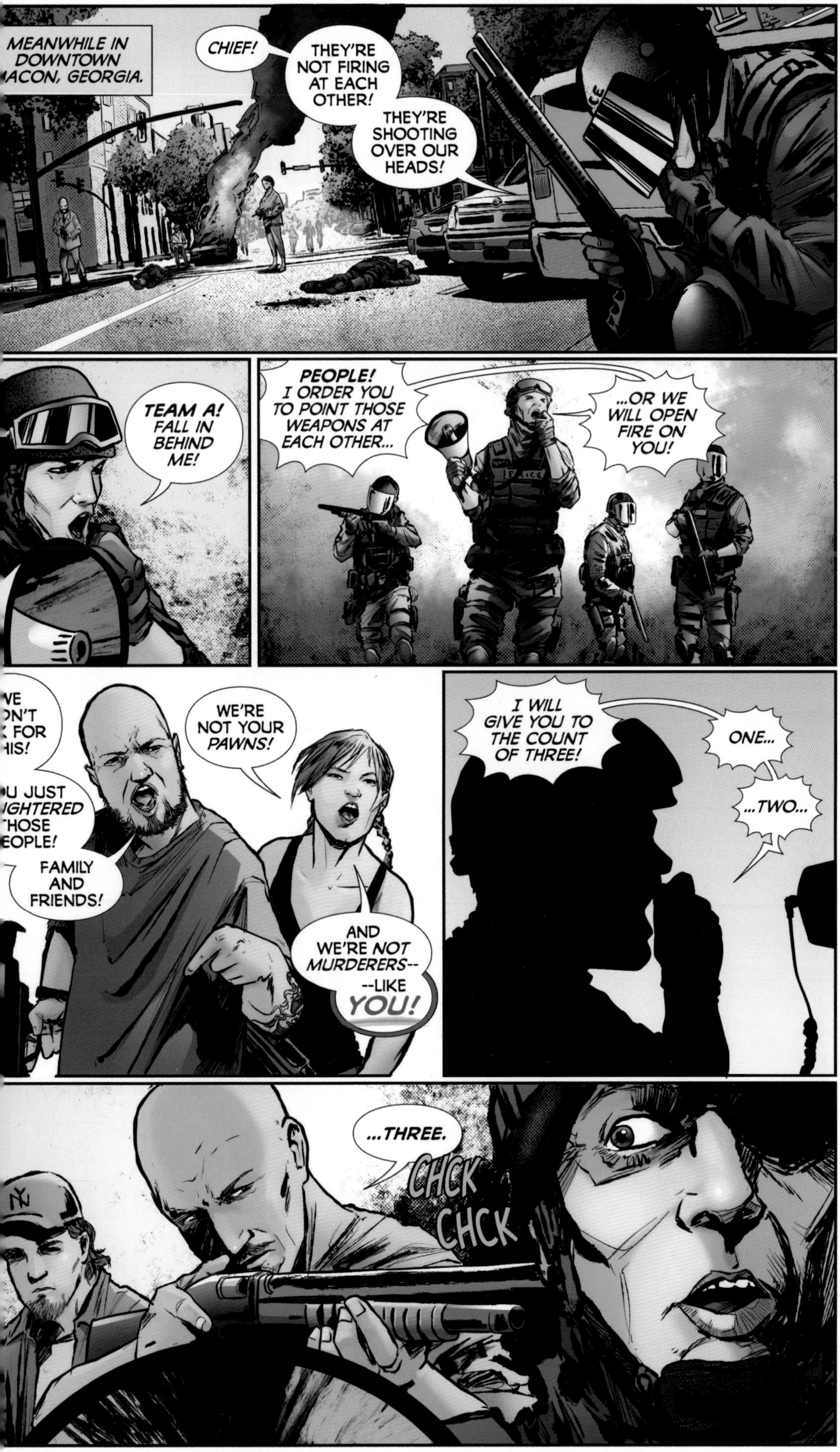

MEANWHILE IN DOWNTOWN ACON, GEORGIA.
CHIEF!
THEY'RE NOT FIRING AT EACH OTHER!
THEY'RE SHOOTING OVER OUR HEADS!
TEAM A! FALL IN BEHIND ME!
PEOPLE! I ORDER YOU TO POINT THOSE WEAPONS AT EACH OTHER...
...OR WE WILL OPEN FIRE ON YOU!
VE N'T FOR HIS!
U JUST IGHTERED THOSE EOPLE!
FAMILY AND FRIENDS!
WE'RE NOT YOUR PAWNS!
AND WE'RE NOT MURDERERS--
--LIKE YOU!
I WILL GIVE YOU TO THE COUNT OF THREE!
ONE...
...TWO...
...THREE.
CHCK CHCK

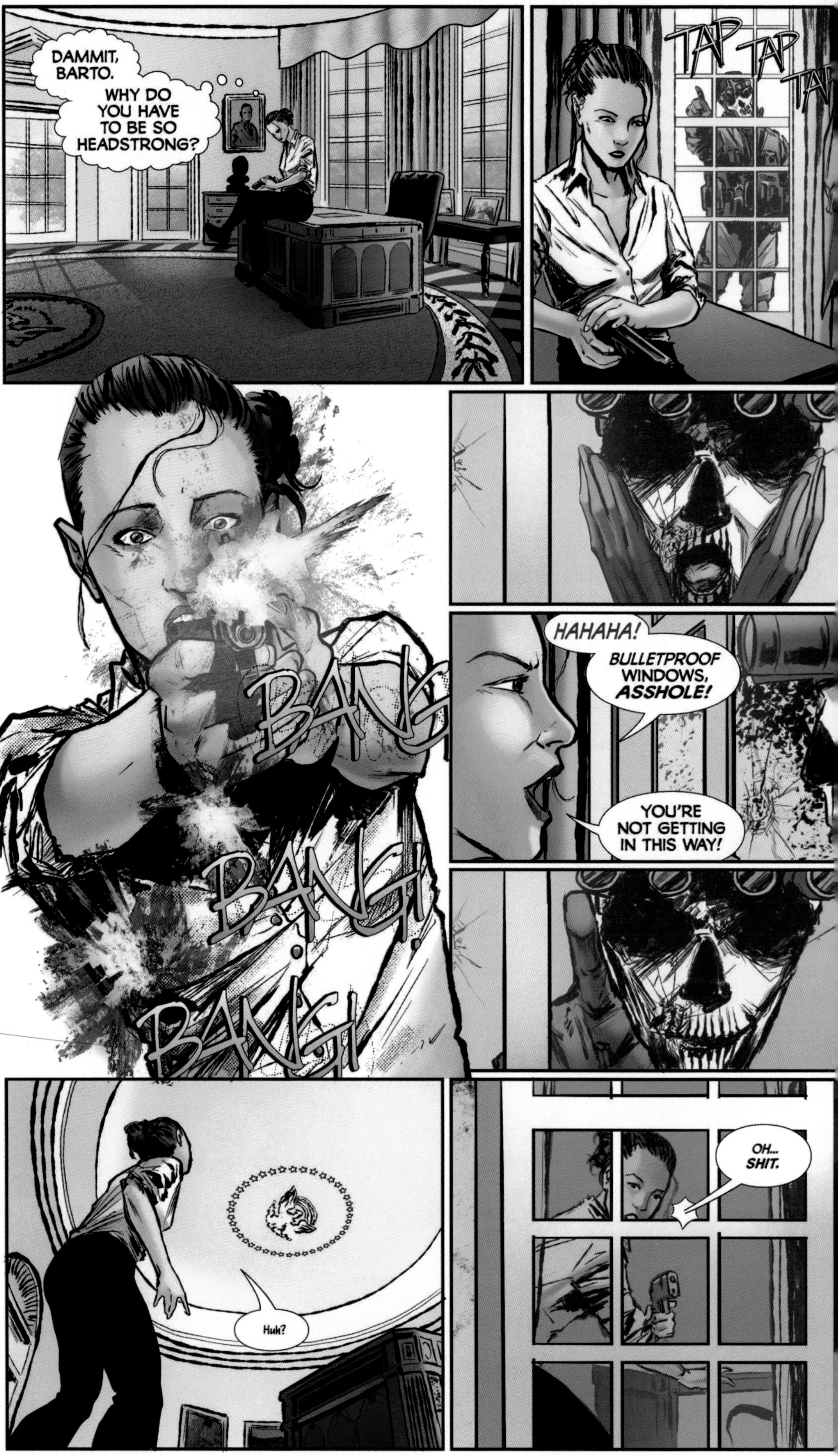
DAMMIT, BARTO.
WHY DO YOU HAVE TO BE SO HEADSTRONG?
TAP TAP TAP
BANG
BANG
BANG
HAHAHA!
BULLETPROOF WINDOWS, ASSHOLE!
YOU'RE NOT GETTING IN THIS WAY!
Huh?
OH... SHIT.

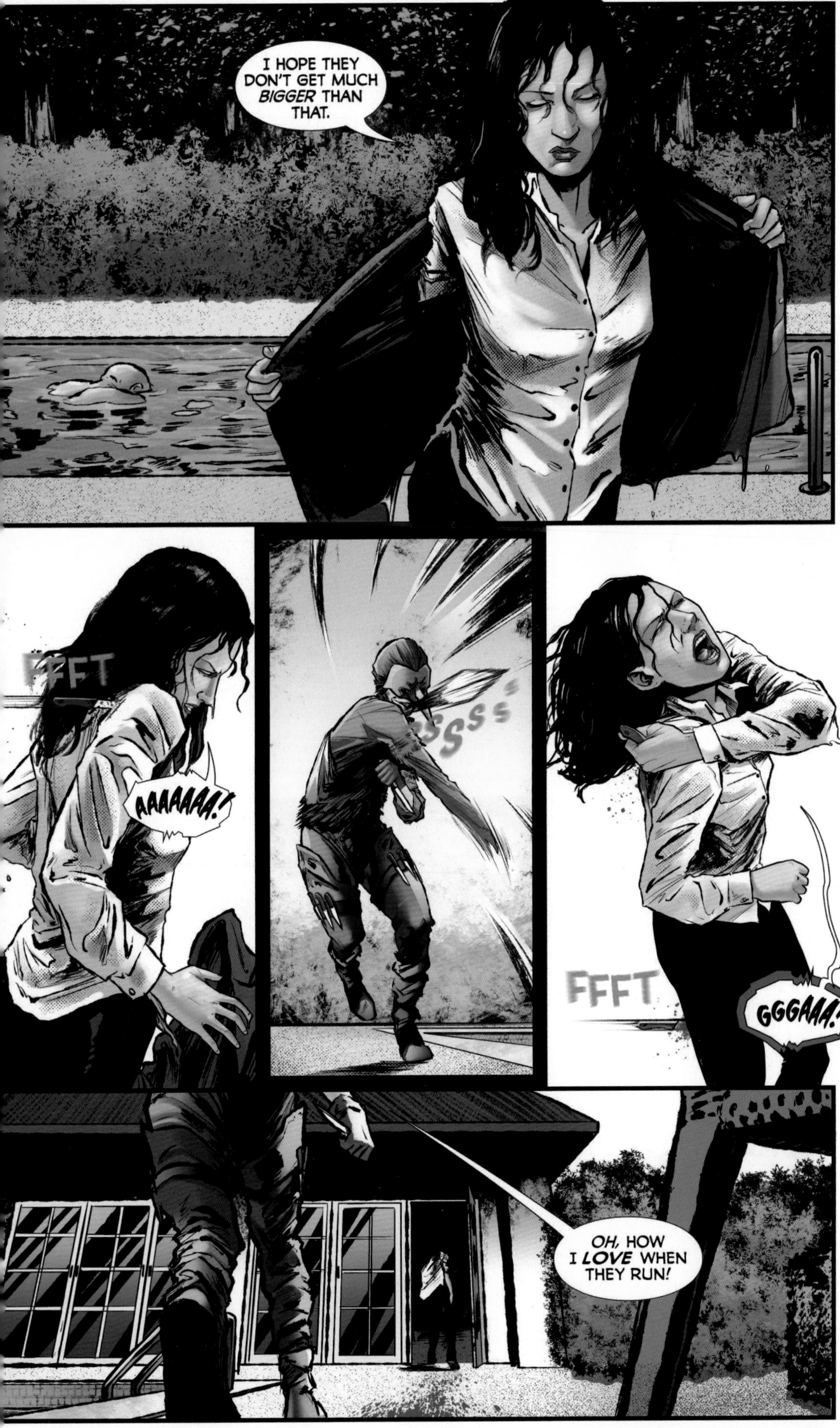

I HOPE THEY DON'T GET MUCH *BIGGER* THAN THAT.
FFFT
AAAAAAA!
SSSSSS
FFFT
GGGAAA!
OH, HOW I *LOVE* WHEN THEY RUN!

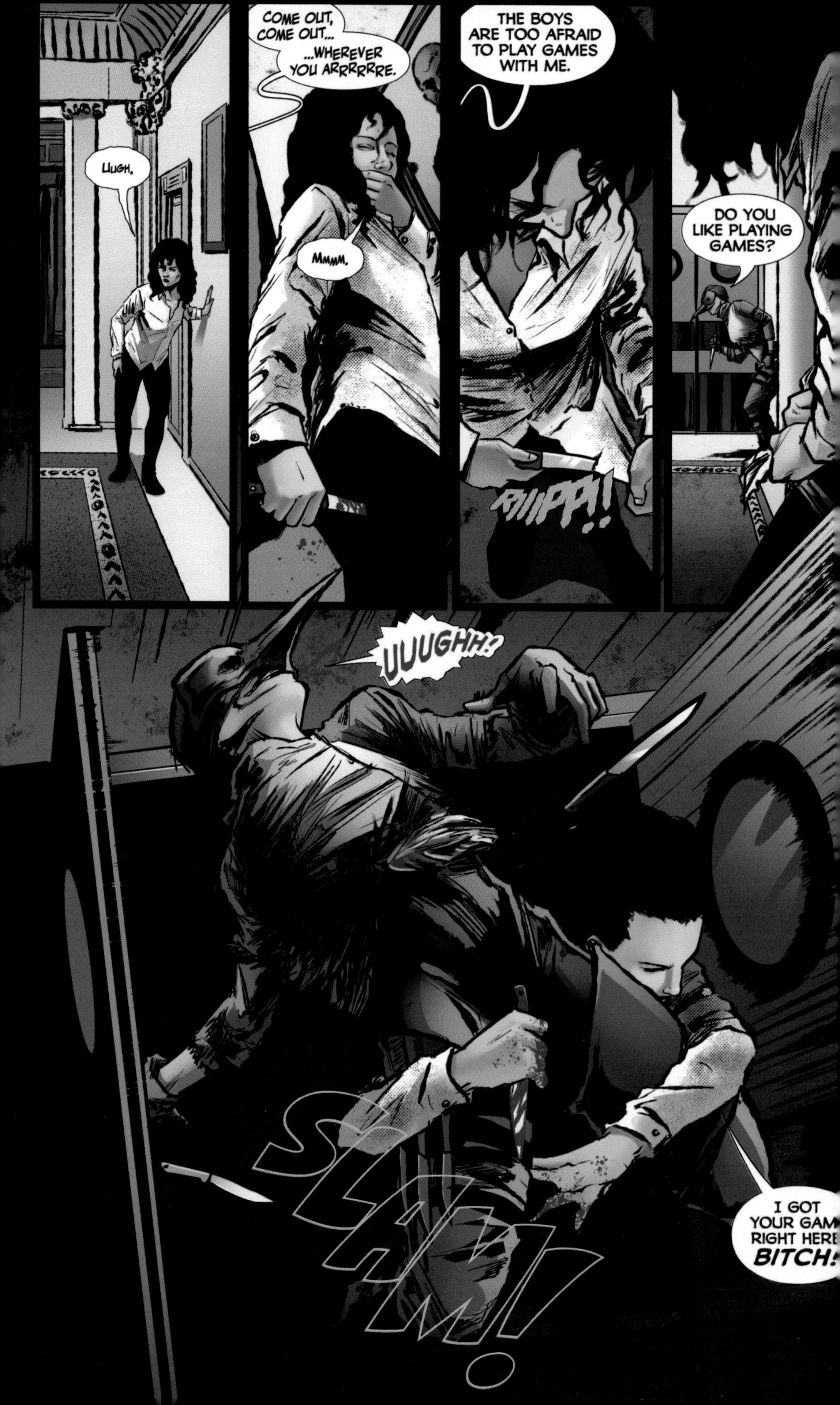

UUGH.
COME OUT, COME OUT...
...WHEREVER YOU ARRRRRRE.
MMMM.
THE BOYS ARE TOO AFRAID TO PLAY GAMES WITH ME.
RIIIPP!!
DO YOU LIKE PLAYING GAMES?
UUUGHH!
SLAM!
I GOT YOUR GAM RIGHT HERE BITCH!

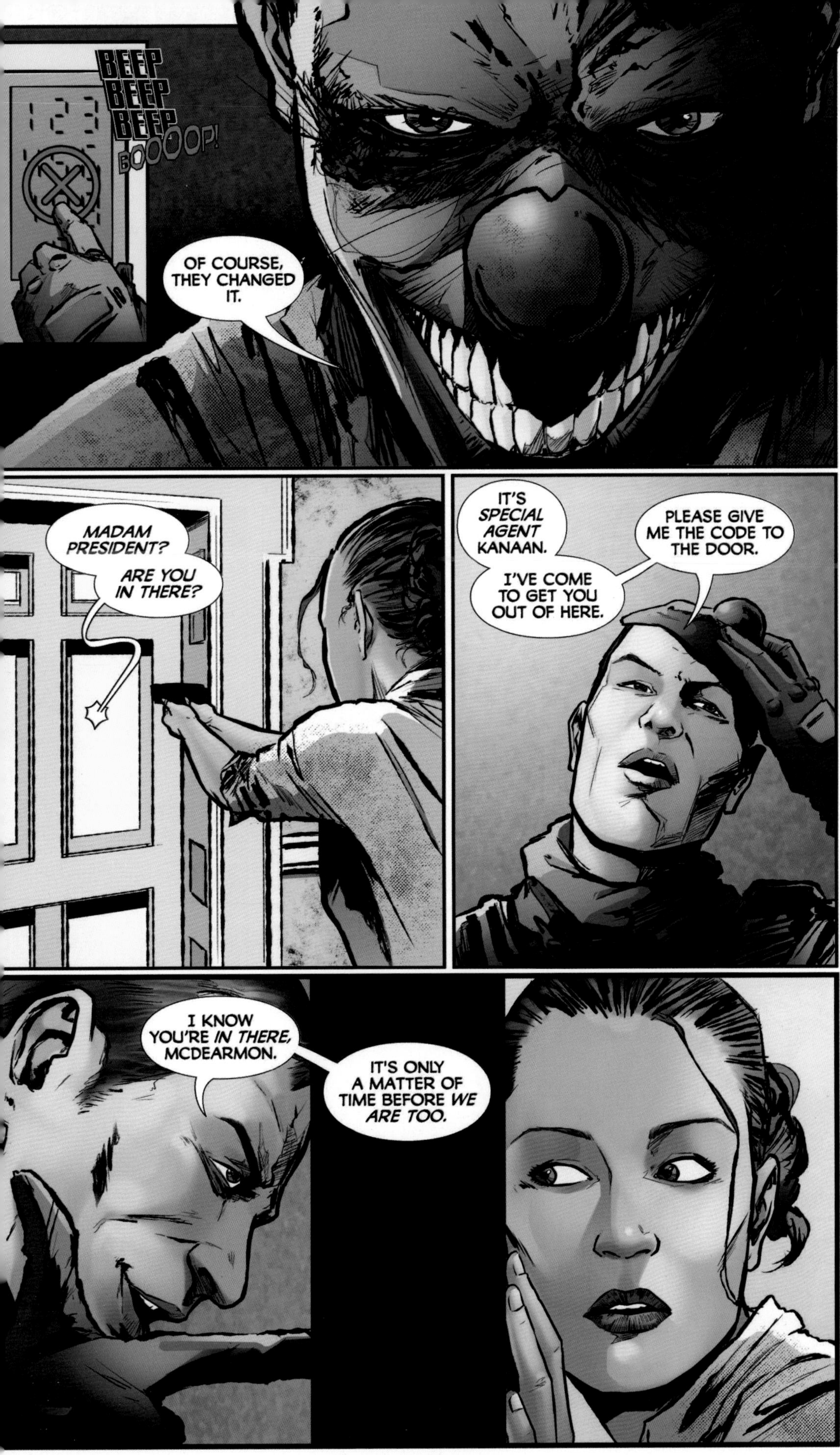
BEEP
BEEP
BEEP
BOOOOP!
OF COURSE, THEY CHANGED IT.
MADAM PRESIDENT?
ARE YOU IN THERE?
IT'S SPECIAL AGENT KANAAN.
I'VE COME TO GET YOU OUT OF HERE.
PLEASE GIVE ME THE CODE TO THE DOOR.
I KNOW YOU'RE IN THERE, MCDEARMON.
IT'S ONLY A MATTER OF TIME BEFORE WE ARE TOO.

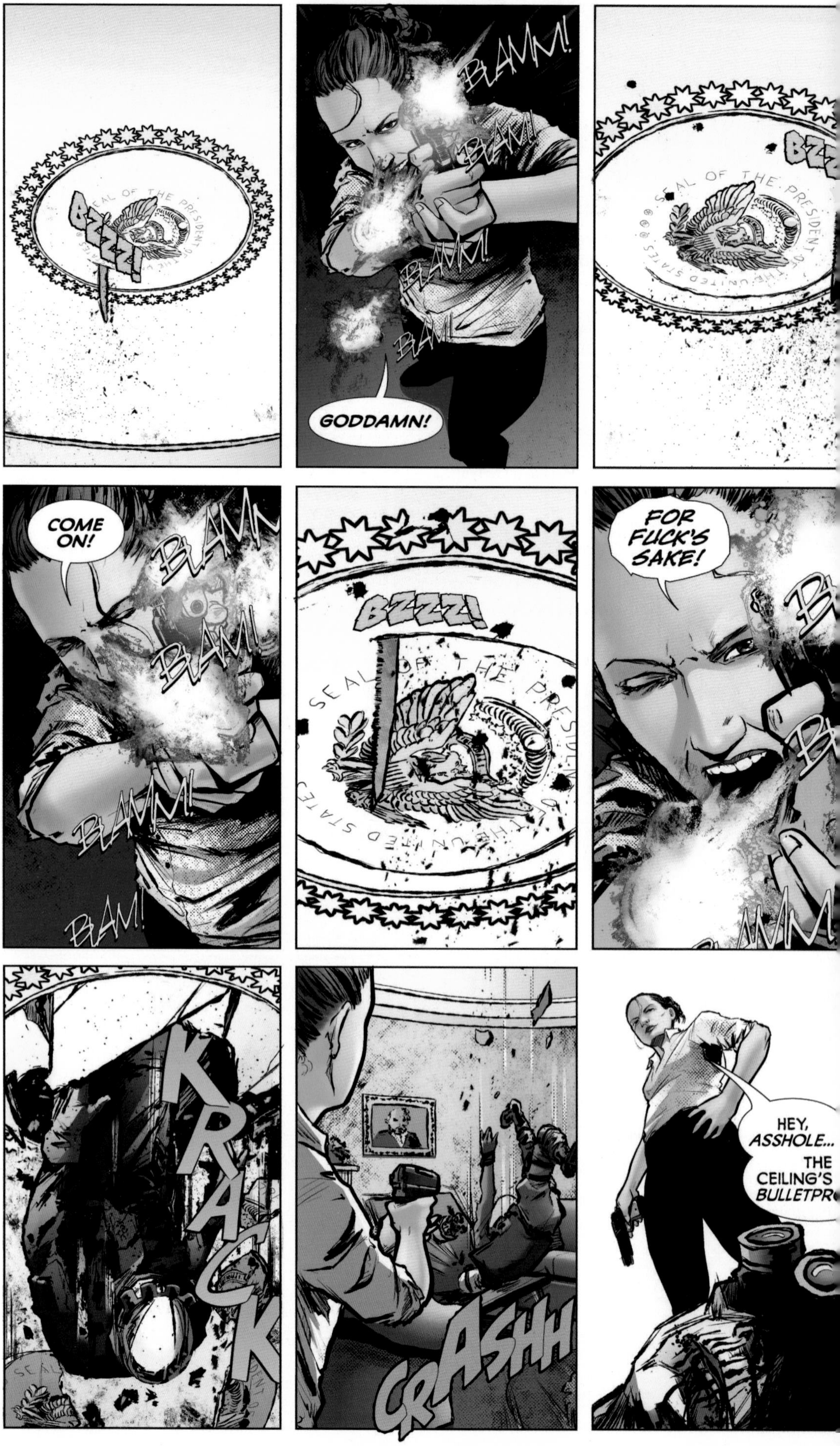
BZZZ!
BLAMM!
BLAM!
BLAMM!
BLAM!
GODDAMN!
BZZ
COME ON!
BLAMM
BLAM!
BLAMM!
BLAM!
BZZZ!
SEAL OF THE PRESIDENT OF THE UNITED STATES
FOR FUCK'S SAKE!
KRACK
CRASHH
HEY, ASSHOLE...
THE CEILING'S BULLETPR

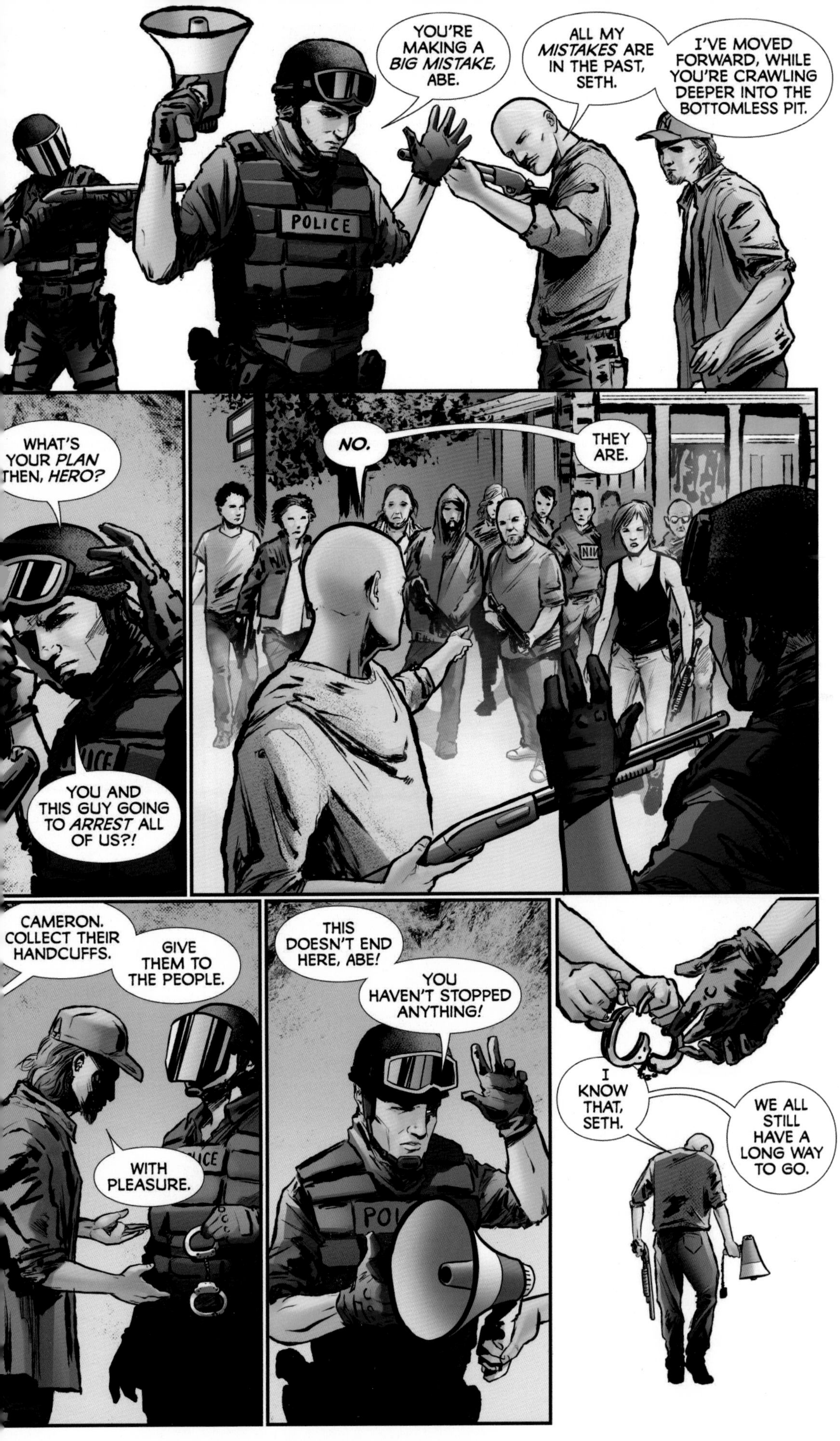
YOU'RE MAKING A BIG MISTAKE, ABE.
ALL MY MISTAKES ARE IN THE PAST, SETH.
I'VE MOVED FORWARD, WHILE YOU'RE CRAWLING DEEPER INTO THE BOTTOMLESS PIT.
WHAT'S YOUR PLAN THEN, HERO?
YOU AND THIS GUY GOING TO ARREST ALL OF US?!
NO.
THEY ARE.
CAMERON. COLLECT THEIR HANDCUFFS.
GIVE THEM TO THE PEOPLE.
WITH PLEASURE.
THIS DOESN'T END HERE, ABE!
YOU HAVEN'T STOPPED ANYTHING!
I KNOW THAT, SETH.
WE ALL STILL HAVE A LONG WAY TO GO.

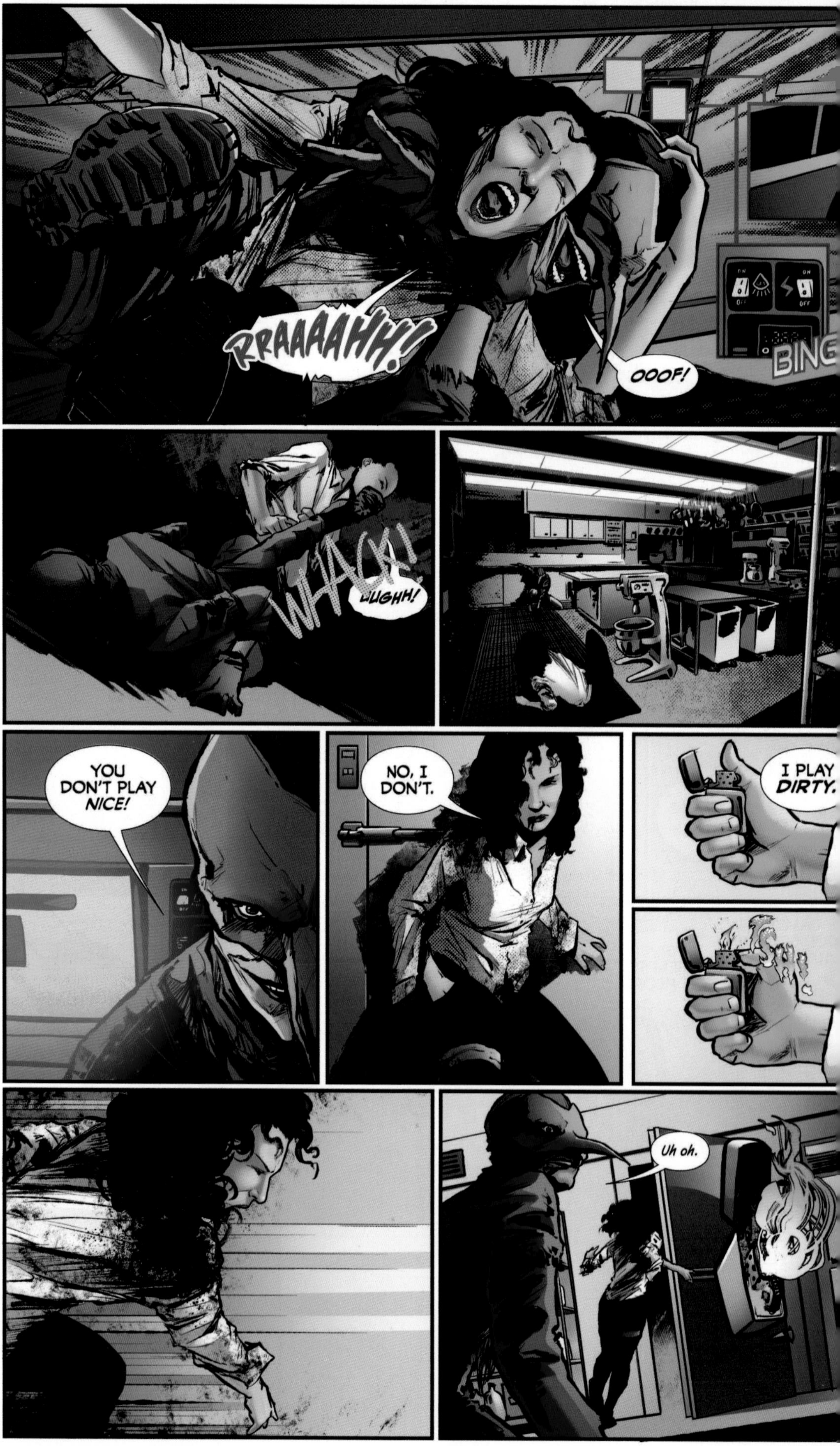
RRAAAAHH!
OOOF!
BING
WHACK!
UGHH!
YOU DON'T PLAY NICE!
NO, I DON'T.
I PLAY DIRTY.
Uh oh.

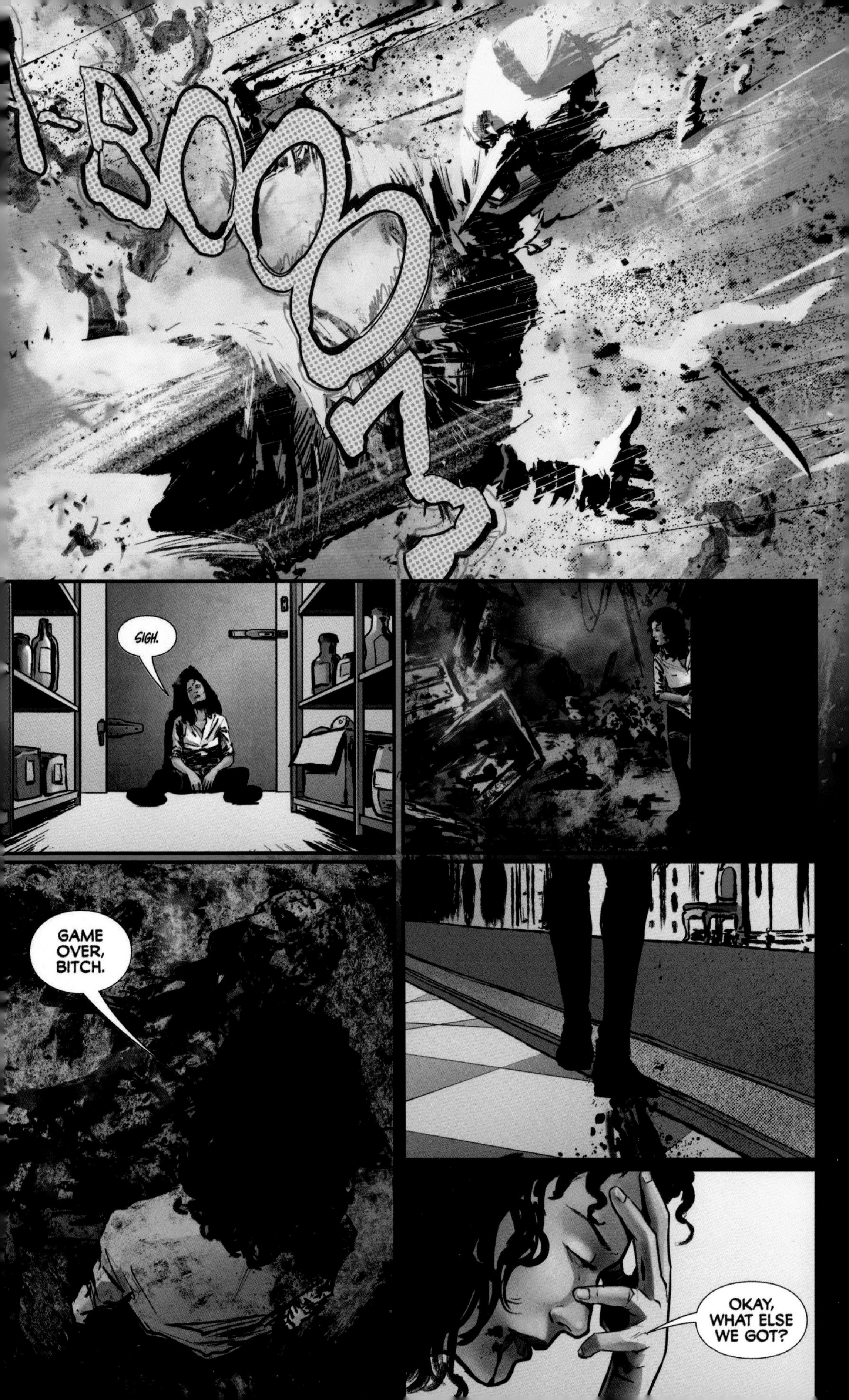

K-BOOOOM
SIGH.
GAME OVER, BITCH.
OKAY, WHAT ELSE WE GOT?

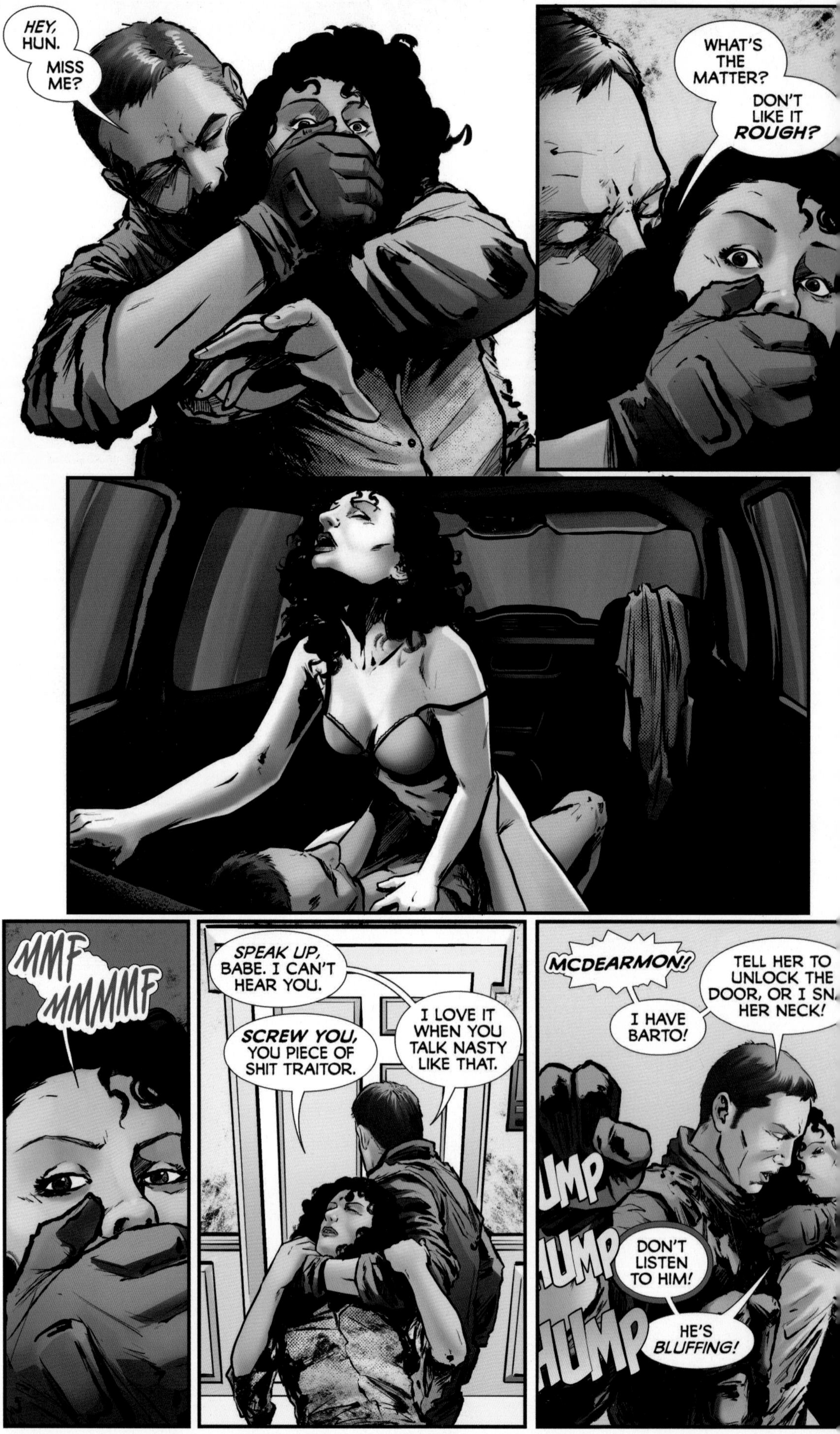
HEY, HUN.
MISS ME?
WHAT'S THE MATTER?
DON'T LIKE IT ROUGH?
MMF MMMMF
SPEAK UP, BABE. I CAN'T HEAR YOU.
SCREW YOU, YOU PIECE OF SHIT TRAITOR.
I LOVE IT WHEN YOU TALK NASTY LIKE THAT.
MCDEARMON!
I HAVE BARTO!
TELL HER TO UNLOCK THE DOOR, OR I SN HER NECK!
DON'T LISTEN TO HIM!
HE'S BLUFFING!

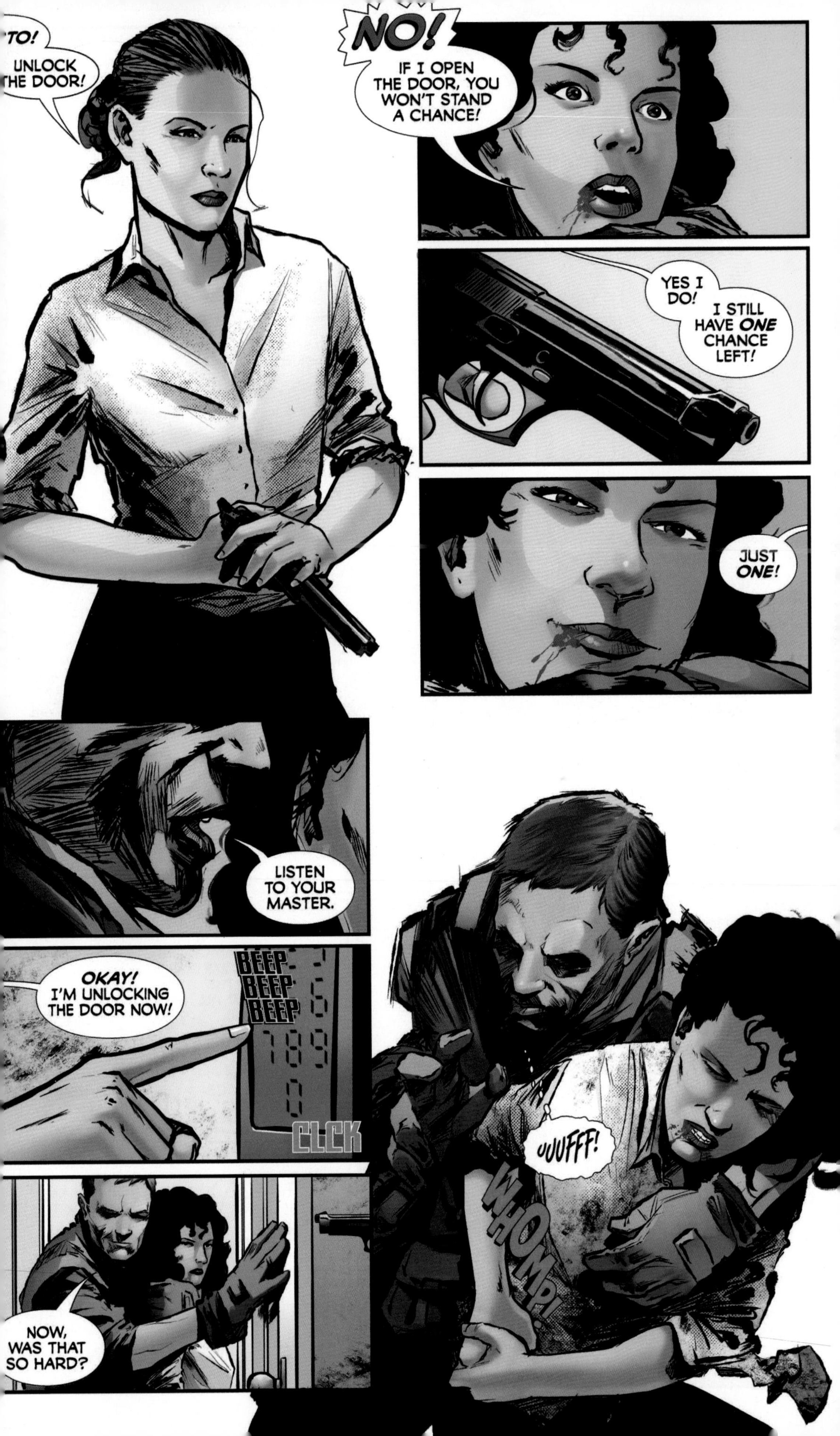

TO! UNLOCK THE DOOR!
NO!
IF I OPEN THE DOOR, YOU WON'T STAND A CHANCE!
YES I DO! I STILL HAVE *ONE* CHANCE LEFT!
JUST *ONE*!
LISTEN TO YOUR MASTER.
OKAY! I'M UNLOCKING THE DOOR NOW!
BEEP BEEP BEEP
CLCK
NOW, WAS THAT SO HARD?
UUUFFF!
WHOMP!

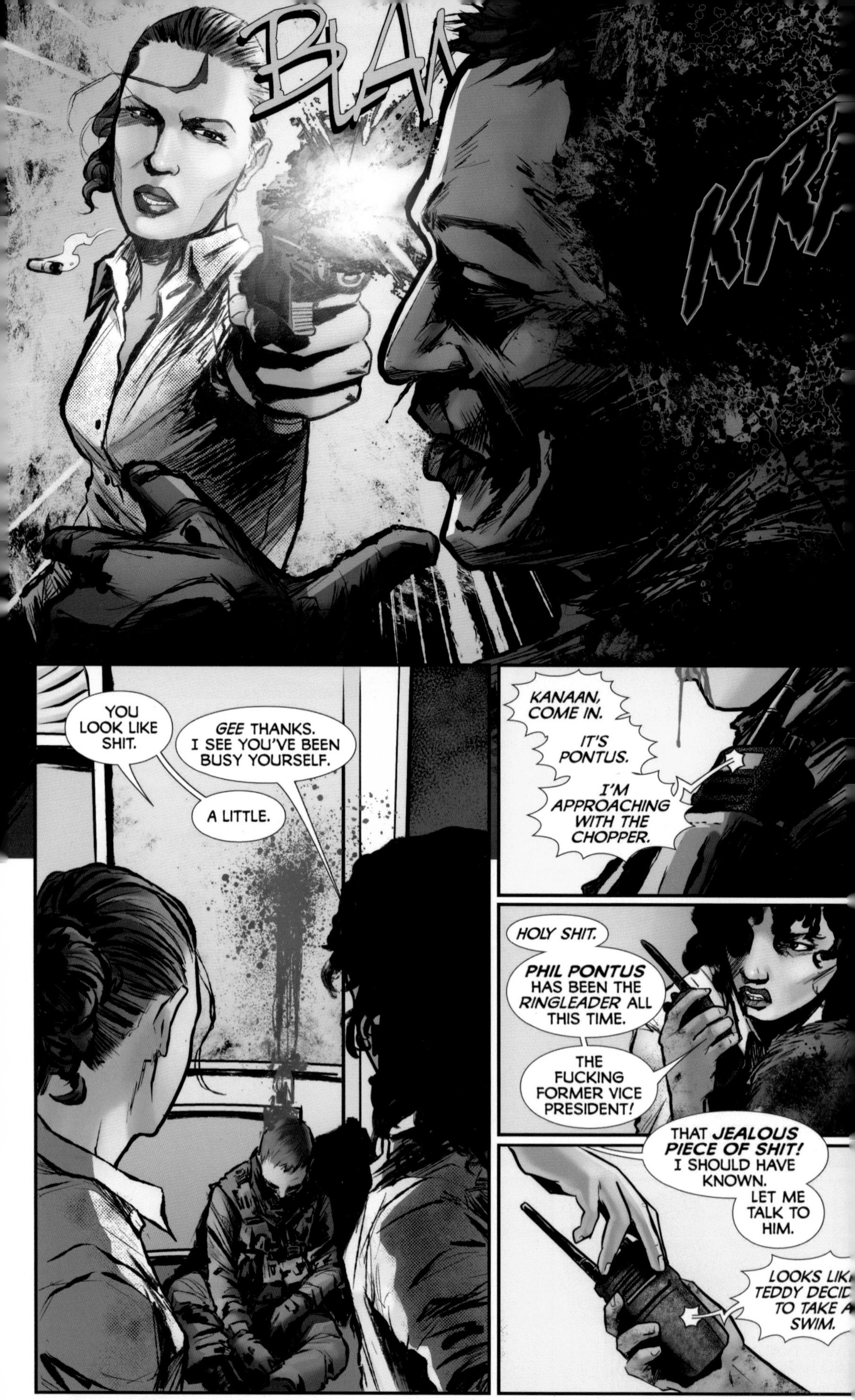
YOU LOOK LIKE SHIT.
GEE THANKS. I SEE YOU'VE BEEN BUSY YOURSELF.
A LITTLE.
KANAAN, COME IN.
IT'S PONTUS.
I'M APPROACHING WITH THE CHOPPER.
HOLY SHIT.
PHIL PONTUS HAS BEEN THE RINGLEADER ALL THIS TIME.
THE FUCKING FORMER VICE PRESIDENT!
THAT JEALOUS PIECE OF SHIT! I SHOULD HAVE KNOWN.
LET ME TALK TO HIM.
LOOKS LIK TEDDY DECID TO TAKE A SWIM.

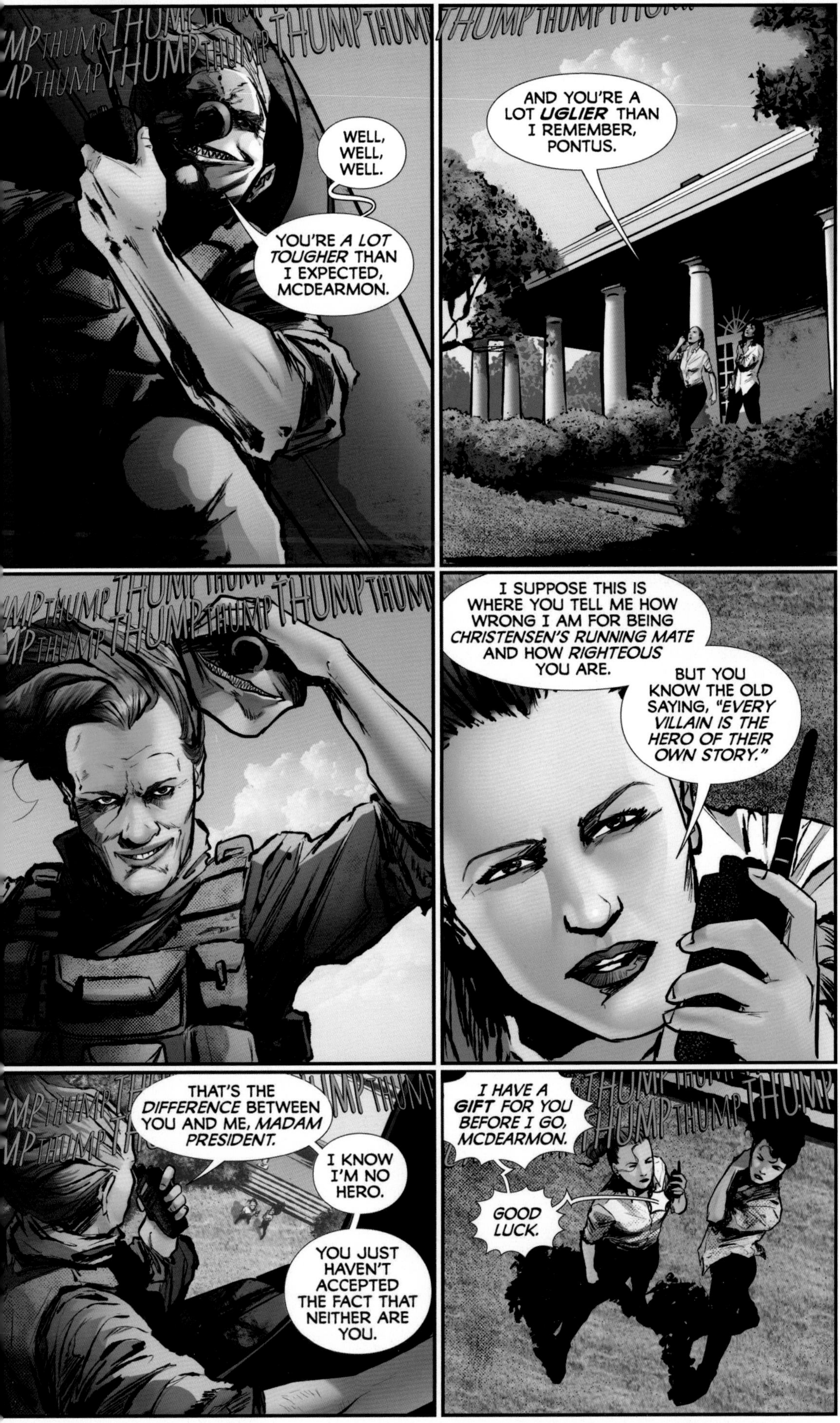
THUMP THUMP THUMP THUMP THUMP THUMP
WELL, WELL, WELL.
YOU'RE A LOT TOUGHER THAN I EXPECTED, MCDEARMON.
AND YOU'RE A LOT UGLIER THAN I REMEMBER, PONTUS.
THUMP THUMP THUMP THUMP THUMP THUMP
I SUPPOSE THIS IS WHERE YOU TELL ME HOW WRONG I AM FOR BEING CHRISTENSEN'S RUNNING MATE AND HOW RIGHTEOUS YOU ARE.
BUT YOU KNOW THE OLD SAYING, "EVERY VILLAIN IS THE HERO OF THEIR OWN STORY."
THAT'S THE DIFFERENCE BETWEEN YOU AND ME, MADAM PRESIDENT.
I KNOW I'M NO HERO.
YOU JUST HAVEN'T ACCEPTED THE FACT THAT NEITHER ARE YOU.
I HAVE A GIFT FOR YOU BEFORE I GO, MCDEARMON.
GOOD LUCK.

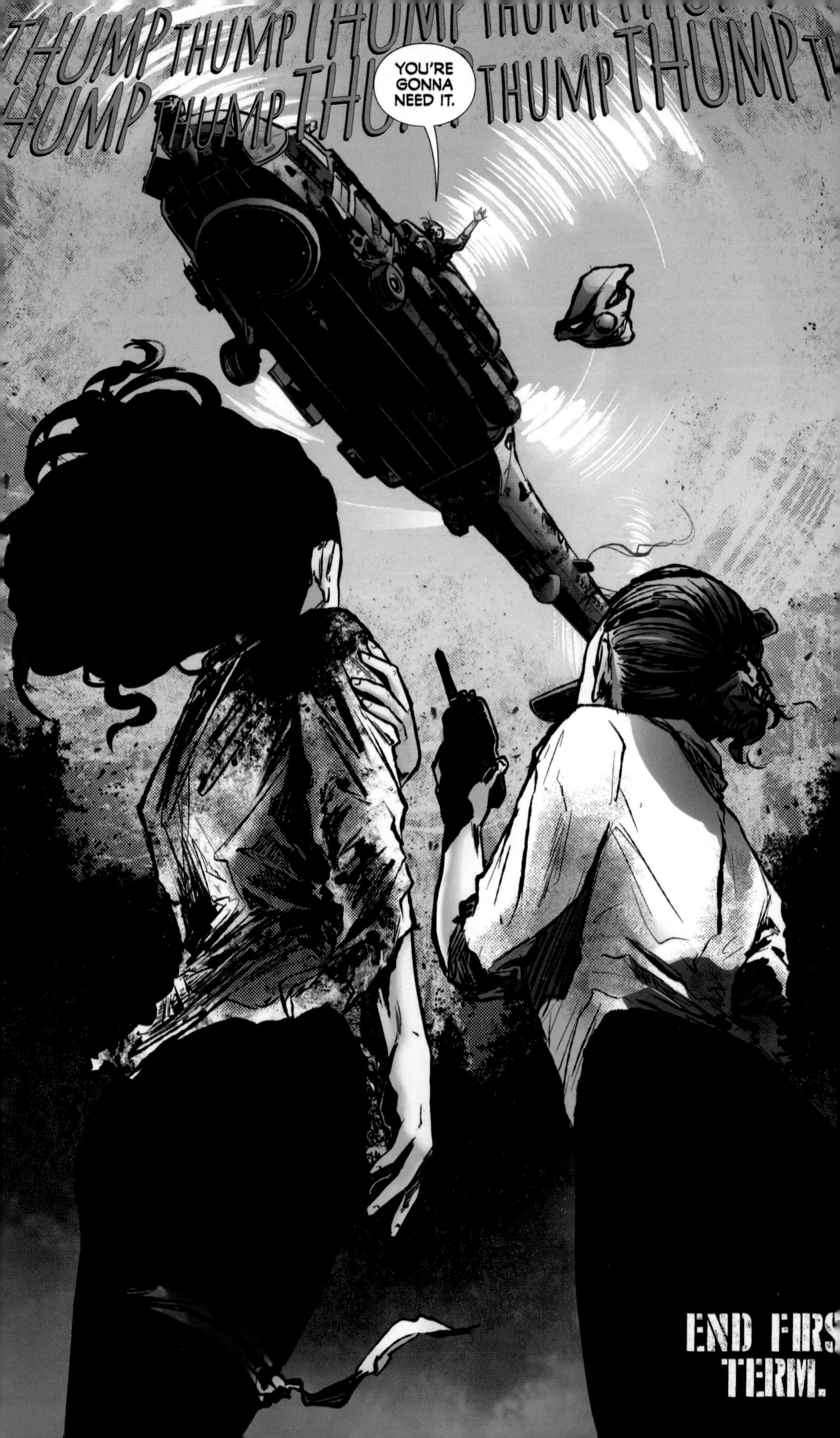
THUMP THUMP THUMP THUMP
THUMP THUMP THUMP THUMP THUMP
YOU'RE GONNA NEED IT.
END FIRS TERM.

EPILOGUE.

ONE DAY LATER.

MADAM PRESIDENT!

PRESIDENT MCDEARMON!

PRESIDENT MCDEARMON

MADAM PRESIDENT!

MADAM PRESIDENT!

PRESIDENT MCDEARMON!

I HAVE A FEW THINGS TO SAY, AND THEN I'LL OPEN IT UP TO QUESTIONS.

OVER THE PAST FEW DAYS, A TERRORIST ORGANIZATION KNOWN AS *"THE MASSES"* HAS COORDINATED AND CARRIED OUT DOZENS OF ATTACKS AGAINST OUR NATION.

YESTERDAY, MEMBERS OF THEIR GROUP ATTEMPTED AN ATTACK HERE AT *THE WHITE HOUSE.*

THEY FAILED. AND IT WAS REVEALED THAT THEIR LEADER IS FORMER *VICE PRESIDENT PHIL PONTUS.*

GASP!

AS THIS IS STILL A DEVELOPING SITUATION, I'LL ONLY TAKE A *FEW* QUESTIONS.

OBVIOUSLY, WITH REGARD TO CERTAIN THINGS, I WILL NOT BE ABLE TO COMMENT AT THIS TIME.

CHRIS, YOU FIRST.

MADAM PRESIDENT!

MADAM PRESIDENT!

MADAM PRESIDEN

WHAT IS KNOWN ABOUT THE FORMER VICE PRESIDENT'S WHEREABOUTS?

DUE TO SECURITY ISSUES, WE CANNOT COMMENT ON WHAT WE KNOW AT THIS JUNCTURE.

HOWEVER, I CAN SAY THAT AN *INTERNATIONAL MANHUNT* IS UNDER WAY WITH THE COOPERATION OF SEVERAL OF OUR *CLOSEST ALLIES.*

JESSICA.

MADAM PRESIDENT!

MADAM PRESIDENT!

ARE YOU ABLE TO COMMENT ON THE EVENTS THAT OCCURRED IN MACON?

YES. I WAS JUST BRIEFED ON THAT THIS MORNING.

FOR THOSE OF YOU WHO MAY NOT BE AWARE, *THE MACON, GEORGIA POLICE DEPARTMENT* WAS INFILTRATED BY *THE MASSES.*

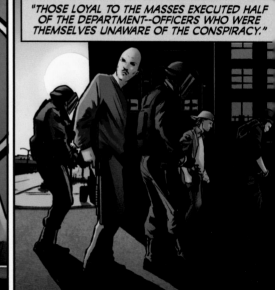

"*THOSE LOYAL TO THE MASSES EXECUTED HALF OF THE DEPARTMENT--OFFICERS WHO WERE THEMSELVES UNAWARE OF THE CONSPIRACY.*"

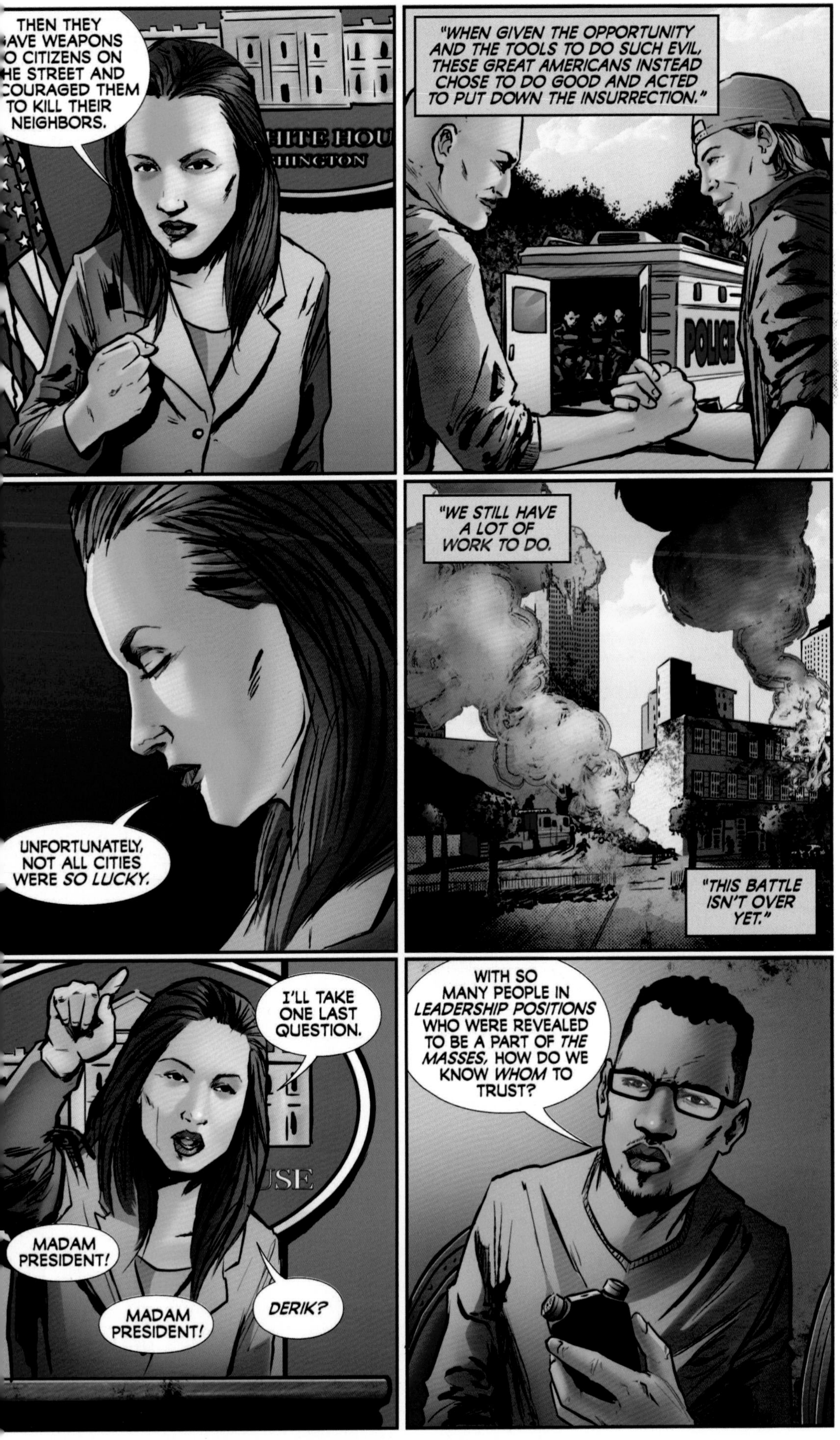
THEN THEY AVE WEAPONS O CITIZENS ON HE STREET AND COURAGED THEM TO KILL THEIR NEIGHBORS.
"WHEN GIVEN THE OPPORTUNITY AND THE TOOLS TO DO SUCH EVIL, THESE GREAT AMERICANS INSTEAD CHOSE TO DO GOOD AND ACTED TO PUT DOWN THE INSURRECTION."
POLICE
UNFORTUNATELY, NOT ALL CITIES WERE *SO LUCKY*.
"WE STILL HAVE A LOT OF WORK TO DO.
"THIS BATTLE ISN'T OVER YET."
I'LL TAKE ONE LAST QUESTION.
MADAM PRESIDENT!
MADAM PRESIDENT!
DERIK?
WITH SO MANY PEOPLE IN *LEADERSHIP POSITIONS* WHO WERE REVEALED TO BE A PART OF *THE MASSES,* HOW DO WE KNOW *WHOM* TO TRUST?

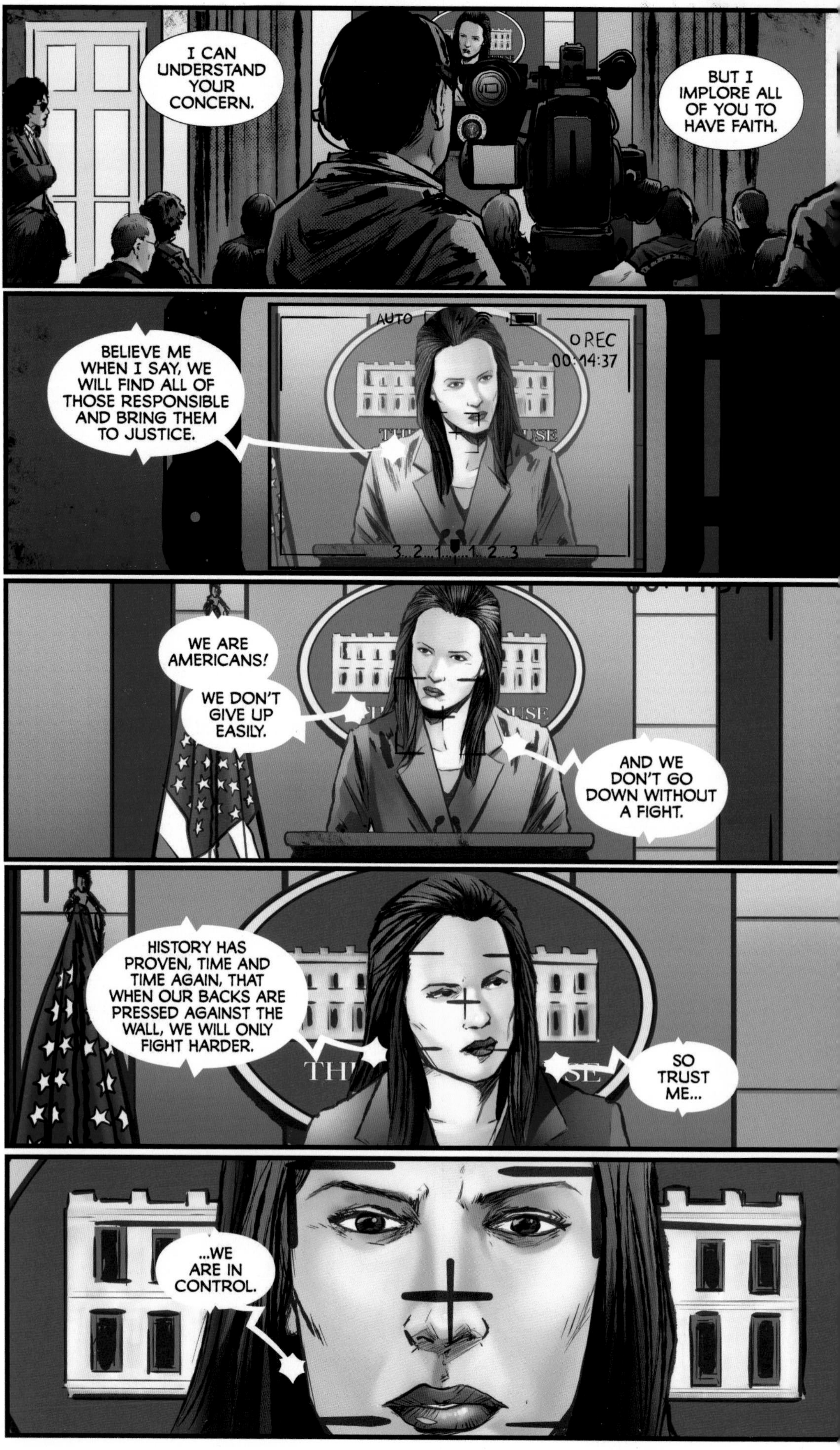
I CAN UNDERSTAND YOUR CONCERN.
BUT I IMPLORE ALL OF YOU TO HAVE FAITH.
AUTO
O REC
00:14:37
BELIEVE ME WHEN I SAY, WE WILL FIND ALL OF THOSE RESPONSIBLE AND BRING THEM TO JUSTICE.
3..2..1....1..2..3
WE ARE AMERICANS!
WE DON'T GIVE UP EASILY.
AND WE DON'T GO DOWN WITHOUT A FIGHT.
HISTORY HAS PROVEN, TIME AND TIME AGAIN, THAT WHEN OUR BACKS ARE PRESSED AGAINST THE WALL, WE WILL ONLY FIGHT HARDER.
SO TRUST ME...
...WE ARE IN CONTROL.

CREATOR BIOS

NATHAN HEDRICK WRITER/ CREATOR

...han Hedrick is a comic book writer/creator born and raised in Brevard County, Florida. Comics has always ... a passion of his and he recently began self-publishing his own titles. His current work includes the zombie ...shots Freakshow Princess & Freakshow Knight *(from Second Sight Publishing)*, a superhero story called ...able, and the political thriller The Recount *(from Scout Comics)*. In addition to being a writer, Jonathan is an ...y veteran and a licensed radiologic technologist. He resides in Melbourne, FL with his cat, Tessa.

GABRIEL IBARRA-NÚÑEZ PENCILS/ INKS

...abriel is a Chilean comic book artist and graduate from the University of Arts and Social Sciences *(UARCIS)*. ...e has worked on Sacred Six *(Dynamite)*, Graveland *(Scout Comics)*, Nanits Chronicles *(Nanits Comics)*, and ...ollaborated on a short story in Zinnober *(Scout Comics)*. He co-created a graphic novel called Juan Valiente ...Liberalia) with his friend and mentor Kote Carvajal. His most recent work is The Recount written by his friend ...onathan Hedrick. Currently, he is making comics, preparing coffee, and writing stories in a little town near ...antiago. During his weekends he lives with his son, painting, and taking occasional photographs.

...E BOCARDO PENCILS/ INKS

...was born in Cádiz, Spain in 1980, but now lives in Seville with his wife and two children. He has always ...n fascinated by drawing and comics, but becoming a father was what pushed him to achieve his dream of ...g an artist. He has been published in 1937, La Desbandá from Carmona en viñetas, and Sangre Barbara ...Karraş Comics, both with a script by El Torres *(The Veil, IDW)*. He and El Torres also created Phantasma- ...a *(forthcoming from Scout Comics)*. Future projects include work on The Shepherd with Andrea Lorenzo ...nari and another miniseries with Scout Comics.

SUNIL GHAGRE COLORIST

Sunil Ghagre is a freelance comic book colorist and artist from Nagpur, India. Over his 11+ professional years he has worked for many publishers such as Disney, Archie, IDW, DC, Avatar Press, and Boom Studios.

...RISTIAN DOCOLOMANSKY LETTERER

...istian was born in Barcelona, 1977, though he now lives in Santiago, Chile. He currently works ... an inker or letterer for several American, New Zealand, Spanish and UK publishers, including ...eavy Metal Magazine, Scout Comics, Advent Comics, Mythopoeia, Blue Roo Comics, Crow Hill ...omics, Arcano IV and Ariete Producciones among others. He is also a comic book teacher for ...ds and the sole creator for his series In.jvsticia, published now on Ariete Producciones.

ANDREA LORENZO MOLINARI, PH.D. EDITOR

Andrea is co-writer/ co-creator of The Shepherd, OGN series with Scout Comics. Molinari serves as editorial director for Scout Comics, and works with many creative teams from around the world. He has worked as both submissions editor and project editor for Caliber Comics, as an editor for the Spanish publisher Amigo Comics (Málaga, Spain), and has edited books for Action Lab Entertainment, Behemoth, and the Canadian publisher Chapterhouse.

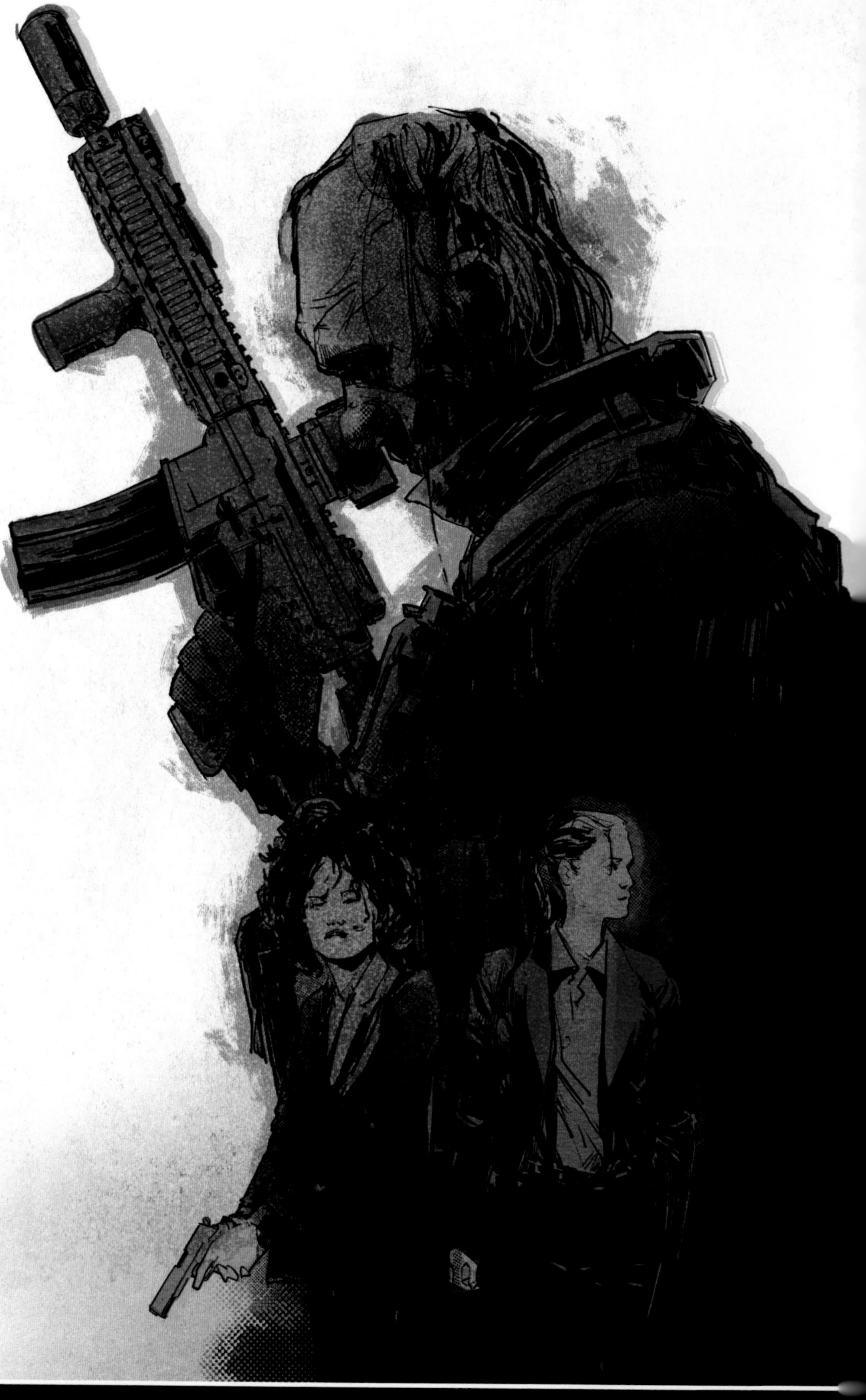

ISSUE 1 COVER A
GABRIEL IBARRA-NUÑEZ

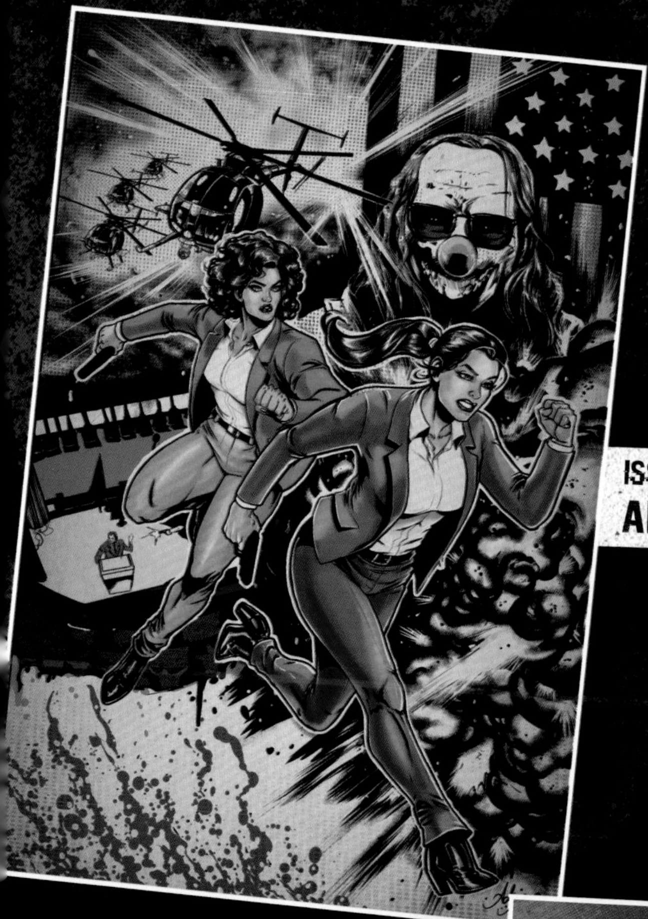

ISSUE 1 HANAHAN VARIANT
ADRIANA MELO

ISSUE 1 WEBSTORE VARIANT
RICH WOODALL

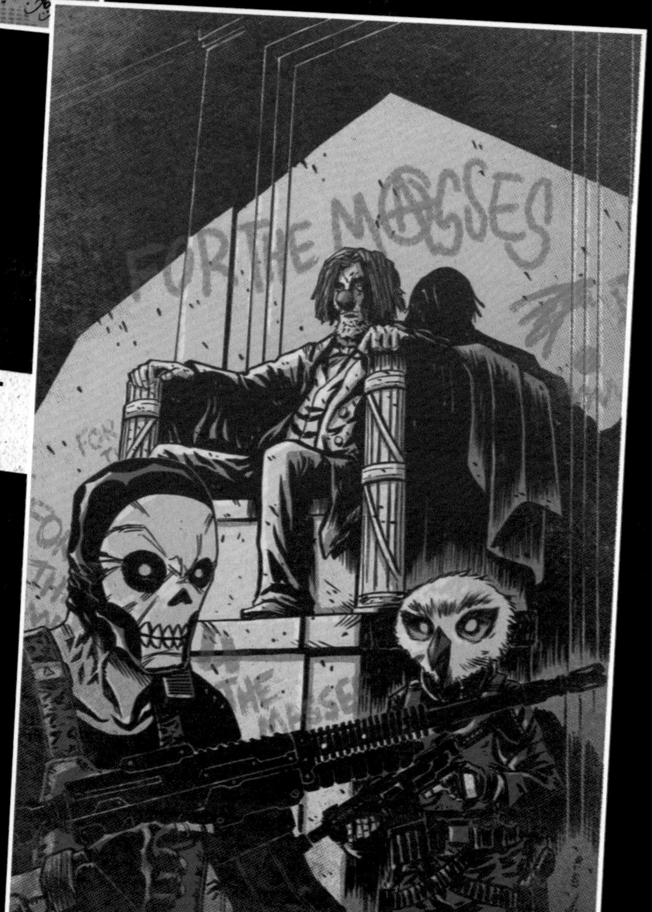

ISSUE 1 SLAB CITY VARIANT
BEN TEMPLESMITH

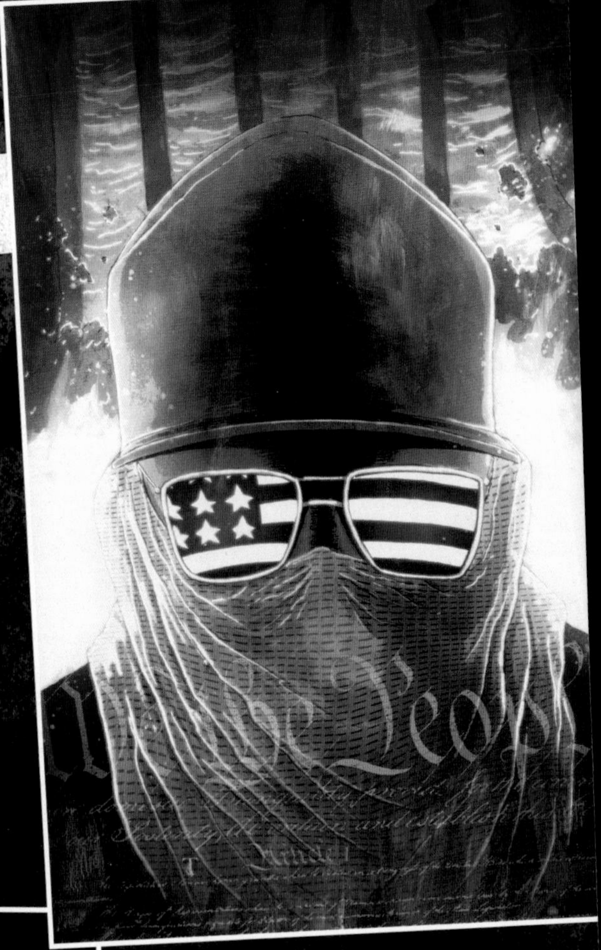

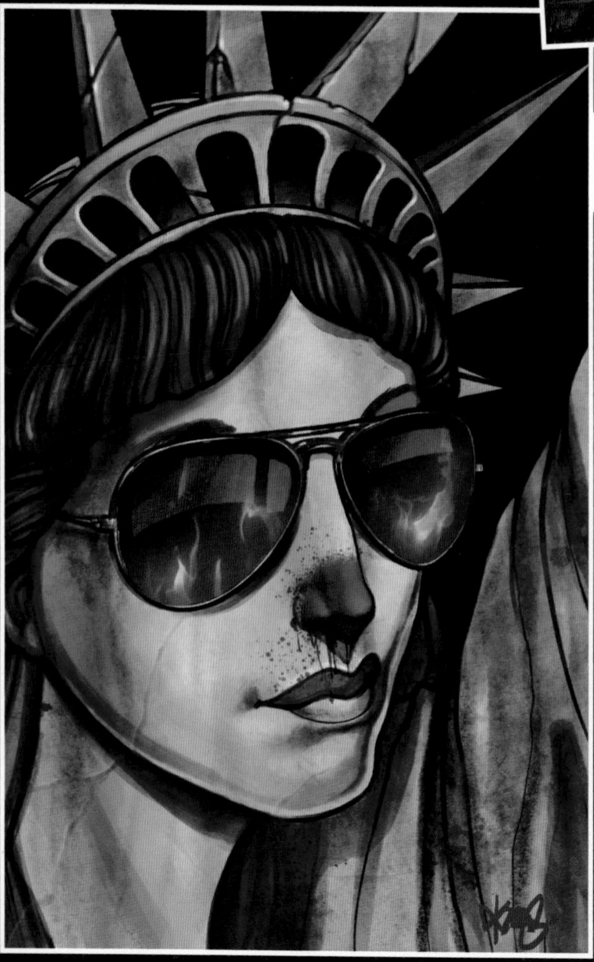

ISSUE 1 1 STOP SHOPVARIANT
NEIL NELSON

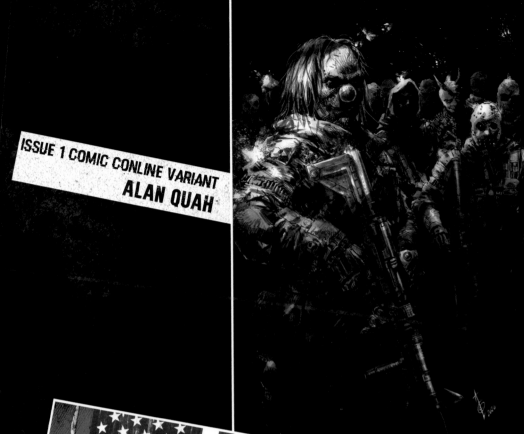

ISSUE 1 COMIC CONLINE VARIANT
ALAN QUAH

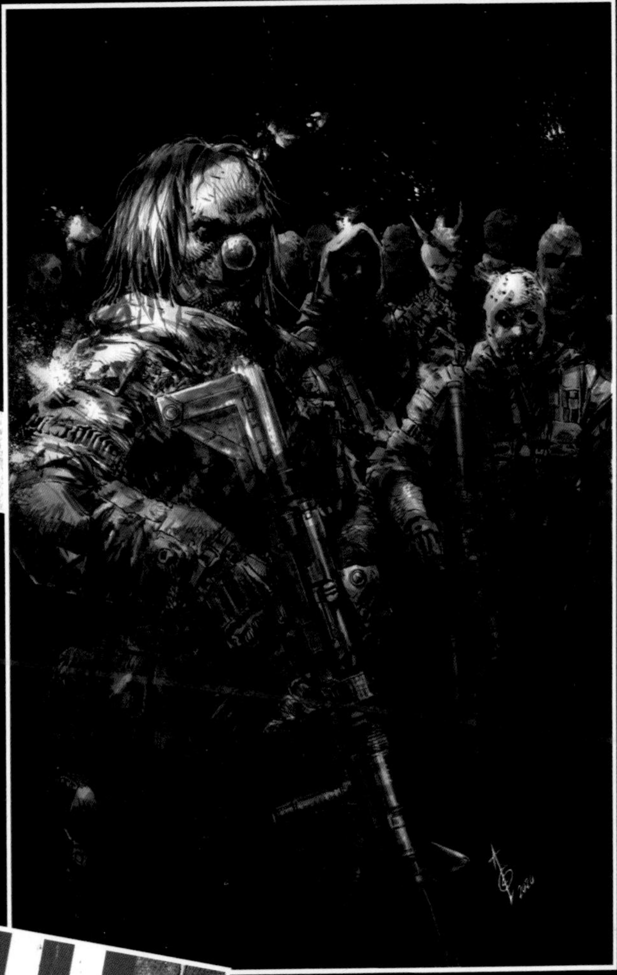

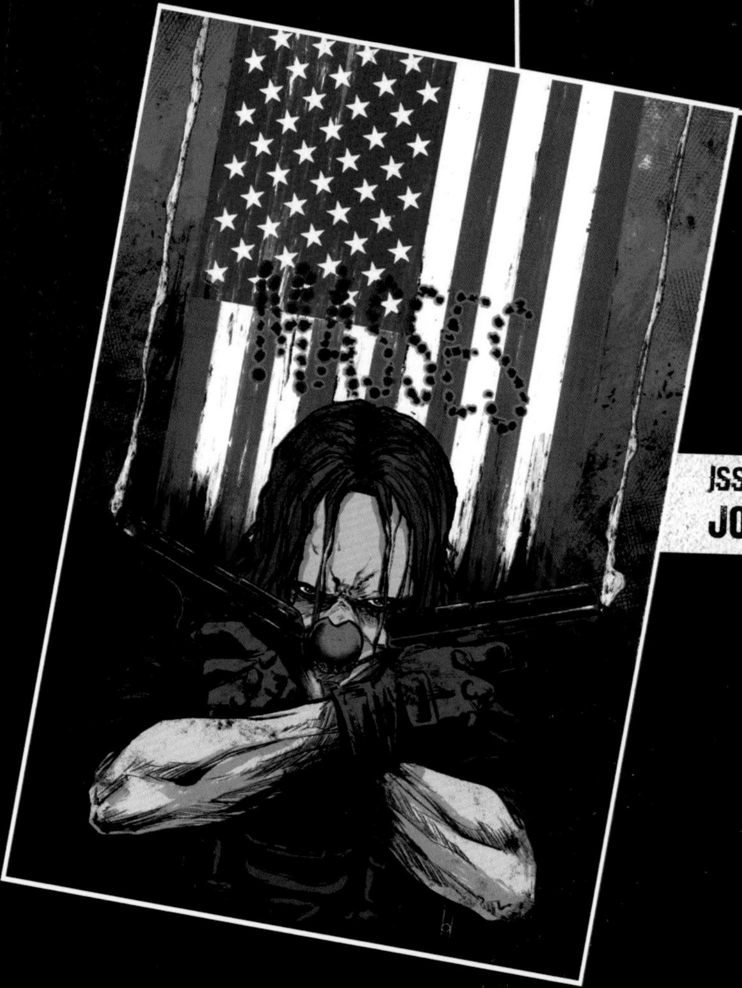

ISSUE 1 METAL VARIANT
JOE BOCARDO

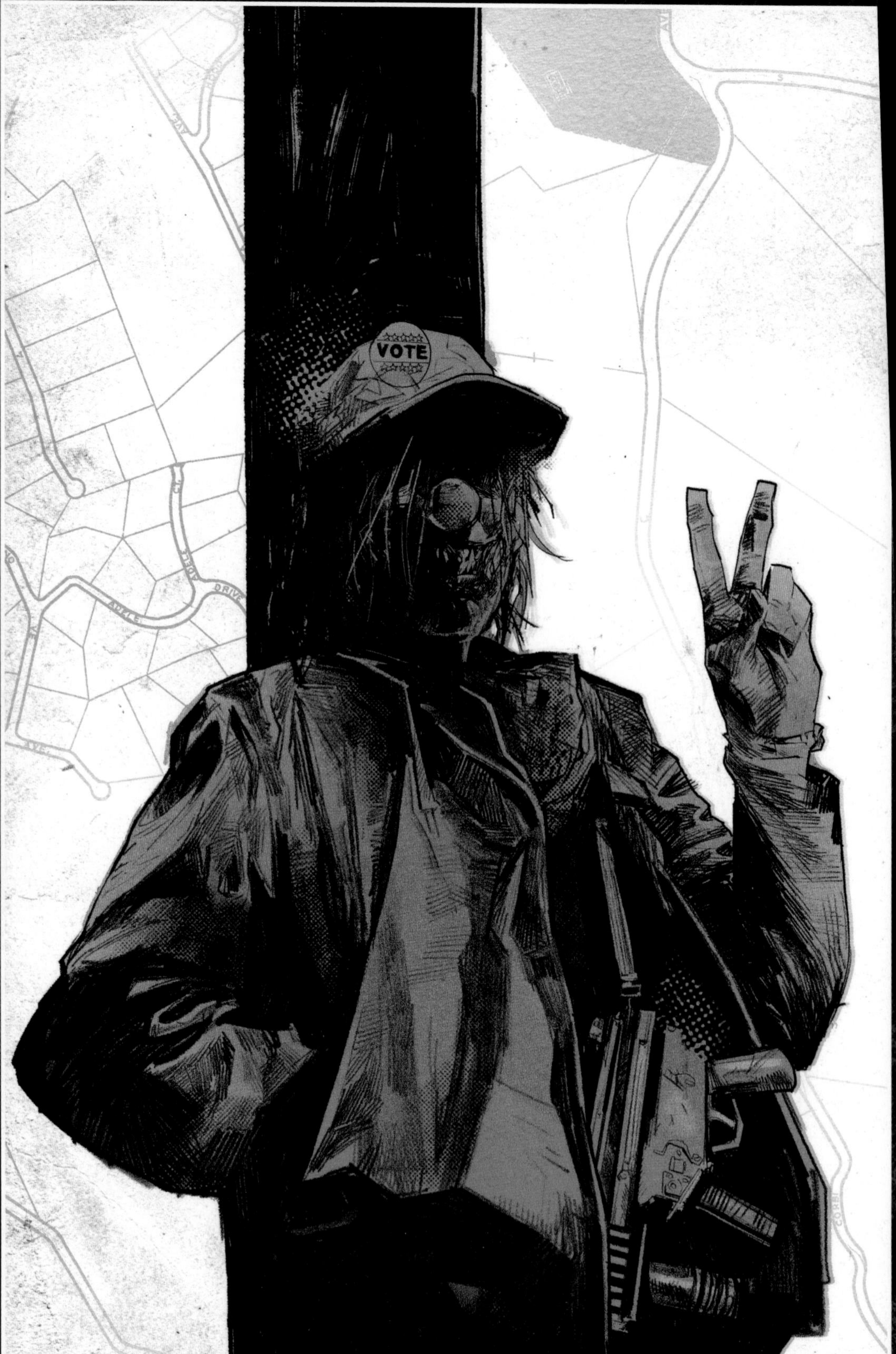
VOTE

ISSUE 1 2ND PRINTING
GABRIEL IBARRA-NUÑEZ

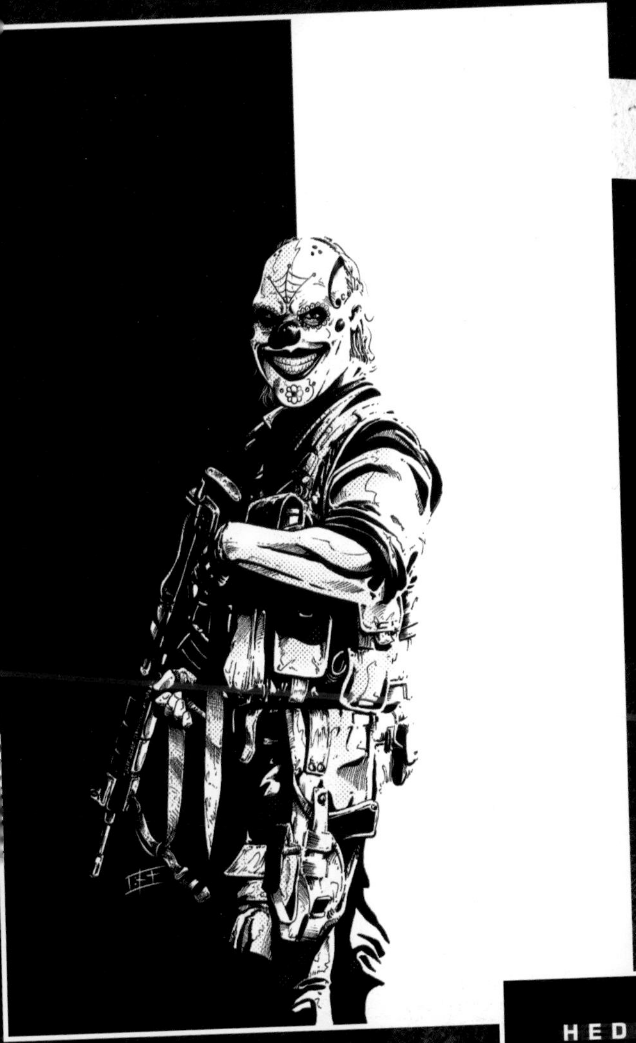

ISSUE 1 COVER B
BRYAN SILVERBAX

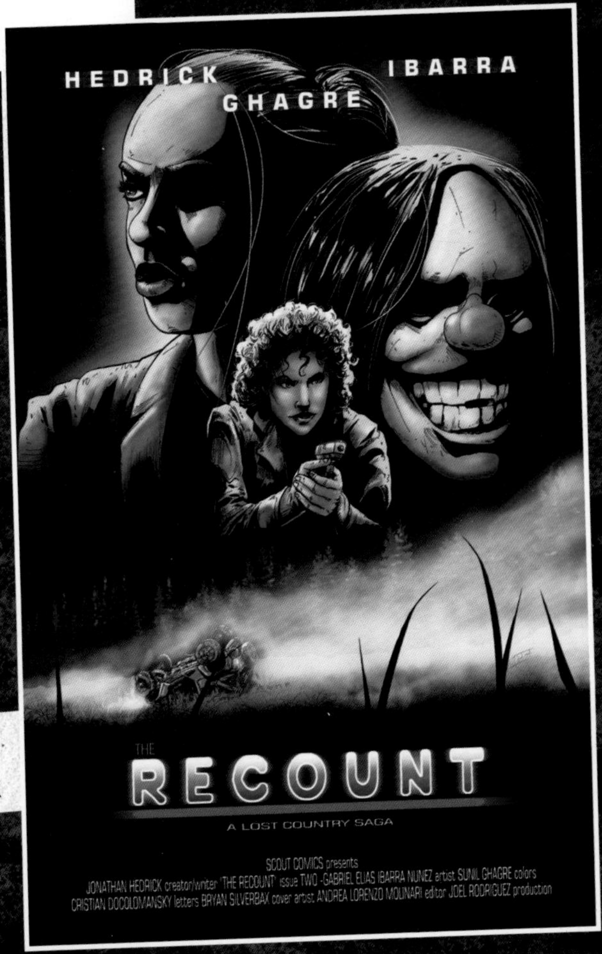

HEDRICK
GHAGRE
IBARRA
THE RECOUNT
A LOST COUNTRY SAGA
SCOUT COMICS presents
JONATHAN HEDRICK creator/writer 'THE RECOUNT' issue TWO -GABRIEL ELIAS IBARRA NUNEZ artist SUNIL GHAGRE colors
CRISTIAN DOCOLOMANSKY letters BRYAN SILVERBAX cover artist ANDREA LORENZO MOLINARI editor JOEL RODRIGUEZ production

ISSUE 2 KINGDOM OF COMICS VARIANT
BRYAN SILVERBAX

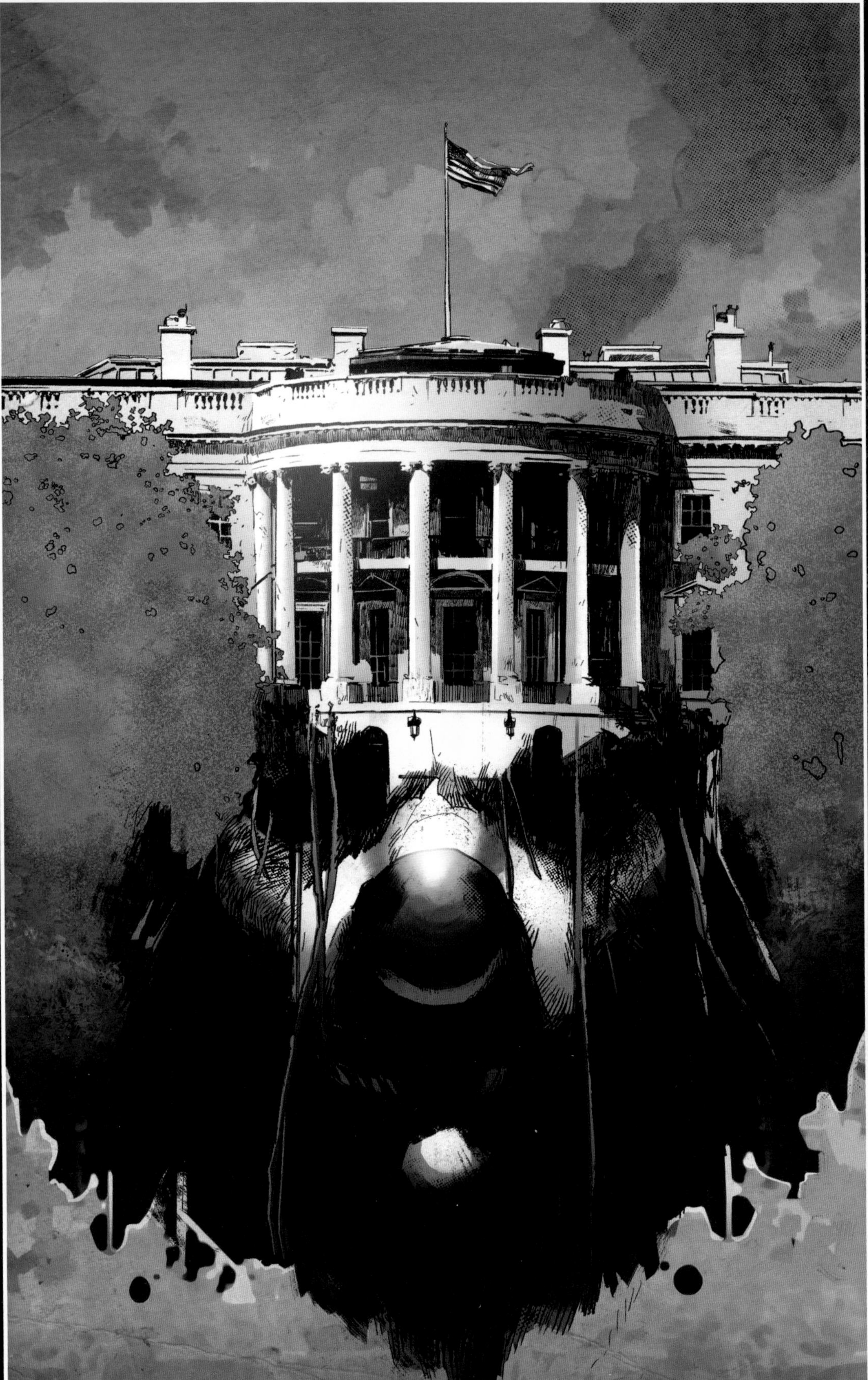

ISSUE 2 STANDARD COVER
GABRIEL IBARRA-NUÑEZ

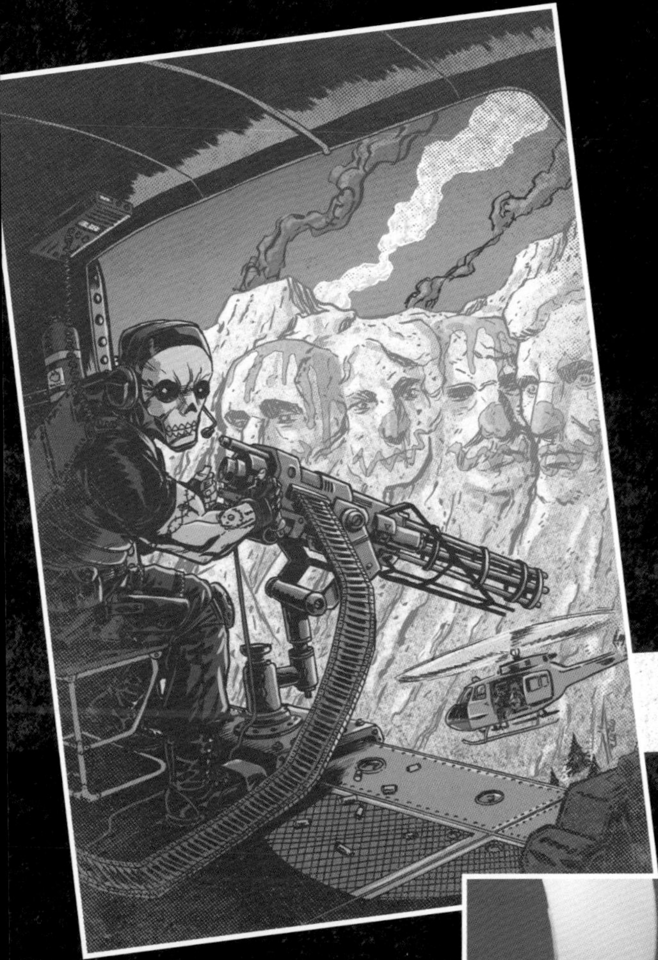

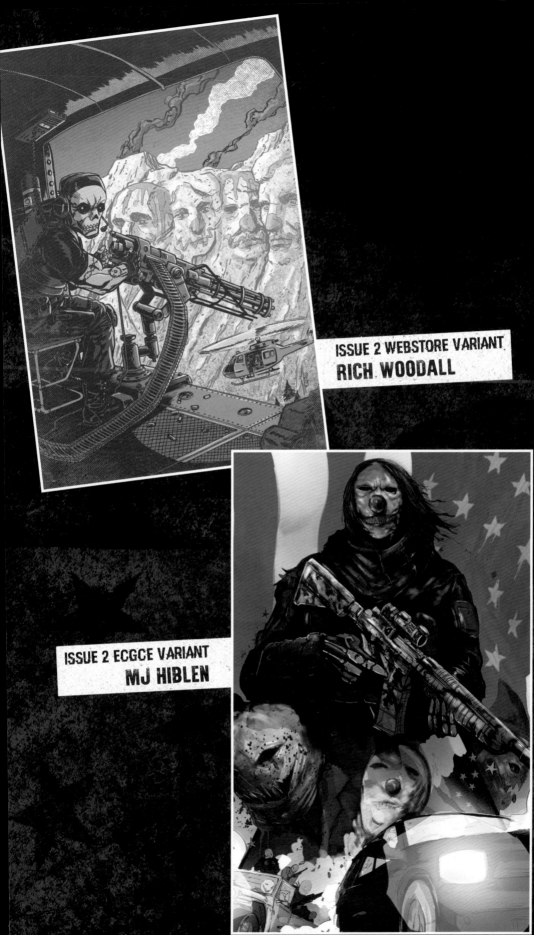

ISSUE 2 WEBSTORE VARIANT
RICH WOODALL

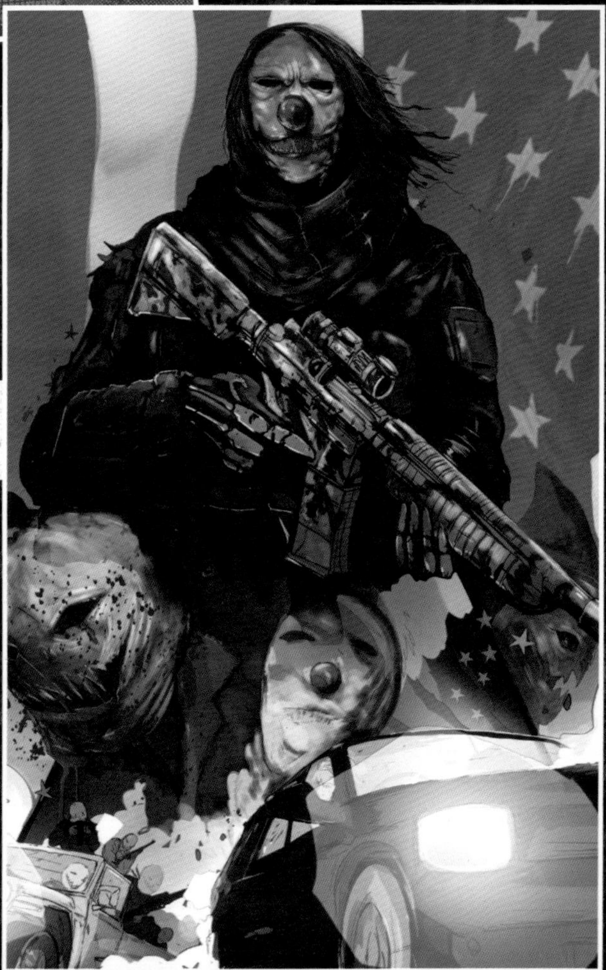

ISSUE 2 ECGCE VARIANT
MJ HIBLEN

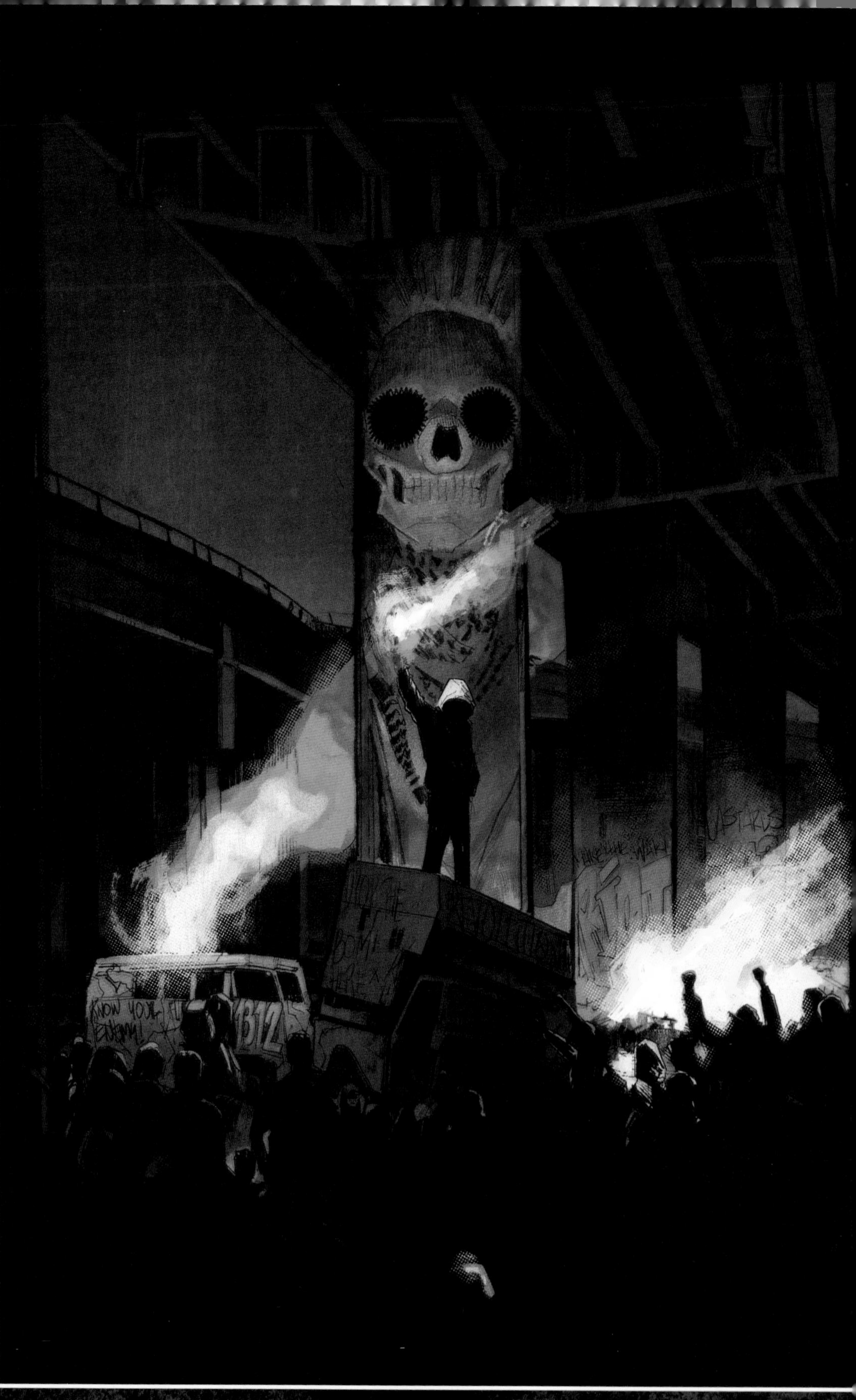
1312

ISSUE 3 STANDARD
GABRIEL IBARRA-NUÑEZ

ISSUE 3 WEBSTORE VARIANT
RICH WOODALL

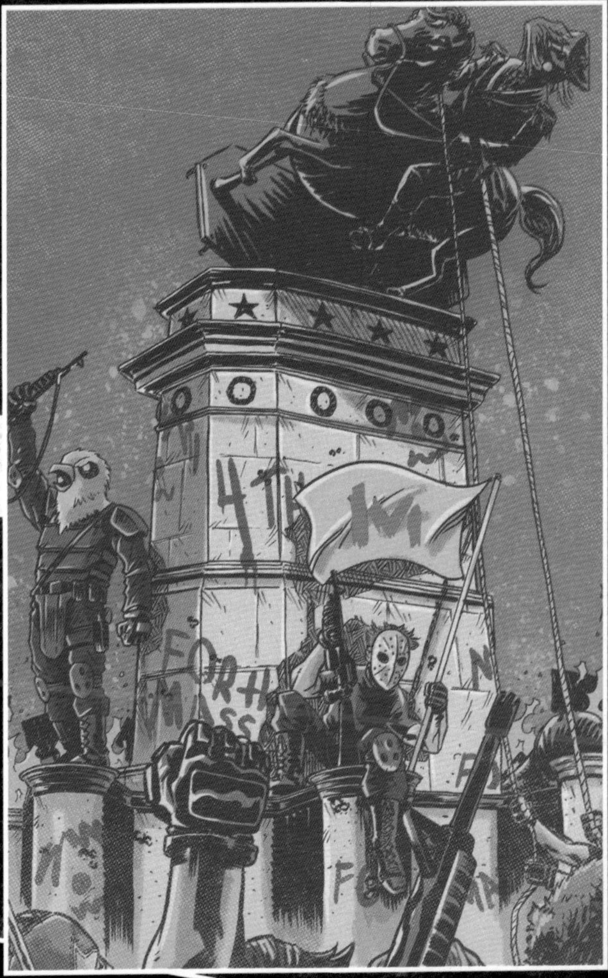

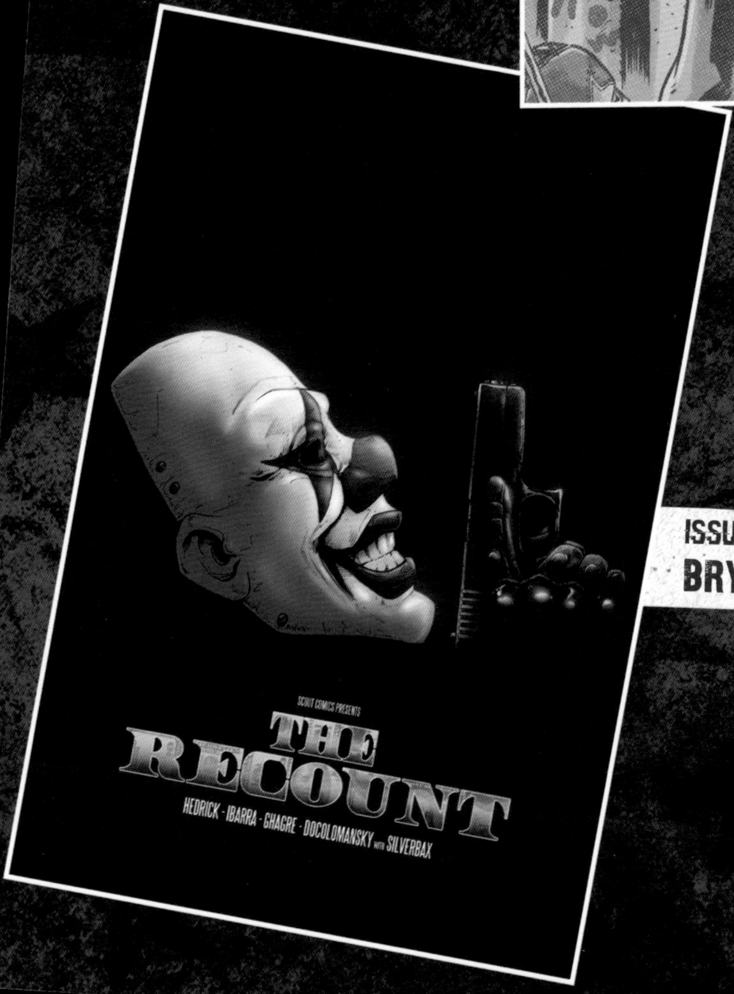
SCOUT COMICS PRESENTS
THE RECOUNT
HEDRICK - IBARRA - GHAGRE - DOCOLOMANSKY WITH SILVERBAX

ISSUE 3 IZZY'S VARIANT
BRYAN SILVERBAX

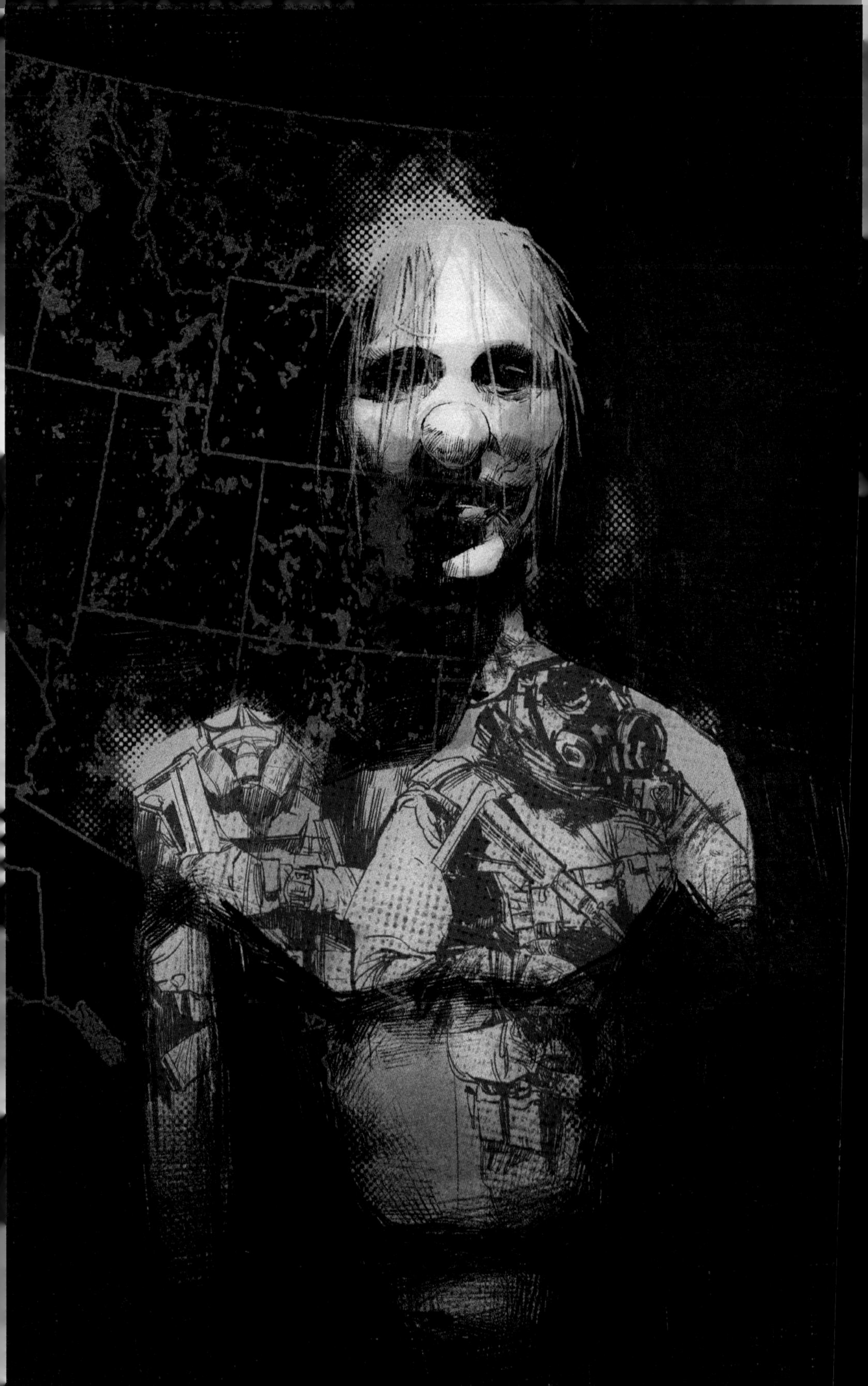

ISSUE 4 STANDARD COVER
GABRIEL IBARRA-NUÑEZ

ISSUE 4 WEBSTORE VARIANT
RICH WOODALL

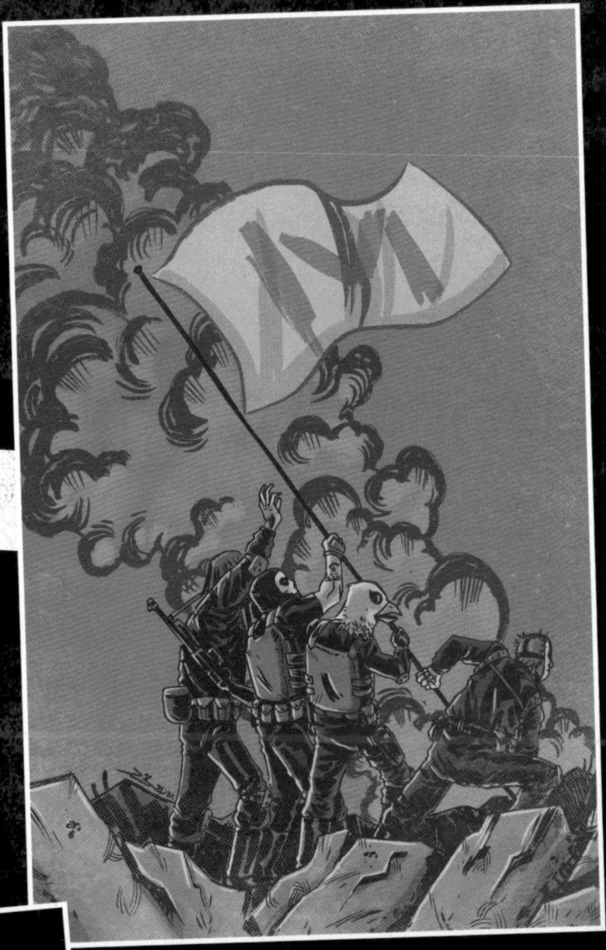

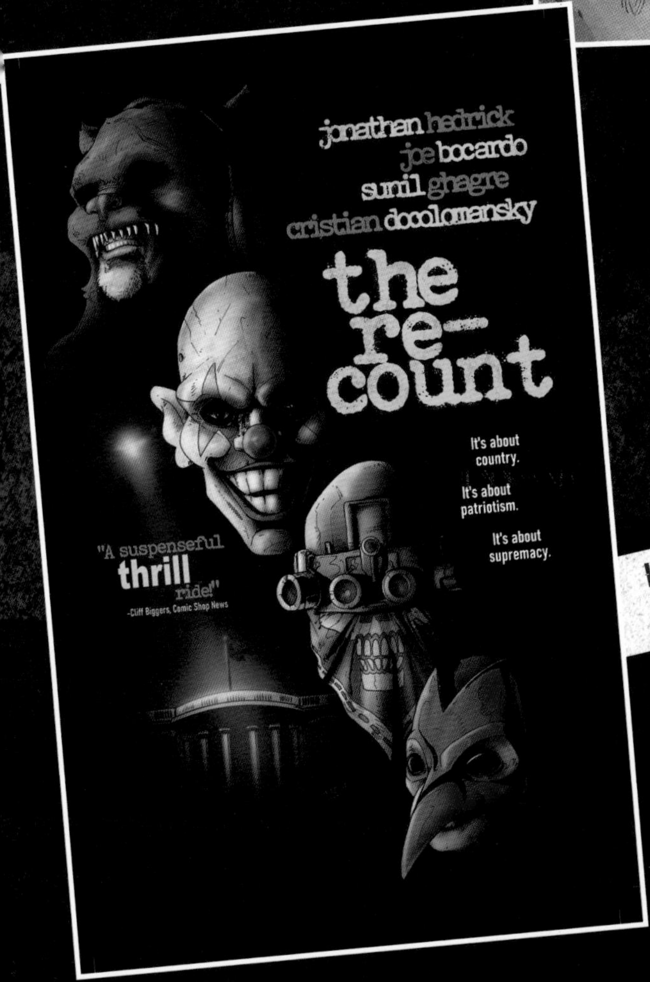
jonathan hedrick
joe bocardo
sunil ghagre
cristian docolomansky
the re-count
It's about country.
It's about patriotism.
It's about supremacy.
"A suspenseful thrill ride!"
-Cliff Biggers, Comic Shop News

ISSUE 4 VARIANT
BRYAN SILVERBAX